MIND, MATERIALITY AND HISTORY

How do we become who we are? How is it that people are so similar in the ways they differ from one another, and so different in the ways they are the same?

Christina Toren's theory of mind as not only a physical phenomenon, but an historical one, sets out to answer these questions by examining how the material world of objects and other people informs the constitution of mind in persons over time.

Toren's theory of embodied mind as a microhistorical process is set out in the first chapter, providing a context for the nine papers that follow. Questions explored include the way meaning-making processes reference an historically specific world and are responsible at once for continuity and change, how ritual informs children's constitution of the categories adults use to describe the world, and how people represent their relationships with one another and in so doing come to embody history.

Mind, Materiality and History has direct relevance to current debates on the nature of mind and consciousness, and demonstrates the centrality of the study of children to social analysis. It will be a valuable resource for students and scholars with an interest in anthropological theory and methodology, as well as those engaged in material culture studies.

Christina Toren is Reader in Social Anthropology and Psychology at Brunel University. She has done extensive fieldwork in Fiji, and is the author of *Making Sense of Hierarchy: Cognition as Social Process in Fiji*, as well as numerous papers.

MATERIAL CULTURES

Interdisciplinary studies in the material construction of social worlds

Series Editors: Michael Rowlands, *Department of Anthropology, University College, London*; Christopher Tilley, *Department of Anthropology, University College, London*; Fred Myers, *Department of Anthropology, New York University.*

MIND, MATERIALITY AND HISTORY

Explorations in Fijian Ethnography

Christina Toren

London and New York

First published 1999
by Routledge
2 Park Square, Milton Park, Abingdon, Oxon, OX14 4RN

Simultaneously published in the USA and Canada
by Routledge
270 Madison Ave, New York NY 10016

Routledge is an imprint of the Taylor & Francis Group

Transferred to Digital Printing 2006

© 1999 Christina Toren

Typeset in Bembo by Routledge

All rights reserved. No part of this book may be reprinted or reproduced or utilised in
any form or by any electronic, mechanical, or other means, now known or hereafter
invented, including photocopying and recording, or in any information storage or
retrieval system, without permission in writing from the publishers.

British Library Cataloguing in Publication Data
A catalogue record for this book is available from the British Library

Library of Congress Cataloging in Publication Data
A catalogue record for this book has been requested

ISBN 0–415–19576–4 (hbk)
ISBN 0–415–19577–2 (pbk)

Printed and bound by Antony Rowe Ltd, Eastbourne

FOR MANUEL TOREN

CONTENTS

CONTENTS

ILLUSTRATIONS

ACKNOWLEDGEMENTS

Fieldwork in Fiji occupied twenty months from July 1981 to February 1983, eighteen months being spent in the chiefly village of Sawaieke on the island of Gau, supported by an SSRC Studentship. Subsequent field trips occupied five months in 1990 – May to September, supported by a Brief Award from Brunel University – and two months in 1993, supported by the Macquarie University Fellowship in the 'Politics of Tradition in the Pacific' and the Australian Research Council. Many thanks to Margaret Jolly, Robert Norton, Caroline Ralston and Nick Thomas for their generous support during my time in Australia.

I am grateful to Ms Taufa Vakatale whose interest and help sent me to Sawaieke in the first place and for the generous kindness and hospitality of villagers there, who always made me feel welcome. I have to thank especially Takalaigau, Ratu Marika Uluinadawa, and his wife Radini Takalaigau and sister Adi Ateca Tui; also special thanks to my teacher Tunitoga, Savenaca Waqa and to the Tabaisa family – especially Ratu Marika Tokalauvere and Adi Mulonaivalu. I have to remember too Serupepeli Vuetanavanua and others who were so helpful to me: Ratu Sefanaia Laua Lewanavanua and his wife Adi Makareta and all his family, Sakiusa Damudamu Vererusa and his wife Salote, and Marika Tagicakibau, his wife Mere and their grandson, Manueli Christian – one of the many, many children of the villages of Sawaieke and Somosomo who made such an invaluable contribution to my work.

The papers collected here were written over the past twelve years, since I received my doctorate in 1986 from the London School of Economics. I want to thank my former teachers there who set my feet firmly on the anthropological path – especially my Ph.D. supervisor, Maurice Bloch, and my first tutors, James Woodburn and the late Alfred Gell. Various friends and colleagues provided constructive comment on early drafts of certain papers: Maurice Bloch, Hastings Donnan, Judith Ennew, Ronnie Frankenberg, Penny Harvey, Susan Hiller, Eric Hirsch, Adam Kuper, Andrew Jones, Jean La Fontaine, Liz Nissen, Mike O'Hanlon, Jonathan Parry. I am thankful too to Maria Phylactou and Marilyn Strathern for remarkably enlightening remarks made in the course of discussion and to George Milner who generously helped me in linguistic matters whenever

I asked. My deepest gratitude however has to be reserved for three close friends and colleagues with whom I have spent many, many hours in passionate discussion and argument, whose comments on early drafts are always enlightening and whose scholarship and intellectual commitment are a continuing source of inspiration: Peter Gow, Jadran Mimica and Alexandra Ouroussoff.

And finally, heartfelt thanks to my dear son, Manuel, who lived this adventure too.

SOURCE ACKNOWLEDGEMENTS

The author and publisher would like to thank the following copyright holders for permission to reproduce papers: chapters 1 and 4 Cambridge University Press; chapter 3 Oxford University Press; chapters 2 and 5 the Royal Anthropological Institute of Great Britain and Ireland; chapter 6 *Journal of Contemporary Legal Issues*; chapter 8 Berg Publishers; chapter 9 Oceania Publications, University of Sydney.

Chapter 1: Toren, C. (1989) 'Drinking cash: the purification of money in ceremonial exchange in Fiji', in J. Parry and M. Bloch (eds) *Money and the Morality of Exchange*, New York and London: Cambridge University Press.

Chapter 2: (1988) 'Making the present, revealing the past: the mutability and continuity of tradition as process', *Man, The Journal of the Royal Anthropological Institute* (NS) 23: 696–717.

Chapter 3: (1995a) 'Seeing the ancestral sites: transformations in Fijian notions of the land', in E. Hirsch and M. O'Hanlon (eds) *Anthropology of the Landscape*, Oxford: Clarendon Press.

Chapter 4: (1993b) 'Sign into symbol, symbol as sign: cognitive aspects of a social process', in P. Boyer (ed.) *Cognitive Aspects of Religious Symbolism*, Cambridge: Cambridge University Press.

Chapter 5: (1993a) 'Making history: the significance of childhood cognition for a comparative anthropology of mind', *Man, The Journal of the Royal Anthropological Institute* (NS) 28: 461–478.

Chapter 6: (1995b) 'Ritual, rule and cognitive scheme', in Paul Wohlmuth (ed.) *The Crisis in Text, Journal of Contemporary Legal Issues* 6: 521–533, University of San Diego.

Chapter 7: (1994a) 'Transforming love, representing Fijian hierarchy', in P. Gow and P. Harvey (eds) *Sexuality and Violence. Issues in Representation and Experience*, London: Routledge.

Chapter 8: (1995c) 'Cosmogonic aspects of desire and compassion in Fiji', in D. de Coppet and A. Iteanu (eds) *Cosmos and Society*, London: Berg.

Chapter 9: (1994c) ' "All things go in pairs or the sharks will bite": the antithetical nature of Fijian chiefship' *Oceania* 64 (3): 197–216.

INTRODUCTION
Mind, materiality and history

How do we become who we are? This question lies at the base of all the human sciences. And for all the vast literature that exists on the subject, it is a question we have hardly begun to answer. Moreover, how exactly, we might address it is an epistemological issue, that is to say, it concerns the theory of the method or grounds of knowledge.

How do we become who we are? An anthropologist's answer begins with the recognition that it cannot adequately be answered in the abstract because that pan-human 'we' has to be broken up into its constituent parts: Inuit babies grow up to be Inuit adults and English babies to be English and moreover, what it is to be Inuit or English at the close of the twentieth century is something rather different from what it was a generation before, or four generations before, or eight. So an anthropologist's answer begins inevitably with an appeal to history, to the particular histories of particular peoples. Implicit in this answer is a further appeal to the specific nature of personal histories, for the anthropologist's answer encompasses an awareness that any English or Inuit person is bound to be uniquely him or herself.

It is clear then that a satisfactory answer has to address at once 'sameness' and 'difference' as fused aspects of the phenomenon of being human. I try to show how, if we take the view that the task of anthropology is to understand how people become who they are, then we can arrive too at a model of mind that is able to encompass at once the commonality and the singularity of what it is to be human in any place, at any time. This task requires that we focus our enquiry on actual persons – in this case and for the purpose of thinking through the question, on you, the reader of this essay and me, the writer.

I do not know who you are, where you were born, what your age is, the traumas and joys of your childhood, your sex, nationality, family history, educational background, intellectual achievements, political and religious beliefs; in short I do not personally know you. I assume however that you and I have in common our humanity and the kind of educational and intellectual history that leads me to write this chapter and you to read it. And so, whatever the differences between us in respect of the details of our respective *curricula vitae*, I grant to you the same general abilities, understandings and so on that I grant to myself.

1

In short, I assume that your subjectivity is, from moment to moment, being brought into being in much the same way as my own and, this being so, I further assume that you are likewise allowing me too to be something more than a mere object in your world, that you allow my subjectivity.

Inter-subjectivity is a fundamental condition of human being: we recognise one another as human and in so doing we take it for granted that we may at least try to communicate with one another and that mutual understanding is likely enough. The core of our understanding of one another is our common knowledge of the fundamentals of human existence, of heat and cold, day and night, hunger and satisfaction, laughter and sex, the wetness of water and the heat of the sun, birth and death, pain and joy, all the many subtle gradations of emotion that we humans experience. And when you think about me the author and I think of you the reader we assume further that each of us has a sense of her or himself as a particular person with a particular history – one that unites us in its commonality with those closest to us, our parents perhaps or our siblings, our children, our spouses, or our friends – and in its particularity separates us from them. In other words, in writing this essay I cannot help but assume fundamental similarities between you and me, and in reading it you do the same, even while we also know that our differences are bound to be profound.

In addressing you, the reader whom I do not know, in acknowledging your subjectivity, I grant you a history, for humans are in their nature historical (or, as some would prefer to say, cultural) beings. We literally embody our history, that is the history of our relations with all those others whom we have encountered in our lives. And through them we tap into their histories too, and not only theirs, but the histories of all those whom they encountered, and so on and on, back through time.

In other words, the history of our ancestors' relations with one another in the world has informed both who we are as particular persons and the conditions of our collective existence: our belonging to this group or that, the appearance of our bodies, the languages we speak, our susceptibility to particular illnesses and disease, our access to particular technologies, our relative riches or poverty, our ideas about ourselves and the world we live. Literally everything about us, from our genes to our most secret and never-to-be-revealed private thoughts have been, and continue to be, informed by a past that at once unites and differentiates us.

It can be difficult to think of yourself as manifesting history in the making, but when we recognise that humans have to bring into being the very ideas and practices of which they are supposed to be the product, we can begin to understand the nature of human being. The challenge then, at the outset, is to arrive at an idea of human being that is rooted in inter-subjectivity and the history that is its artefact, and to show how, exactly, we humans can be understood to embody the history of our own making.

Any idea of human being entails a theory of mind; so even where it is not the focus of discussion, an implicit theory of mind is to be found in all human science texts. Often enough this theory renders the brain or nervous system as a computer in which certain mental structures are regarded as 'hard-wired' products of biological evolution and thus as universal, and others as relative because they are the artefact of a cognitive program that governs acquisition of social or cultural knowledge. The model itself rests on a set of theoretical distinctions (between biology and culture, for example) that I show below to be untenable. A further problem, however, is that it is extraordinarily difficult to delineate with any precision what features of mind are universal to all humans and what features are relative. And no wonder, because the more one reads ethnography and the more experience one has of doing one's own research, the more it becomes apparent that not only do we humans differ from each other in the ways we are the same, but we are remarkably similar too to one another in the ways we are different. The mind–computer analogy does not allow us to explain this conundrum. To arrive at a formulation that is capable of addressing it, we have to begin by acknowledging fully that the human mind and the human body are aspects of a single phenomenon that is the living human being.

The idea that mind is embodied is common to a number of theorists.[1] I want to argue further that mind is the emergent product of a continual process of becoming, one that is mediated by our lived engagement in the peopled world. In other words, our relations with those others whom we encounter in the course of daily life, from birth to death, inform the processes through which, over time, we constitute our ideas of the lived world of objects and other people. In this view, mind is *the* fundamental historical phenomenon. It becomes apparent too that children are crucial to our understanding of embodied mind; for it is by studying how, over time, they constitute their ideas of the world that we can come to have some insight into the historical nature of our own epistemological and ontological certainties.

Re-thinking analytical categories

As anthropologists we know that our concepts of biology – like anyone else's ideas of the material substance of living things – have a history, so we know that our biological descriptions of what it is to be human cannot be taken to be transparently true, even if they may be argued to be more or less valid. In other words, our biological concepts are historically constituted – that is to say, just as cultural as any other ideas. Contemporary anthropologists have devoted a good deal of time and effort to explicating ideas of the person held by people of other than European origin, so we know too that the idea of the person as 'an individual in society' is by no means universal. Moreover, given that as yet we have no ethnography concerning the idea of the individual as held by people who *do* make use of it, we should also suspect that there will be wide variation in what it means to different people, even within a relatively limited group, e.g. white, middle-class Londoners. So the idea of the individual in society cannot be taken to be self-evident. Rather it has to be viewed as just one, historically specific, idea

3

of the person and sociality and as such it can be compared with all those other, equally valid, but very different, ideas of the person held by other peoples. Ideas of the person and sociality are always crucial to any ethnographic analysis because inevitably they inform people's day-to-day relationships and their collective life as this may be described in terms of political economy, religion, kinship, and so on.

These points are already well understood. If I reiterate them here it is only to remind the reader that theoretical distinctions of the biology/culture variety continue to be a problem for anthropological analyses. As does the equally well-known 'dialectical relation' that is supposed to resolve that problem. This supposed resolution suggests a reciprocal interaction between biology and culture, individual and society, body and mind – but note that there is no place here for transformation, except as a function of an encounter with external forces. And these ideas continue to hold force (they underlie, for example, theories of cultural or social construction) even though their proponents know that there are no definable empirical entities to which any of the terms can be applied. Nevertheless, the argument goes, humans everywhere have the same kind of material substance and this justifies our delimiting of the domain of 'biology' from which it follows that the manifest behavioural differences between humans have to be relegated to another domain – that of 'culture'. Moreover, considered as discrete biological entities, each one of us is an individual which means that there must be some other force – society – that binds us together. And because it seems that mind is in the domain of culture it can in theory be abstracted from particular bodies such that mind and body can be analysed as if they are separate entities *in dialectical relation to* one another.

But why remain wedded to this idea of dialectical relations between abstract entities when it manifestly violates our own experience? The theoretical synthesis I propose here is intended to force a genuine shift in the way we, as anthropologists and human scientists, conceive of ourselves and other human beings and, willy nilly, in the way we do our research. It proposes that we take seriously our understanding that body and mind, the biological and the cultural, the material and the ideal, are aspects of one another, rather than separate and dialectically related phenomena. But to do this we have, firstly, to re-think the analytical categories we have been used to take for granted and, secondly, to arrive at an understanding of the processes in and through which each of us, in any given time or place, is the unique and always emergent product of our relations with others.

The suggestion that we re-think our analytical categories is not new. It resides in an awareness that certain widely accepted theoretical distinctions do not adequately capture our day-to-day experience of the world and our relations with others: culture/biology, society/individual, mind/body, ideal/material, objective/subjective, structure/process. I have already pointed out that all the terms in these theoretical distinctions are abstractions, but we do not usually consider them as such. Rather in each case we are more likely to assert that a real, material phenomenon is set against an abstraction; for example we may seem to have no problem in pointing at 'biology', at 'individuals', at 'bodies', but when it comes to 'culture', 'society', 'mind', all definitions become more obviously a matter of debate because we cannot point to the concrete entities they might denote. But let's say that we are generally aware that both terms in any of these oppositions are abstractions; for the human scientist (here an anthropologist) the problem then is how exactly to characterise an interaction between abstract terms such that it is adequate to describe phenomena like you and me.

So when we pause to consider any one of these distinctions we come up against a number of immediate theoretical and practical problems (i.e. epistemological problems). My general aim in this essay is to suggest a theoretical synthesis that is able to overcome the problems posed by theories of mind and learning that rest on ideas of a dialectical relation between abstract terms. So let us look at the set of theoretical distinctions cited above and see what happens when we collapse them into one another. Then it becomes plain that:

1   *We are individually social and socially individual.* We are social beings in our very nature and it is because we are, that the history of our relations with others informs who we are as particular persons.

2   *We are biologically cultural and culturally biological.* All human behaviour – including of course linguistic behaviour – is culturally patterned and, by the same token, all our many and various ideas of the substance of living things, including ourselves, are historically constituted. So, for example, given our different ideas of the body and of what constitutes health and illness, it follows that Chinese medicine differs significantly from Ayurvedic medicine and orthodox Western medicine.

3   *Mind is embodied and the body manifests mind.* The workings of the brain cannot be understood apart from the workings of the nervous system and the body to which they are intrinsic. It is as an integrated whole that embodied mind functions; it follows that mind is evident in bodily praxis.

4   *The ideal and the material are mutually specifying.* Our ideas are constituted in material relations with one another and we communicate with one another in and through the materiality of the world, its manifold objects, and awareness of our common humanity. Thus our understanding of what is material is always mediated by our relations with others and, likewise, the material stuff of the peopled world confirms our ideas of what those relations are and should be. Or, in other words, all the world's objects whether they be natural or made by humans and all its processes – the seasons, day and night, growing things, the very earth itself in all its aspects – always have in human understanding a symbolic dimension, and what is symbolic inevitably has material implications.

5   *Our subjective and objective perspectives guarantee each other.* The validity of our objective descriptions of the world is guaranteed via inter-subjectivity; so, for example, the success of any new idea requires that one convince others

that it is viable. By the same token, we can without difficulty render our subjective views as warranted by reference to an apparently unassailable concrete logic; for example we might thus argue that rising rates of violence in American schools are caused by children's exposure to violence on television or that astrological analyses really do reveal people's underlying characteristics.

6 *Structure and process are aspects of one another.* For most of us the term 'structure', when applied to a concrete entity, tends to denote something that is fixed, static. Biologically speaking however, structures such as a geranium, a frog, a human being are constituted in and through transformation. So, for example, any of us begins as a single-celled entity – the zygote that is formed out of the union of our father's sperm with our mother's ovum; all our subsequent physical development is a function of the differentiation via cell division that takes place within that entity. Our environing world evokes responses in us, but it is the structure of the embodied nervous system that at any given time specifies what is evocative for us; so certain neurobiologists have argued that, for example, the environment we visually perceive is determined largely by the activity in which we are currently engaged.[2] So we cannot adequately describe the structure that is the human being without invoking the complexity of the continuing transformations that constitute the process we call 'living'.

My reasons for insisting on the necessity of our doing away with the above taken-for-granted theoretical distinctions are not arbitrary. Rather this necessity, as I see it, arises out of my experience of trying to make sense of ethnographic studies in the light of psychological theories of cognition and, conversely, of trying to make sense of psychological theories in the light of ethnographic studies of different peoples. It follows that there are plenty of empirical, as well as theoretical, reasons for undertaking a radical re-working of cognitive theory in both psychology and anthropology.[3] But perhaps the most fundamental observation in favour of such a proceeding is that humans (like all other living things) are 'autopoietic systems'.

Humans as autopoietic systems

We embody the history of our own making because, like other living systems, we are autopoietic – that is to say, self-creating or self-producing. I take this idea from the great Chilean neurobiologist, Humberto Maturana, and his colleague Francisco Varela.[4] It is autopoiesis that gives rise to the autonomy of living systems, including ourselves. To return to the example above: you and I started as single-cell beings – zygotes. From that moment onwards foetal development was a function of structural transformations occurring within the zygote – itself an autonomous living system. It was this system itself that governed what structural changes occurred, specified what constituted viable environing conditions, and what happened when they were threatened or upset. The conditions of our mothers' existence were important for our respective development in the womb in so far as their good health promoted our own, but it was not our mothers who determined how, precisely, we developed. So, for example, while an illness such as German measles in a pregnant woman is likely to cause damage to the developing foetus, the sort of damage it causes – deafness, for example – is a function of what changes are occurring in foetal growth at the time the illness strikes. At any time, how we respond to a disease is going to be a function of our general condition at the time we contract it. All this seems obvious enough, as does the way that, in later life, when we first sign on with a new clinic, the doctor takes a medical history – i.e. notes down not only what illnesses we've had and when they occurred, but also any serious health problems encountered by our parents or siblings or other close relatives. In this sense, the idea that you literally embody your history seems fairly straightforward. It becomes more difficult and more complicated when you have to take in, too, the idea that you personally embody the history of your relations with all those others whom you have encountered from birth onwards. These relations with others are crucial to the human autopoietic process.

You are a biologically social being and because you are, you cannot help but engage others in the process of becoming yourself: indeed throughout infancy others were necessary to keep you alive, but even when you were an infant, these others could not entirely determine what happened to you, nor did they have absolute control over the relations between you. Because, even in infancy, even as a newborn, your responses to those others were just that – *your* responses, and as such they contributed to the precise nature of the inter-subjective relations in which you were engaged.[5]

This is precisely *not* an argument for a radical individualism. The process of becoming oneself can cease only with death, but this does not mean that we are independently the authors of our own being; we do not control the conditions of our own existence. What I am arguing for here is merely the inevitable autonomy of each and every human being that is given by the process of autopoiesis.

Let us return to you, the newborn baby. Once out of the womb you were immediately engaged in relations with others; indeed one can argue that even before birth you were positioned *vis-à-vis* those others in the sense that they had certain expectations about you. The ideas about newborn babies held by your parents and other carers – your siblings or grandparents or nanny for instance – structured the conditions of your early life: how often you were fed and how you were weaned; whether you were picked up as soon as you cried, whether or not you were talked to; the kind of language used to you and around you; the way you were clothed, where you were taken and how you were carried about; and so on. And as you grew older, became a toddler, learned to talk, arrived at nursery age, went to pre-school, graduated into infants, attended primary school, arrived at puberty and secondary school, then adulthood and university – throughout all your existence – you have encountered and been inducted into manifold kinds of relations with others. Kinship relations: parent–child, siblings, cousins, grandparent–grandchild, spouses, step-kin and so on. Teacher–pupil relations. Friends. Buyer–seller relations. Lovers. Relations with those who perform services for you, or for whom you do likewise. Mentors. Sexual partners. Colleagues. And so on.

Beyond these immediate, face-to-face relations are all those more distant ones that are brought into being through television, radio and other media and/or mediated by what we generally call 'institutions'. In so far, for example, that you hold certain ideas about politicians, film stars and other public figures, you stand in a particular relation to them – as voter or fan, for instance. In short, you were born into a set of relations with others and the ideas held by those others and the practices with which they are associated have informed, and continue to inform, the process of your becoming.

I have to emphasise here that this process of becoming is *not* correctly characterised as 'socialisation'. I am arguing here for a process of human autopoiesis in which, willy nilly, we engage others in the processes of our own becoming. In bringing you into the world, your parents quite literally constituted themselves as such, as your parents, even as you constituted yourself their child – and a particular child at that, for even if you have an identical twin you cannot help but be uniquely yourself. This uniqueness is a function of human autopoiesis, for even if you are one of genetically identical twins, your understanding of the peopled world as you grow up has to be brought into being by you; however close you are, your twin cannot do this for you and the specificity of your experience, the sheer fact that it is *yours*, constitutes the difference between you and your twin.

So if, as I am arguing, you were not 'socialised', how did you become who you are? The process is complex, but it can, in essence, be stated quite simply. In the course of growing up you could not help but enter into manifold relations with others and, in so doing, you made meaning (or what might also be called knowledge) out of your experience in the world. Other people had structured the conditions of your existence, indeed other people explicitly instructed you about certain aspects of the world, but it was you who made meaning out of the meanings they presented you with. So, to take but one example, when first you went to school you were engaged for the first time in a formal pupil–teacher relation; that first teacher's ideas of pedagogy and the proper nature of pupil–teacher relations, along with the behaviour of your peers and the nature of the school itself (its appearance, for example, and how classroom and playground were organised) structured the conditions in which you formed your own idea of what it is to be a pupil or a teacher, of what school is, of learning and so on. And in all your subsequent relations with all your many teachers in a variety of settings – school, music lessons, drama club, learning to drive – you continued to constitute anew your idea of what this teacher–pupil relation is and should be, and at any given point in time your ideas informed your formal learning, its relative success or failure.

This process of making meaning is the psychological aspect of human

8

autopoiesis. The constituting process is not willed by you, you do not have to be explicitly conscious of it, and nor can you escape it – it is a function of being human. Like the process of physical development, the meaning- or knowledge-making process should be understood as giving rise to psychological structures that are at once dynamic and stable over time. These psychological structures are usually referred to as 'schemas' or 'schemes'. This term has come to be used with some frequency in contemporary social psychology and certain sub-disciplinary areas of anthropology and sociology so I have to emphasise here that Piaget's idea of the scheme is my referent here. This brilliant and essentially simple idea is the core of Piaget's work. Just how very clever it is is rarely acknowledged.

Piaget's cognitive scheme is 'a self-regulating transformational system'; in other words, it is autopoietic. Originally a biologist, Piaget argued that 'only self-regulating transformational systems are structures' (1971: 113) and that, because the character of structured wholes depends on their laws of composition, these laws must in their nature be structuring.[6] This gives rise to the dual attributes of structured wholes – that is, that they are simultaneously structured and structuring. If a structured whole has stable boundaries and conserves adaptation, these features themselves presuppose that structures are self-regulating or, to use Maturana and Varela's term, autopoietic. Piaget argued moreover that 'the idea of *structure* as a system of transformations [is] continuous with that of *construction* as continual formation' (ibid.: 34) and demonstrated his argument via his studies of children's cognitive construction of fundamental categories of quantity, space, time, number and so on.

In Piaget's theory of cognitive development, the newborn child starts off with only a few 'reflex-like' behaviours at its disposal – for example, sucking, swallowing, crying, grasping and so on. The primitive psychological structures that govern these behaviours become differentiated through functioning. So, for example, the scheme for grasping rapidly becomes differentiated via the baby's experience of grasping different objects – a finger, a dummy, a piece of cloth; the baby assimilates the feel, as it were, of each new object to its grasping scheme and in so doing accommodates to the feel-aspect of that particular object. And when the baby grasps the dummy and gets it into its mouth, the assimilation schemes of grasping and sucking are assimilated to one another in such a way as to produce a qualitatively different, more highly differentiated, scheme that provides for a new and more complex accommodation to the world.

So, for Piaget, all behaviour has innate roots, but becomes differentiated through functioning; and all behaviour contains the same functional factors and the same structural elements. The functional factors are assimilation, accommodation and equilibration. Psychologically assimilation is a process whereby a function, once exercised, presses towards repetition; in assimilation an action is actively reproduced and comes to incorporate new objects into itself (e.g. sucking incorporates the thumb, the nipple, the teat of a bottle, a piece of cloth, a dummy, someone's finger, a spoon and so on); this is an assimilation scheme. In accommodation, schemes of assimilation become modified in being applied to a diversity of objects. Equilibration is the process by which assimilation schemes become mutually co-ordinated in such a way as to produce an 'equilibrated structure' that yields a necessity that is a non-temporal, because reversible, law. An example might be the scheme that is constituted via the cross-modal matching of the sound of people's voices and what they look like; the particular sound of mother's voice is very rapidly associated with the particular configuration of her face such that the perception of either necessarily suggests its complement.[7]

The structural elements in behaviour are order relations: e.g. the order of movements in an habitual act; subordination schemes: e.g. grasping is subordinate to pulling when an infant gets hold of your finger and pulls it towards its mouth; and correspondences: e.g. what Piaget calls 'recognitory assimilation', for instance, the kind of motor recognition a baby evinces when its physical movements mimic those of the person to whom it is attending.

> So assimilation, the process or activity common to all forms of life, is the source of that continual relating, setting up of correspondences, establishing of functional connections, and so on, which characterizes the early stages of intelligence. And it is assimilation, again, which finally gives rise to those general schemata we called structures. But assimilation *itself* is *not* a structure. Assimilation is the functional aspect of structure-formation, intervening in each particular case of constructive activity, but sooner or later leading to the mutual assimilation of structures to one another, and so establishing ever more intimate inter-structural connnections.
>
> (ibid.: 71, italics in the original)

Autopoiesis entails that structure and process be recognised as aspects of one another. Thus to say that a cognitive scheme becomes differentiated through functioning suggests at once an increasing fineness and subtlety in the differentiating process *and* increasing stability in structure. Perhaps it is useful to point out here, in passing, that it is because structure and process are aspects of one another that if we concentrate on the processual aspect to the exclusion of the structural it appears as if all is transformation; and if we ignore process it seems that what is structural is also static. That structure and process are inextricable and mutually defining means that the process that Piaget called 'genetic epistemology', while it produces stable and mutually confirming sets of ideas about the peopled world, is never in principle finished but open always to further elaboration. So, meaning is always emergent, never fixed. And this would be true even if each of us acted directly on the world and made meaning in isolation from other persons – as Piaget so often seems to suggest. When we incorporate inter-subjectivity into his model, it becomes plain that the meanings we make of the peopled world are themselves constituted in an encounter with the meanings already made, and still being made, by others.

The idea of the scheme as a self-regulating transformational system in which structure and process are aspects of one another has not, so far as I can see, been widely understood. It follows that its theoretical usefulness has not been recognised. As used by researchers other than Piaget himself the term 'scheme' usually denotes a *mental representation* of experience. The formation, continuity over time, and transformation of these so-called schemes (also referred to by cognitive anthropologists as 'cultural models') are treated as separable aspects; moreover the structure and transformation of any given scheme are by and large taken to be a function of pressures from an environment that can itself be objectively specified because it is held to be separable from the person in whose head the representation is supposed to be stored. This peculiarly static idea of the scheme has long militated against the development of a model of embodied mind that is phenomenologically sound.[8] Contemporary connexionist models of mind do, however, attempt to make computational theory consistent with what we know of the workings of the human nervous system; they employ an idea of parallel distributed processing that allows for a cognitive scheme that is always emergent, never fixed. In this narrow sense, the connexionist scheme is consistent with Piaget's.[9]

The answer one gets to any question is a function of the terms in which the question is stated. So any scientific hypothesis contains a more or less explicit theory that structures the terms in which it can be answered. The distinctions between biology and culture, body and mind, and individual and society have helped produce disciplinary distinctions in which, crudely speaking, the physical substance of living things is the province of biology, mind and individuality the province of psychology, and culture and society the province of anthropology and sociology. An artefact of these disciplinary distinctions is that biological questions are held to be more basic than 'higher level' psychological questions which, in their turn, are said to be at a less inclusive level than sociological questions. So disciplinary distinctions structure the kinds of questions that researchers ask and so-called inter-disciplinary research tends to produce ever more specialised sub-disciplines – e.g. cognitive anthropology, social psychology, psychological anthropology, evolutionary psychology.

Irrespective, however, of their disciplinary or sub-disciplinary identification, theorists of cognition continue to take for granted as their starting point the universal epistemic subject, the ahistorical individual. It follows that for cognitivists of all persuasions (including connexionists who, not unreasonably, like to distinguish themselves as followers of a new paradigm) it seems obvious that 'culture' or 'society' is a variable. So they cannot help but find attractive the idea that there has to be a substrate, at the very least, of innately given, domain-specific, cognitive universals that taken together define the mind of the universal epistemic subject. The trick then, is to find them.

A series of wonderfully ingenious and interesting experiments suggest that neonates and very young babies have abilities at their disposal that may have surprised Piaget.[10] It seems that babies are born with a body scheme, a scheme for human voices, for human faces – all of which seems reasonable enough, given that sociality or inter-subjectivity must, in some minimal sense, be given if its particular forms are to be achieved. Indeed one might say the same for infants' abilities to conceive of objects in the world as solid and stable across time, and to demonstrate cross-modal matching – for example, of a particular sound with the sight of a particular object. But these latter abilities do not appear before three to four months old, and given the extraordinary complexity of the human nervous system, the infant's immersion in a world of highly differentiated sensation, and the rapid growth of inter-neuronal connections, this is surely ample time for their autopoietic development out of much more primitive beginnings.[11] Moreover, as a 'self-regulating transformational system', a Piagetian scheme, even in its early stages, is going to 'look like' what cognitive psychologists call a module.

But let's say one accepts the thesis of innate modularity, that is, that we are born with certain minimally defined cognitive modules at our disposal – a language acquisition device for instance, a module for the perception of colour, or depth, or other living kinds, or humans, or solid objects – we have still, given the autopoietic nature of human being and the infant's orientational bias towards other humans, to conceive of these structures of mind as self-regulating transformational systems that are elaborated, if not constituted, in and through inter-subjectivity. Proponents of massive modularity cannot accept such a view because it threatens the vaunted objectivity of their model with its own historical specificity. So the massive modularity thesis entails that cognition about people (so-called social cognition) can be axiomatically separated from other kinds of cognition (e.g. ideas about number, space, time and so on) such that sociality cannot be held to have contaminated the logic that justifies as objectively given the modularity theorists' own perspective.[12]

Mind and inter-subjectivity

The theoretical synthesis I am proposing here can be encapsulated in the following formulation. *Mind is a function of the whole person constituted over time in inter-subjective relations with others in the environing world.* This radically phenomenological perspective on mind is derived in part from my reading of the work of Merleau-Ponty.

Merleau-Ponty's view that '[t]he body is our general medium for having a world' (1962: 146) accords with Piaget's insistence on sensori-motor or practical intelligence as the foundation for the subsequent development of logical categories. Piaget's driving interest was to understand how the necessity that seems to be given in our categories of space, time, number and so on, could be the outcome of a process of cognitive construction, rather than an innate function of mind as Kant had argued – a project that is at least related to Merleau-Ponty's inheritance of Husserl's concern to render human science phenomenologically sound.[13] Piaget, however, appears to have been, at least initially, untroubled by any awareness that history might constitute a problem for the human sciences; thus Piaget's subject is the universal epistemic subject who acts on a world whose material properties can be directly apprehended. By contrast, for Merleau-Ponty subjectivity pre-supposes inter-subjectivity and the self has to be understood as the always emergent product of the history of its becoming: 'I am installed on a pyramid of time which has been me' (1964: 14).

A crucial aspect of this process is that Merleau-Ponty's subject is for itself an other; in other words, the self-conscious awareness of oneself as the subject of one's being in the world (for example, I-the-writer-of-this-essay or you-the-reader) entails a conscious awareness of one's otherness or, to give a simple example, a consciousness of the distance that enables any one of us to ask ourselves questions such as, why did I do that? Or, why do I have this quality and not that one? Or, why can't I be more ...? The problem here for any one of us is that even while we embody our particular past, we do not have access to it except from the perspective of who we are now. We can, for example, remember the details of our childhood more or less well; what we cannot do is again be in the world *as that child*. It follows that we cannot have access to how we came to know what we know; this opaqueness of our own past – and its density – is further intensified by our having lived the peopled world, and ourselves as given in it, in manifold and ever more complex ways hour-by-hour, day-by-day, for a good twelve months or so before we speak our first word and, in so doing, for the first time indicate something in speech.

A key element in Merleau-Ponty's analysis of the fundamentals of human perception is his idea of intentionality. This has two components: (i) that all consciousness is consciousness of something and (ii) that 'the unity of the world – before being posited by knowledge in a specific act of identification – is "lived" as readymade or already there' (1962: xvii). Merleau-Ponty's idea of intention-ality is important too for the theoretical synthesis I am proposing here because it asserts both that consciousness is a material phenomenon and that what we take for granted as given in the very stuff of the world (what some might call a 'belief system' or a 'cultural model') is brought into being by ourselves as a function of our lived experience of the peopled world and of ourselves as given in it. So for example, for some years before I begin consciously to posit my own existence *as an object of knowledge* – who am I? where did I come from? what am I doing here? – I have already embodied a sense of the spatiotemporal dimensions of the world I live. I come to consciousness of myself and other people and all the manifold objects of the world by virtue of the motility of my body, whose move-ments bring the object-laden world into direct contact with me and me into consciousness of myself, and I embody particular spaces in so far as I am able, as it were, to command them. So it makes sense that a park that is unimaginably large to a 4-year-old is more-or-less average-sized in the view of the child's 7-year-old sibling. Likewise, rather than being in time, I am myself the embodiment of the time I have lived. And so, for instance, it follows that a year is experientially longer for a 7-year-old than for a 14-year-old because it consti-tutes one-seventh of his or her life rather than one-fourteenth.

I come into awareness of myself in a world I take for granted as including myself and as being, quite simply, the way the world is. It is perhaps a world where going to nursery or to infant school is what we children do from nine till three-thirty Monday to Friday, where piano or swimming lessons or after-school club or just playing is what we do when school's over, where shopping with mother in the supermarket and playing in the park is what we do on Saturday and church is where we all go on Sundays, where by and large I get to choose the food I want to eat and the clothes I want to put on. We live in a house with a big back garden and three bedrooms where I share a room with my big sister and my baby brother has a little room all to himself. While I'm at school Mummy is at home looking after the baby and Daddy is at work. Like all the other kids I know, I watch lots of cartoon shows on TV, have lots of brightly coloured toys and games, go out to eat at fast food restaurants with my parents, go on holiday in the summer and so on. I have lived this world and have developed a complex and highly differentiated embodied knowledge of it as the way the world *is* before, as a 4-year-old, I begin to ask why?[14]

Thus for Merleau-Ponty intentionality denotes a mode of being-in-the-world that, in the case of humans, is in its nature historical because human being-in-the-world entails a consciousness that not only lives the world, but explicitly reflects on itself and the world. My ability explicitly to posit the world and to question it and my own existence is, at any given time, a function of the depth and complexity of my explicit knowledge at that time – i.e. the knowledge I can articulate. But however profound that knowledge, however subtle and pene-trating my gaze, however incisive or sceptical my questions, I can neither access nor do away with the lived, embodied consciousness of myself in the world that I knew as an inarticulate infant and young child – it is the initial radius of the knowledge from which my understanding continues to spiral outwards, and as such it is always with me. Of course, all knowledge, including explicit knowledge, is embodied; here I am referring however to that visceral, felt knowledge that itself becomes ever more highly differentiated with increasing experience, but cannot be easily justified in language.[15]

The embodied but inarticulate structures of consciousness that constitute the lived knowledge of the infant and young child continue inevitably to assimilate new experiences and in so doing arrive at new accommodations to the world that are shaped by those earliest experiences. Because they are and will always continue to be, quite literally, inaccessible in language, and because the sheer fact of living renders them ever more complex, these embodied but inarticulate structures of consciousness may be likened to, or perhaps even equated with, the 'unconscious' of psychoanalysis. I cannot here explore the implications of this observation but only suggest, in passing, that Merleau-Ponty's idea of intention-ality does not rule out a psychodynamic perspective on development.

In the preface to the *Phenomenology of Perception* Merleau-Ponty observes that '[t]he world is not what I think but what I live through. I am open to the world, I have no doubt that I am in communication with it, but I do not possess it; it is inexhaustible' (1962: xvi–xvii). It is because the world is 'what we live through' that we are able both to assert with confidence the reality of our own particular experience and to assume that others are bound to experience the world as we do ourselves. This latter assumption is of course problematic (though we may live our lives in such a way that we never find it out, or if we do, put it down to the other's ignorance) but it is not unjustified.

After all, suppose you are lost in the Amazonian rainforest of Brazil and there have the good luck to meet with a group of indigenous people. No doubt you will have the sense to try to show them by appropriately submissive signs that you are not armed and mean no harm, that you are human too and in desperate need of food and water, that you've come a great distance, are very tired and want to sleep. You might even try to communicate the fact that you're lost because you had to parachute out of the small plane in which you were flying and so on. They decide that you are indeed some kind of human and for all your bizarre appearance and behaviour not obviously dangerous and on this account give you food, drink and a place to sleep. They might even adopt you and, because you're open-minded and keen to make the best of things you become, over the next few months, reasonably knowledgeable of their language – at least in so far as you're able to name many different aspects of the world and human experience. By now you have a vocabulary of nearly a thousand words. You can greet people appropriately, ask innumerable questions about things, exclaim enjoyably over the size and taste of the fish you ate that day for dinner, flirt with attractive potential sexual partners, and so on. The people live a life with which you are not familiar at all, one that includes various rituals and other practices you find it difficult to make sense of, but you're getting on very well in the language and have reason therefore to think that in time all will become plain.

Your problems begin precisely at that point where your hosts have revised their initial views and are beginning to take for granted that you know what they know and to tell one another that you are amazingly like themselves, and you in turn are discovering that your knowledge of them, which had seemed so good, is merely superficial. You were using the same words as your hosts to name things and you assumed that agreement on reference was the same as agreement on meaning. Only with time do you begin to realise that they understand the world and human being to be characterised by processes that differ significantly from the processes you yourself take to be self-evident. At first you are inclined to think that their ideas are a function of their ignorance of Western science and technology, but the more you get to know about the world they live, the more aware you become that their ideas are in their view materially justified by the world and logically coherent, for all that they differ so much from your own.

Your respect and liking for these hospitable people and your knowledge of them grows daily, but you cannot live the world they live because your own taken-for-granted was constituted under very different conditions. Nor can you, when you have returned due to a chance meeting with deep forest loggers to your own home place in a major European city, really convince your friends and family that the world lived by the people who had looked after you makes as much sense as their own. You've already told them that this is a world where, for instance, the ancestors can appear as certain animals whom it is extraordinarily dangerous to kill and the mention of a man's mother-in-law's name in his presence is cause for justifiable homicide. You argue, lamely, that these ideas are 'valid for them because that's what their culture tells them' but this argument is in bad faith. For a start, if you really hold this view, it is more or less bound to precipitate an existential crisis in which all your previous certainties are undone and the world becomes terrifyingly unstable. But this is unlikely because, for all your protestations that 'it's all relative', you yourself remain secretly absolutely certain that animals are just animals and that one could hardly justify killing someone for such a trivial reason.

This form of bad faith is common enough in contemporary anthropology where, in its most extreme form, it has given rise to the idea that without actually being one of them, the anthropologist can have nothing valid to say about the people with whom he or she works; the corollary of which is that 'being one of them' is itself impossible if only because of the distance that is an inevitable function of the analytical gaze. Like certain other problems referred to above, this quandary is an artefact of analytical distinctions between the real and the symbolic, biology and culture, and so on. The solution lies, I suggest, in trying to understand how it is that humans are able at one and the same time to have the world in common and to live it as a function of their own particular histories. And we can do this by complementing our studies of what adults have to say about the world with a contemporaneous study of how, exactly, children are constituting over time the concepts their elders are using. And here method becomes an important issue.

The language aspect of becoming who we are

Participant observation remains the primary method of anthropology because it provides for the possibility that the researcher has neglected crucial questions – not out of stupidity or laziness, but because he or she did not know they were there to be asked. By contrast, psychologists set out to test definite hypotheses or to answer definite questions. Studies of cognitive development tend therefore to focus on children in convenient settings where it is possible to film their responses to certain stimuli or to a play task that bears on the research question; the filmed behaviour then becomes the focus of study. If, however, the researcher has been influenced by the work of the Russian psychologist Vygotsky, the filmed sequence may include the child's mother, teacher or other adult. This difference in the conditions of the experimental situation reflects a difference in developmental theory; in the latter case, the researcher may be interested in understanding what Vygotsky called 'the zone of proximal development'. This developmental domain is created by the way that, at any given time, adult interventions explicitly or implicitly address the gap between a child's present knowledge and its potential knowledge. Via observation the child internalises what an adult is saying and/or doing and in the process arrives at a greater depth of understanding. This idea has obvious implications for any study of how people become who they are, but it is just as obvious from an anthropological perspective that this same study demands participant observation as its primary method, a matter I return to below.

Vygotsky's contribution to our understanding of how people become who they are lies primarily in his insistence that language, considered as the symbolic form par excellence, is rooted in historically specific material relations between people.[16] His observations concerning the functional implications of speech in infants and young children led him, in 1934, to argue that:

> Words and other signs are those means that direct our mental operations, control their course, and channel them toward the solution of the problem confronting us.
>
> ...
>
> Real concepts are impossible without words, and thinking in concepts does not exist beyond verbal thinking. That is why the central moment in concept formation, and its generative cause, is a specific use of words as functional 'tools'.
>
> (1986: 106–107)

Vygotsky made considerable use of a distinction between what is 'natural' or 'biological' and what is 'sociohistorical' or 'cultural'; thus he believed that because the child's initial use of language is directed towards communication with another, it is language that transforms the child from a natural into a cultural being.

> Every function in the child's cultural development appears twice: first, on the social level, and later, on the individual level: first, *between* people (*interpsychological*), and then *inside* the child (*intrapsychological*). This applies equally to voluntary attention, to logical memory, and to the formation of concepts. All the higher functions originate as actual relations between human individuals.
>
> ...
>
> The internalisation of cultural forms of behavior involves the reconstruction of psychological activity on the basis of sign operations.
>
> (1978: 57)

Internalisation is not, however, a matter of 'received meaning', rather Vygotsky maintained that 'it goes without saying that internalisation transforms the process itself and changes its structure and functions' (1981a: 163, quoted in

Wertsch and Stone 1985). Moreover, he observed that during the early years of the child's use of its native language, 'The child's and the adult's meanings of a word often "meet", as it were, in the same concrete object, and this suffices to ensure mutual understanding' (1986: 111).[17] From an anthropological perspective, this is an immensely useful insight because, of course, it can apply just as much to communicative exchanges between adults as it does to those between children and adults – especially when those adults have significantly different histories, for example, an Australian and a Fijian or, within a particular language group, a man and a woman or people of different class and/or regional backgrounds. No doubt we have none of us to think very hard to remember numerous experiences of the way that agreement on reference to objects, processes and visceral experiences such as hunger, anger or jealousy can be mistaken for agreement on meaning.

From my point of view 'internalisation' is not a useful term because it too easily implies (contra Vygotsky's own view) that knowledge or meaning is received. Because every child has itself to make meanings anew, and because meanings are transformed in the very process of being conserved, I prefer to talk of constituting meaning or of making sense. The key point here, however, is that if as anthropologists we can show in what respects the child's meanings differ from the adult's, and chart the transformations through which the child arrives eventually at a complexly nuanced understanding of what adults mean by what they say, this analysis will have profound implications for our own understanding of how history informs the processes in and through which the manifold forms of human intentionality are constituted. Or, in other words, it will enable us to show how the process of constituting meaning over time itself produces, for any one of us, an abiding sense that the world conforms to our understanding of it.

The phenomenology of learning

Participant observation will have to be the primary method for such studies because, given that it is adults who structure the conditions in which children live, the researcher must also be gathering data on relations between adults and the world as they live it. As I pointed out above, adults cannot have access to how they came to know what they know. And given that what they are able to articulate is founded in what is taken for granted, the meaning of what adults say goes well beyond what they can make explicit. So, for example, a study of white, middle-class American children's ideas of personhood and social relations would require not only a long period of participant observation in suitable settings such as pre-school and elementary school (where teachers and auxiliary staff as well as children would be the object of study), but a lot of contact with their parents, a lot of television viewing, a lot of hanging out in people's houses, a lot of eating in fast-food restaurants and so on. In other words, in order to understand the conditions lived by the children, the researcher would have to gather extensive data on adults' practices and their ideas of the person and relations between people and, as good ethnography demonstrates over and over again, the interview method is not adequate for this purpose.

Extended participant observation is essential even if I the researcher am a white, middle-class American, because only systematic participant observation, and the discipline of writing field notes that it entails, is capable of revealing to me what I myself take for granted. In such a case, to be able to lay bare what is taken for granted and to ground one's analysis there requires, for example, *systematic* data on the way that relations between people are projected into the spatiotemporal dimensions of their lives and made concrete in the rhythm of the day as this is lived in one's own house and the houses of one's friends and neighbours, in the streets along which we drive, in the classrooms and gym and playground of the children's schools, in the shopping malls, the church and so on. The embodied understanding of a certain spatiotemporal dimension as given in the conditions of existence is an aspect of the taken-for-granted that is fundamental to ideas of person and collectivity. How, exactly, it is constituted over time and in the process informs our ideas of the world, ourselves, other people and human relations requires, for example, that one map the layout of these different spaces and the objects in them and, throughout the period of participant observation, record how they are used by children and adults and what they have to say, in passing, about what they're doing, and the spaces where they are. One has also to pay careful attention to the ritualised behaviour that characterises day-to-day life – for example, greetings and politeness; the conduct of meals; hospitality of various kinds; birthday parties; the conduct of staff and children at school and the etiquette appropriate to relations between them, between peers of various ages, and between children of different ages; Halloween, Christmas Day, Thanksgiving and so on.

Towards the end of a year or so of participant observation, these accumulated data will enable the researcher to begin to see what should be the focus of diagnostic tasks with a balanced sample of children of different ages (from say, 3 to 12 years old) and of interviews with their parents and teachers. Note however, that these diagnostic tasks and interviews are not designed with a hypothesis in mind; they are designed in the hope that they will reveal aspects of children's and adults' ideas and the process of their understanding that have not, previously, been obvious to the researcher.

Thus interviews with adults will be largely unstructured and open-ended; they might propose, for example, a topic such as what the interviewee likes and dislikes about his or her neighbourhood or how they think children should be reared and educated, their views on abortion and/or assisted conception, or why it's important to observe Christmas and other holidays. A content analysis of these interviews will not only reveal a particular idea of person, sociality and kinship, but may also bring to light, for example, a perspective on political economy that conflicts with the same interviewees' overt opinions on democracy. Children might be asked, for example, to 'draw where you live' and subsequently asked to 'tell me about your drawing' or, if they are literate, to label their drawing or write a story about what it depicts. (Note that children's drawing is not a useful research tool unless it is supplemented with the children's own accounts of the various features of what they have drawn.) A content analysis of these drawings and the children's commentary on them is likely to reveal not only how children's ideas of 'where I live' are transformed over time, but are also how they implicate ideas of the person and social relations.

Thus, in this imaginary case, a year to fifteen months' research should produce richly complex and varied data from long and careful participant observation, systematic interviews with adults and older children on various topics, and the systematic use with younger children of a number of different diagnostic tasks that bear on ideas of the person and social relations. The resulting ethnographic analysis of these data should be able to lay bear the concrete logic of adults' and children's ideas of person and sociality and show how exactly it is made material in the spatiotemporal dimensions of their day-to-day lives, there to be continually constituted anew by each succeeding generation, and in the process at once maintained and transformed. It should show in what respects the children's ideas differ from each other and from those of adults; these differences may well be unforeseen and, if they follow a particular pattern, are likely to make a significant difference to the analysis. It should reveal any reliable features of the constituting process – particular stages for instance, or gender – and how it is that the oldest children in the sample (i.e. those around 12) have come to hold ideas that are closer to those of adults' than to those of 5-year-olds. In sum, it should be able to reveal what ideas of person, kinship and collectivity are held by a certain population of middle-class white Americans and how these ideas come to be taken for granted as, by and large, given in the nature of human being.

Only this kind of study is capable, I would argue, of revealing the microhistory of how people come to be who they are, how they come to embody the ideas and practices of which they appear to be the product. The empirical validity of such research rests not on assertions of its objectivity, but in its capacity to reveal in any given case the complexity of the constituting process, and how it produces the taken-for-granted. So, in the imaginary case of research into middle-class, white Americans' ideas of the person, kinship and collectivity, the study is likely to have profound implications for the development of theory in the human sciences. Our notion that the world is objectively given to us is not peculiar to ourselves; everyone, everywhere thinks the same – the problem being of course that what is objectively given for example, for a white, middle-class Londoner may not be what is objectively given for a black middle-class Londoner, and this in spite of their easy agreement on reference. And both would be likely to reject as entirely unwarranted a great deal of what is objectively given to say, a Bimin Kuskusmin or Kashinaua person.

Conclusion

This introductory chapter has argued for a theoretical synthesis that allows us to understand that *mind is a function of the whole person that is constituted over time in inter-subjective relations with others in the environing world*. This model is, I argue, good for anthropologists because it has at its core a perspective on humans as at once products and producers of history. And because transformation and continuity are intrinsic to it, this model is a good basis too for our attempts to understand other peoples and their different responses to, for example, the various forms of colonisation. By the same token, we can use it to understand ourselves and the historical specificity of our own models of human being and how their conti-nuity is an aspect of their transformation.

My imaginary ethnographic examples have by and large concerned ourselves – a rhetorical device that is intended to emphasise that the model of human being we use has to be as good for understanding ourselves as it is for under-standing others. My own fieldwork, however, has been carried out entirely in the chiefly *vanua* (country) of Sawaieke, on the island of Gau, central Fiji. The ethnographic questions explored in the various essays that follow led me, by degrees, to the point where I felt it necessary to propose the model suggested above. Or, to put it another way, my attempts to answer the questions that arose out of long and repeated participant observation have, over the years, brought me ever closer to understanding how it is that I and the Fijian villagers with whom I work come to be remarkably similar to one another in the ways we are different, and wonderfully different in the ways we are the same.

Part I

OBJECTIFYING HISTORY,
MATERIAL MIND

My introductory essay above attempts to resolve theoretical problems which have nagged at me since first I became conscious of them during the postgraduate qualifying year that converted me from a psychologist to an anthropologist, and which crystallised during the writing of my doctoral dissertation – completed in 1986. At any given time – both then and later – what I was writing focused on an attempt to understand the ideas and practices that inform everyday life in Sawaieke and in so doing to gain a degree of access to my own taken-for-granted. All three essays in this first part provide examples of how the knowledge that is a product of mind is made material in practices like *yaqona*-drinking, in objects such as tapestry reproductions of 'The Last Supper', in the very land itself. In this process history is rendered objective by virtue of its instantiation in the concrete – a process that itself suggests that 'the real and the symbolic are aspects of one another.

As will become clear to the reader of the essays in this volume, my understanding of life in Sawaieke has shifted with the years – a shift I attribute in part to the way new data gathered during additional field-trips threw up new questions and in part to an increasing awareness of what ethnography can contribute to human knowledge. As a scientist, I am interested in explanation. Fijians do not need me to interpret them to the world; should they see any need for this they are well able to do it themselves. But I have reason to be grateful to Sawaieke people, because they let me be a participant observer in their midst and so gather the material that would allow me to provide an empirical demonstration of how it is that people come to be enchanted, as Bourdieu would say, by an idea they themselves have made – in this case, the Fijian idea that hierarchy is a principle of social relations.

The reader who recoils at the mere thought of 'an empirical demonstration' is perhaps owed a brief explanation here and this is easiest done via a little auto-biographical detour. I was spared the post-modernist crisis – in part because I was fortunately in the field from 1981 until 1983 when the eye of the storm passed over UK anthropology departments and in part because the analytical

23

problems that precipitated it had been the focus of intense informal discussion *outside* the classroom among pre-fieldwork graduate students in the LSE in the early 1980s. Neither I nor any of my peers went into the field as naïve empiricists. We knew that any answers we found would be a function of the questions we asked and that the questions we asked were our own product and *as such* a product of our personal and collective history. But we did think that anthropology – i.e. 'the whole science of man' – was possible. We did think that ethnography could claim to be explanation and that some explanations were demonstrably better than others. It was a question of how we were to deal with history, and not just other people's history, but our own. In my own case it became ever more plain that the challenge was to derive a model of human being that was as good for explaining me and my certainties about the world as it was for explaining the others and their, perhaps very different, certainties.

It is worth noting that the influential post-modernist texts in anthropology were produced by people who did their graduate work in the late 1960s and early 1970s and who either then or later lost faith in the positivist tradition in which they had been educated and in whose spirit they had, presumably, carried out all their early work. The existential crisis to which this loss of faith gave rise seems, by and large, to have resulted either in a new positivism (tending to be ever more abstracted from the rigours of fieldwork and to take a cognitivist form) or in an attempt to persuade a younger generation that ethnography is the art and ethics of 'writing culture'. Indeed it seems to me that the crux of the problem for a number of this senior generation was that they at once relinquished the positivist dogma and held to it in their hearts – a form of bad faith that has proved disastrous for those who came into anthropology from the late 1980s onwards and were led to believe that interpretation (itself held to be impossible except as a kind of art form) was the only justification for ethnography. My peers and I were lucky enough to have more inspiring objects of intellectual interest, in particular Marilyn Strathern's *The Gender of the Gift* which, still in manuscript form, was the focus of a near- and post-doctoral reading group in the LSE some time around 1987.

To return then, to my own work. The essays here are more or less adequate, empirically based, explanations of how Fijians become who they are; they are all founded on systematic fieldwork and they all have as background the data and analysis I produced in my doctoral dissertation, later edited and published (in 1990) as *Making Sense of Hierarchy: Cognition as Social Process in Fiji*. The first two essays in this part were written while I was still in the throes of my dissertation, and revised for publication shortly after it was finished. At this time I was still mired in a distinction between the real and the symbolic and so, when Fijians told me that clan chiefs are above others and therefore always – even in reference to a single plane – seated above others who, in any gathering, both sit below them and face upwards towards them, I interpreted this in my own mind as 'symbolic above/below' and used single quotes around 'above', 'below' and 'upwards' to indicate their symbolic status. (Single quotes are fine, of course, to indicate that one is quoting or translating an indigenous term; it's another matter, however, when they are used to suggest that people don't really mean what they say.) I felt uneasy about this usage, but held to it in part because, given that Fijians also used the terms above and below to distinguish between *different* planes, it seemed to me they must be making the same kind of distinction that I was making myself between the real and the symbolic or the literal and the metaphorical. Nowadays I would use the data in these first two essays to show how the material and the ideal, the real and the symbolic, the literal and the metaphorical are, in each case, aspects of one another. In other words, while I would hold to the data themselves and to the explanatory core of each analysis, each paper would be in itself both more coherent and phenomenologically more sound.

Here the important thing to note is that my endeavour in each case would be to find out what happens, as it were, when one *really sticks to* the terms in which Fijians talk about their lives and the world they live. This is emphatically *not* to argue that the people with whom one works are better at analysing their own lives than any anthropologist. After all, this is not their project – they live their lives and by and large are not concerned to produce a social analysis of what they live. But by the same token, if someone tells you, for example, that one transaction involving money is a gift and that another, in your view remarkably similar, transaction is payment, it makes sound ethnographic sense to credit what you're told. So, for example, in 'Drinking cash' I should no longer argue that the ideal contrast between the Fijian and the European ways 'does not reflect an empirical reality'; instead I should show how this distinction is warranted by the lived experience of Sawaieke villagers and how it can be understood as a transformation of historically earlier ideas that was mediated by the Fijian colonial encounter, whose manifold features were assimilated to the existing structures of Fijian dualism. In so doing I should hold hard, however, to what might some might take to be a now superseded structural analysis. As will become plain, especially in Part III, Fijians are thorough-going dualists; indeed, in elaborating his own ideas of structural transformation Lévi-Strauss made frequent use of Hocart's data on Fiji. Moreover, as is clear in Peter Gow's study of transformations in Amazonian responses to historical contingency, a structural analysis is inevitably an analysis of historical transformation. See Gow (forthcoming, and related works 1989 and 1991).

I leave it to the reader to spot other points where these first two papers clash with the model of mind I proposed in my introduction – the third paper in this section being rather more closely in line with it.

It will be apparent that I am not sympathetic to the notion that ethnography is the outcome of a 'dialogical process'; in my view this would be the case only were I working with a Fijian anthropologist and the two of us were constantly talking things through and writing papers together – a crucial point here being that each of us could then claim the same academic credit. Any ethnographic endeavour entails making other people the object of one's gaze and there is little point in adopting cosmetic methods that pretend otherwise. On the other hand, one has a duty to check whether what one has written makes any sense to the people one is writing about – which is not to say they have to agree with every-thing one writes. In my own case I have been content, for example, to hear two Fijians arguing with one another as to whether or not I was justified in making certain inferences about chiefship out of my field data – one being for my anal-ysis and another against and neither one disagreeing with the data themselves. On the other hand, it is wonderful to receive whole-hearted approbation as when a Fijian Methodist minister, having read 'Making the present ... ' told me that it should be set as required reading for students in all Fijian Methodist training colleges.

1

DRINKING CASH

The purification of money through ceremonial exchange in Fiji

Many times during the eighteen months of my fieldwork in the village of Sawaieke on the island of Gau, Central Fiji, I listened to one or other of my hosts champion *na i vakarau ni bula vakaViti*, 'the Fijian way of life' which he or she contrasted with *na i vakarau ni bula vakailavo se vakavavalagi*, 'a way of life in the manner of money or in the European way'. Virtually all Fijian villagers remark on this contrast to visiting Europeans and they do so in an entirely predictable way. The speech below is that of the elderly man who, in the early months of my fieldwork, gave me lessons in Fijian:

> The Fijian way of life is good eh? Nothing is paid for. If you want to eat there are many kinds of food available – taro, cassava, chestnuts, yams, green vegetables, pawpaw, pineapples. The food's not paid for, it is just given. You are hungry? Yes. Fine. Come and eat, come and eat here. Come here and eat fish. You want to drink? Fine, come and drink *yaqona* here. Should a guest come here we look after him. If he wants something it is given to him at once. It is not paid for. No, not at all. This is the Fijian way, the chiefly way, the way according to kinship. Kinship and life in the manner of kinship are good things – there are never any problems. No, not at all. But it is different with you Europeans. Everything is paid for. You all live alone, each family by itself. Not one of your kin is nearby. They are perhaps far away. With us kinship is the most important thing of all, for you it is not.

This succinct statement of an enduring ideal contrasts 'giving' with 'payment'. What is given is food and *yaqona* (*piper methysticum* whose ground root is infused in water to make the mildly intoxicating, but non-alcoholic, drink that is called kava elsewhere in the Pacific) and the giving is made identical with Fijian tradition. So 'the way according to kinship' and 'the chiefly way' are made antithetical to 'the European way' by which kinship is not valued and everything is paid for. The Fijian way is conceived of as highly moral and ordered, the European way as amoral and without order – an association of strangers. Here, by implication, an assertion of the overriding value of money results in the alienation of one's kin.

However, this ideal contrast does not reflect empirical reality; it ignores the practical organisation of contemporary village life in Fiji and denies historical change. The Fijian village economy is a mixed cash and subsistence economy.[1] Villagers today want a secondary education for their children, a Western-style house, furniture, radios and so on. In addition every family needs money to buy a variety of commodities in standard use and to meet their obligations in respect of village funds. The money for these wants is obtained, for the most part, from the sale of cash crops. Moreover, villagers have to engage in monetary transactions with each other – buying and selling, paying for food and other items and even sometimes for labour. *Yaqona* is an important commodity and *yaqona*-drinking too has taken on a modern form – one that reflects profound historical change rather than an unalterable tradition. Nevertheless, villagers are able, with justice, to assert their ideals as reality, even in the face of these apparent contradictions. How they manage to do so is the subject of this chapter.

The gift and the status quo

My teacher's speech does not suggest that there is anything wrong, in itself, with money. Rather, it is money as symbolic of a commodity exchange that is seen as antithetical to the Fijian way. Villagers make a sharp distinction between an ideal commodity exchange, which assumes the independence (and thus a notional equality) of transactors, and an ideal gift exchange, which assumes a relation between them. This distinction is *not* an empirical one; rather it depends on the construction that may be placed on any given transaction. This construction should not challenge the high moral value attached to the recognition of proper social relations 'in the manner of the land'. In other words, the notion of the gift is essential for the maintenance of a status quo that is supposed to depend upon a set of part-ascribed, part-achieved traditional statuses that everyone recognises and accepts.

In the traditional status quo in the chiefly village of Sawaieke the chiefs of ranked clans (*yavusa*) hold sway over their own clan and, to a lesser extent, over villages that are traditionally subject to it.[2] These chiefs are the focus of exchange processes in the kinship/gift economy. Thus one can, to a great extent, map differential status onto differential access to various forms of labour and produce.[3] Clan ranking is ambiguous in that, while everyone believes the clans and the lineages (*mataqali*) within them to be ranked in accordance with their traditional tasks *vakavanua* ('in the manner of the land'), people differ as to the precise order of this ranking according to their view of the place of their own clan within it.[4]

The rank of one's clan is important for one's personal status within the community and interacts with two other equally dominant principles: seniority and gender. These latter principles structure hierarchical kinship relations within the domestic group.[5] The term for kin, *veiwekani*, subsumes affines and friends as well as consanguines; ideally all Fijians are kin to one another. With the exception of the relation between cross-cousins *all* kinship relations are hierarchical. The equality of cross-cousins poses an implicit threat to the assertion of hierarchy as identical with social order. However, this threat is effectively de-fused by the fact that, when two cross-cousins marry (and by definition all marriages are between cross-cousins) the equality between them gives way to the axiomatic hierarchy of husband over wife. In effect this means that kinship hierarchy is able to contain the equality of cross-cousins by subordinating it to the hierarchy of the domestic group. Thus hierarchy is dominant in 'the way according to kinship' which is itself synonymous with 'the Fijian way'.[6]

This traditional organisation is maintained in the face of both governmental aid programmes to encourage village development and individual as well as co-operative businesses, and of people's own desires for manufactured items – desires that in the fulfilling bring people of necessity into the monetary economy and thus into market relations with one another.

The process by which an apparently traditional status quo is maintained in spite of radical changes in village politico-economy during the past 150 years is in essence an uncomplicated one. Fundamentally it consists in a constant reiteration of a clear conceptual distinction between commodity exchange and gift exchange, while simultaneously allowing for the incorporation of money and commercial products into gift exchanges. Money is the primary symbol of commodity exchange, *yaqona* the primary symbol of gift exchange among the community of kin; their meaning as antithetical symbols is examined below.[7]

The ideal distinction between gift and commodity

For Fijians the moral value of money changes according to the construction they place on transactions in which it is included. Money has a neutral, moral value in explicit commodity exchanges because such exchanges are considered irrelevant to the creation, fulfilment or maintenance of social bonds. It is good in a gift exchange because, like any other gift, it marks the continuing obligations between kin. Money becomes problematic only when its exchange threatens to confuse the ideal distinction between commodity and gift and thus to call into question existing social relations. In other words, monetary transactions must not be allowed to confuse the social relations of the market with social relations 'in the manner of the land'.

In any exchange that is understood to come within the ambit of the traditional, one cannot simply pay for a service rendered as if service and payment described the sum total of the social situation. This became apparent to me very early on in my fieldwork in that people absolutely refused to state a monetary value for their services. This was so even when it was clear that they expected payment and had a definite idea of how much that payment should be, but in all cases where I was clearly obliged to make payment, I also had to decide on its amount. I was living with a family – how much was I to pay them for food and rent? I had to decide this for myself because our relationship could not be defined impersonally in terms of landlord and tenant (i.e. as a market relation-ship). Rather, it was defined at the outset as traditional in that I was accepted into their family: it was they who ceremonially presented a *tabua* (whale's tooth) to the chiefs on my behalf and thus publicly affirmed my incorporation into their lineage and into the community. As a quasi-family member then, I was expected to contribute according to my status and my means and not merely to pay a fixed weekly sum for food and shelter.

My teacher, the elderly man mentioned above, refused to be paid daily or weekly for the lessons he gave me, but this did not mean that he refused money. Rather, what was required of me was that I hand over the money at irregular intervals in such a way that it looked like a gift that reciprocated his own gift – that of teaching me. I would hand over the money saying, 'This is just a small thing by way of thanking you for all your help to me' and then would ensue an exchange of thanks in which each of us tried to outdo the other. This minor ritual effectively asserted that our relationship was not entirely encompassed by saying that I paid him money to teach me; it was not an impersonal payment calculated against his labour. Instead, he was helping me and I was showing my appreciation.

In other words, what we would see as commodity transactions are made to take the form of gift. So a woman who pays others to make mats for her invites them to her house, presides over the *yaqona* bowl and compliments them on their work. When she pays over the money, it is a reciprocal gesture in acknowledge-ment of their labour. This transaction does not preclude the possibility, on another occasion, of the same services being performed by and for the same people as part of a gift exchange that does not involve money. The transactors are explicitly recognised as kin and the exchange is seen as an expression of the continuing obligations obtaining between them. As we shall see below, traditional forms of exchange vary according to the relative status of the parties involved.

There are many occasions, large and small, when exchange takes place. The big occasions include all major events in the life cycle, as well as occasions that require some material acknowledgement of gratitude or pleasure as when a group of people visit one of their senior kin in the same or a different village who has recently recovered from a serious illness. Money may be incorporated into all of these exchanges – usually in the form of store-bought goods. Large-scale formal exchanges take place too on grand fund-raising occasions where, for instance, the object might be to raise enough money to build a new church. Then all those one-time villagers who now live in Suva, Levuka, Sigatoka and other towns and who, on a day-to-day basis, might be said to live their lives 'in the manner of money' are invited *en masse* to the village during the Christmas/New Year holiday season. They are expected to give large sums of money and are looked after, feasted, and sent on their way with many mats, whale's teeth and such-like items derived from the subsistence economy, when the days of celebration are over.

One who refuses to take part in such a *soli* or 'giving' is failing publicly to avow a link with the village. In any public fund-raising the amount given by each person or family is noted down and read out to those assembled and any derelictions are noticed and become the subject of criticism. This is true for all money gifts – from the weekly contributions every Sunday in church to those made to school or village. Any large donation is always a public affair: one should be seen to give and those of highest status to give the most. The idea of an anonymous donation is absurd in Fiji where all instances of giving mark the fulfilment of a recognised obligation to one's kin and incur obligations from the receivers. If the giving is generous it can increase one's status in the community and guarantee ones ability to mobilise a large labour force on occasions that require it, e.g. when one builds a new house or marries a child.

One who is covetous (*dau kocokoco*) may attempt to manipulate the conceptual separation between commodity exchange and gift exchange by pretending that it means that money is irrelevant in the village economy. He or she uses the rhetoric whereby in the village 'nothing is paid for' and pretends that the economy is entirely a subsistence one. This is not tolerated for it is not only a clear failure to fulfil one's obligations, but an insult to the intelligence as well. Thus I once heard a woman criticise the behaviour of her elder sister from Suva who, on a visit to the village, exploited her younger sibling's labour and food resources without making any return:

> She thinks I'm crazy. She comes here, brings her children here: 'Oh village life is good, I'm tired of the town.' Yes, it's good for her. She's sharp. She doesn't bring a thing with her: no flour, no food for her children to eat. No money. She says she's sick, she can't work. Only I can. Her children want to eat, they cry out. Only I am doing the cooking. When I ask her for money to go and buy flour there is no cash. But I know she has plenty of money. Her husband is a good man, always gives her money. She thinks I'm stupid. Enough of cooking and washing, I'm not crazy. I refuse.

Despite the overwhelming importance of the gift, certain common transactions are constructed as explicit commodity exchanges. However, such exchanges are in effect relegated to a context symbolically outside the village. Thus, co-operative stores tend to be located on the boundaries of villages and one who sells tomatoes or fish (a relatively rare event since most locally produced foods are not sold) does so at the roadside – not so much because people are passing, but rather because this is the only appropriate place for explicit commodity exchanges.

Money is neutral in what is constructed as an explicit commodity exchange because the kin relation between transactors is ideally seen as irrelevant. While certain commodity exchanges (e.g., payment for mat-making) are routinely transformed into gift exchanges, it is nevertheless considered immoral to confuse the two types of transaction. Thus the behaviour of those who try to exploit a close

31

kin tie with a store manager is frowned on and said to be shameful; it is considered out of place. This is apparently because it attempts to make kin relations relevant to an exchange which, by definition, assumes the independence of transactors. The ideal commodity transaction does not carry forward. If one runs up too large a debt in the village store, credit is simply cut off and the debt published. Such transactions do not disrupt social bonds even though the creditor's debt to the village co-operative is a debt to the village itself. The fact that the store depends for its success on a recognition of obligation to one's kin at large is not acknowledged, because exchanges there are not considered to be 'in the manner of the land'. Being unable to clear one's debt to the store may place one in a somewhat onerous position, but the matter is not particularly a subject for criticism as is failure to contribute to the funds for the church or the village school – these being considered to be 'traditional' obligations.

It should be apparent from the above that, from the analyst's point of view, the distinction between gift exchange and commodity exchange is often artificial. One can easily view the exchange of labour for money as an intrusion of the market economy and as part of 'the way in the manner of money' or, conversely, see the co-operative store as dependent upon notions of traditional obligations and 'the Fijian way'. However, villagers construct an ideal separation between commodity and gift exchange that allows them to behave as if the distinction between the two 'ways' is unambiguous.

Within the village, people tend to privilege gift exchange over commodity exchange – most exchanges are constructed as gift. This is essential if the gift is to retain its power as a constitutive element in hierarchical kin relations. It is the possible ultimate triumph of market relations that makes payment potentially undermining: if 'the European way' were in force, then all social relations would be determined by the market where transactors are presumed to be independent and equal, everything is paid for and one's kin are 'far away'. So it is the market relationship that is resisted by ceremonial exchange which invariably divests money of any moral neutrality and places it firmly within the context of tradition.

I use the term ceremonial exchange very broadly here to cover all exchanges that are accompanied – as it were compulsorily – by ritual formulae, be they of the order of the small but effusive exchange of thanks and self-denigration that regularly accompanied my handing over any money to my teacher, or of the ritual speeches of the imposing *solevu* on the occasion of an arranged marriage or a big fund-raising drive. The construction of the symbolic opposition between market relations and traditional relations, between ideal societies 'in the manner of money' and 'in the manner of kinship', and the substitution of the highly valued morality of gift exchange for the neutral morality of commodity exchange, is nowhere more clearly seen than in the way in which *yaqona* and money are allowed to move against each other. As will be seen below, notions about *yaqona* and the behaviour appropriate to its use are crucial for the construction of the traditional side of the symbolic contrast between 'the Fijian way' and 'the European way'.

Yaqona as gift and tribute

The *yaqona* ceremony and the *sevusevu* – or presentation of the roots of the plant – are the central rituals of Fijian social life. The centrality of *yaqona*-drinking is such that the arrangement of persons in relation to one another as they sit on the mat around the *tanoa* (the large bowl in which the ground root is infused in water and from which it is served) provides an image of a hierarchical society ordered according to an interaction between principles of rank, seniority and gender.

No matter how informal the occasion, persons of the highest status sit in a semi-circle 'above' the *tanoa* – which is so designed that one side may be designated that which 'faces the chiefs' – while those of lower status sit 'below' it, facing the chiefs. The seating position that is called 'above' is defined by its being the place of chiefs, the position 'below' by its being the place of women. This mode of drinking *yaqona* is understood to be *vakavanua* (traditional), and eminently Fijian, in spite of the fact that people are aware that, historically, women and young men were not permitted to drink *yaqona* at all. Women were actually excluded from *yaqona*-drinking groups, while young men were allowed only to prepare and serve the drink to older men, that is, to those classified as *turaga*. This term refers specifically to chiefs but is also used to cover all married men. The image of an ordered and stratified society exemplified in people's positions relative to one another around the *tanoa* is one that is encountered virtually every day in the village of Sawaieke.

Yaqona is prepared by squeezing the pounded root through water to produce a pleasant and slightly astringent brew; on formal occasions the very gestures of the man preparing the drink are highly ritualised and orchestrated by a traditional chant given out by the men. Once the drink is prepared it is served in bowls of polished half-coconut shells one after another to the assembled people according to their position in the social hierarchy, with the highest-status person present being served first. *Yaqona* is drunk on all social occasions ranging from half-a-dozen men getting together for an afternoon or evening of chat around the *tanoa*, through occasions requiring community labour as when a house is built or pandanus stretched to make mats, at all ceremonies attendant upon life-cycle events, as well as during the grand and lengthy ceremonial mounted to install a chief or to welcome a high chief.

When a chief is installed it is the presentation to him within the appropriate ritual context of the chiefly bowl of *yaqona* under the aegis of the chief of that clan that is said to be able to 'make the chief', that actually gives him the 'real power', that is, the spiritual power that confirms and entrenches the political power inherent in the position when he was only designated high chief but had not yet been properly installed. Once he has drunk the chiefly *yaqona* his every command must be fulfilled on pain of his mystical power causing illness to those who fail to do their duty; a high chief does not will this punishment, it simply occurs because *sa tu vei ira na sau*, the command (or prohibition) is his, i.e. has become as it were intrinsic to him and mystically effective so that his will is simply asserted since no dereliction of duty can be concealed from one who now has the powers of a god.

The *sevusevu*, the ceremony that precedes or accompanies the drinking of *yaqona*, involves the presentation of a bundle of *yaqona* roots, or, on grander occasions, an entire uprooted *yaqona* plant six feet or more in length. Essentially the *sevusevu* is a form of tribute to chiefs that, once presented and accepted, confers on those who present it the freedom of the place where they are and entails obligations of hospitality etc. from those who accept it. Thus, one always takes a *sevusevu* when going to another village or, within one's own village, when one wishes to join a group of people who are already drinking. Similarly, if one wishes to ask someone a favour, the use of land or the right to name a child perhaps, or to beg forgiveness for a fault committed, raising one's hand against one's father or one's wife for example, then one asks a senior man to present *yaqona* on one's behalf with a speech that asks the favour or begs forgiveness, and in the acceptance and the subsequent drinking the favour is granted or the fault buried. It should be apparent from this that the *sevusevu*, while always performed, may consist on informal occasions of a few ritual phrases of acceptance, this being a highly attenuated form of the full ceremony where speeches are made by both givers and receivers.

The drinking of *yaqona* being, for Fijian villagers, an act that both expresses and in part constitutes a particular and ritually defined social order, it follows that to accuse someone of drinking *yaqona* alone is to accuse that person of witchcraft. Only one who is intent upon evil magic would prepare and drink *yaqona* alone behind closed doors. By pouring out the first bowl as a libation to one's original ancestor god or *kalou vu* and drinking the second bowl oneself, one summons the god to one's aid and is tested by having to select one of one's nearest kin as first victim to the god's death-dealing power. That person having died one is then able, in subsequent lonely *yaqona* rituals, to ask for aid in acquiring riches, sexual magnetism of an utterly irresistible kind, or whatever else it is that one wants. In pouring out the first bowl as a libation to the god and drinking the second, one places oneself in a position analogous to that of a chief's *matanivanua* (executive, lit. the face of the land), who is traditionally the mouthpiece of the chief in transmitting his orders to the people and has his ear for the asking of favours – a position that traditionally entailed real political and economic power.

Yaqona is a necessary and essential form of gift and/or tribute. However, the conceptual separation between gift exchange and commodity exchange and the importance of *yaqona* ritual has not interfered with the incorporation of *yaqona* into the market economy. Rather it is the source of its status as a valuable commodity. In the last ten to twelve years or so *yaqona* has become an important cash crop.

Nevertheless, the two statuses of *yaqona* as gift/tribute on the one hand and commodity on the other are generally kept as far apart from one another as possible. In *sevusevu* one gives *yaqona* as if its status as commodity was irrelevant. No social occasion can take place without *yaqona*; moreover the obligatory nature of the *sevusevu*, together with the central importance of *yaqona*-drinking itself in constructing the traditional social order, is such that any reference to the high monetary value of the root – a comparatively recent occurrence – would probably be seen as an explicit attack on traditional values.

This is not because Fijians view references to the cost of things as ill-bred but rather because a man is expected to fulfil his obligations to kin and community and these include an adequate production of *yaqona* to meet all day-to-day drinking and ceremonial requirements. He is offering, when he presents *yaqona*, the literal fruits of his labour and any reference to the sale price of *yaqona* would be redundant. It is interesting, by contrast, to note that if *yaqona* is not available in the village store and one has no ready supply of one's own one can, on joining a group that is drinking, *sevusevu* by presenting tobacco, cigarettes, sweets or chewing gum. In this case – and especially if the amount given is large – someone almost always calculates out loud the amount spent and praises the buyer's generosity.

Its status as commodity does not mean that one cannot *kerekere yaqona* (lit. ask for *yaqona*). *Kerekere* is crucial in 'the way according to kinship' and when discussed as such the generosity it entails is usually contrasted to the profit motive in 'the European way'. *Kerekere* is a traditional means of getting hold of something one needs by simply asking for it with varying degrees of formality depending upon what the thing is and what is one's relationship to the owner. Conventionally, the owner should if at all possible, accede to the request. Not to do so is to incur disapproval. However, if the owner is unable, because of personal need, to do so, then no grudge should be borne by the one who asks. People *kerekere* anything from a little salt or a single cigarette to significant sums of money, e.g. $40 to make the return trip on the plane to Suva. One should not expect to be repaid, though sometimes the thing asked for – a spade or a cooking pot for instance – is borrowed and returned rather than kept. People say explicitly of *kerekere* that there is both an obligation to give and an obligation for the receiver to accede to some future *kerekere* on the part of the giver, that is to say a *kerekere* of a similar kind, but that this may not occur until a considerable time has passed.

Despite its being 'in the manner of the land', Fijians complain quite readily about actual instances of *kerekere* and often refuse a request if they can do so without being seen to be mean, i.e. they say they do not have any *yaqona* or salt or money etc. There is therefore a certain tension about *kerekere* that is apparent sometimes when one sees the process itself, but which never appears when people are waxing eloquent about 'true kinship' and the harmonious nature of Fijian village life.

Yaqona and money as material symbols

The symbolic contrast between an ideally moral society 'in the Fijian way' and an ideally amoral society 'in the European way' is, as we have seen, constructed around ideas of kinship, order, generosity etc. and operated by two material symbols: *yaqona* being the positive material symbol and money the negative material symbol. At the level of the symbolic construct the opposition looks like this:

yaqona	money
Fijian	European
gift/tribute	commodity
insiders	outsiders
kinship	no kinship
morality	amorality
order	lack of order
community	independence
hierarchy	equality
generosity	profit motive
traditional	new

However, neither side of this opposition corresponds to an empirical reality.[8]

Yaqona is an important commodity and money is in routine use in the village. Its immediate source is market transactions with other Fijians and with Indians, rather than with Europeans. The notion of 'the European way' is a legacy of British colonisation; however, in the current political situation in an independent Fiji, it also implicitly refers to the way of life of the large indigenous Indian community. Indians are often said both 'to have no kinship' and to be entirely conversant with 'the path of business'.[9] Moreover, the European way is in some respects regarded as entirely moral; the British queen – whose picture hangs in a place of honour in most Fijian houses – is also queen of Fiji and the highest of high chiefs. In accordance with this, Fijians often assert that the stratified order of the British aristocracy is 'the same' as their own.

Thus the village is not a closed world, nor is its economy separate from the wider monetary economy. Kinship, morality and order are not confined to 'the Fijian way' and neither is amorality excluded from it. Indeed, the ideal construct of 'the Fijian way' is not as unambiguous as it appears here, even to those who represent it in terms of the contrast described above. So my teacher, who usually made ancestral practice the precedent for everything 'in the manner of the land', also referred to the pre-colonial era as 'the time of the devils' and to Christianity as 'the light'. These very common expressions suggest that Fijians view their past as amoral, if not immoral, especially with respect to polygamy, witchcraft and cannibalism, which are said to be 'ancestral practices in the manner of the land'.[10]

Perhaps most important however is that what is understood to be most 'traditional' – and I am speaking here of ritual behaviour and particularly of *yaqona*-drinking – is in fact in continuous process of transformation. Not only has the conduct of *yaqona*-drinking itself changed in that women and young men are routinely included, but *yaqona*-drinking appears to be in the process of becoming ever more central to the image of the hierarchically ordered society.

In the past chiefs had real political and economic power, including the power of life and death over their subjects. This power was dependent on the mystical power or *mana* bestowed on any given chief by the *kalou vu* or ancestor god who was the original 'owner' of the land. The chief himself was not thought to be a direct descendant of this ancestral owner, but his own *mana* as one of a line of chiefs was greatly enhanced by virtue of his installation as high chief by those who were considered to be the jural owners of the land.[11] Today, in Sawaieke district, a paramount chief must still depend for his *mana* on proper installation in office by those who are said to be the original owners of the chiefly village of Sawaieke. However, people say that the *mana* of a paramount chief is not what it was and attribute this to their commitment to Christianity. The ancestors are still said to exist, but their power is diminished because 'no one attends on them anymore'. Moreover, in the past the relative status of *yavusa* (clan) and *mataqali* (lineage) was linked to their traditional obligations (as warriors, priests, fishermen, carpenter etc.) to chiefs. Not only have several of these categories of traditional obligation disappeared but those which are observed are a matter of ritual performance only once or twice a year. In addition, today all adults have voting rights – in the weekly meetings of the village council as well as in general elections. So, according to law, all adults are jural equals and matters concerning all should be subject to democratic processes. In the district of Sawaieke the authority that remains to contemporary chiefs and elders is constructed in ritual and largely dependent upon their pre-eminence there.

It is in this context that *yaqona*-drinking has become of central importance; indeed there is said to have been a marked increase in frequency of drinking as well as in inclusiveness of persons involved. *Yaqona*-drinking is today the prime ritual manifestation of the traditional order, where chiefs and elders are paid tribute and are seen to be above others who are seated in their due order below them. Here the imagery of *yaqona*-drinking stresses a hierarchy that depends on political, economic and spiritual inequalities that differ in kind from those that obtained in the recent historical past and at the same time effectively denies that irreversible changes have occurred. Thus 'the way in the manner of the land' is not a mere 'leftover' from an earlier era, but is itself being continuously constructed and transformed.[12]

This contemporary construction of tradition is, as we have seen, taking place over against the concurrent construction of an image of 'the European way'. The experience of the past 150 years, of colonialism, of independence, of insertion into a world-wide capitalist economy, has been drawn on to produce an ideal contrast between 'the gift' as the essence of the Fijian way and 'the commodity' as its antithesis. *Yaqona*-drinking being a crucial form of ceremonial exchange where *yaqona* is at once tribute and gift, it would seem necessary that here *yaqona* and money should be kept entirely separate from one another. In general this is so. However, there is one context in which money and *yaqona* are brought together in ceremonial exchange. This is when people gather for *gunu sede* (drinking cash).

Drinking cash

Gunu sede as opposed to ordinary, everyday *gunu yaqona* (*yaqona*-drinking) is the name given to those occasions where money is raised by buying and drinking *yaqona* together with other members of the community. This is the *only* context inside the village in which money is exchanged for a bowl of ready-prepared *yaqona*.[13]

From late March or so to early August in 1982 villagers in Sawaieke – and in other Gau villages – met once a week to *gunu sede* in order to raise enough money to send all members of the local rugby and basketball teams to Suva for the annual inter-island games. The organisation of the affair never varied. The date and time would be announced in the weekly village meeting and sometimes the village chief (an elected administrator, not a traditional chief) would remind villagers on the evening before by calling out the details as he made a round of the village during the hour of the evening meal. A certain sum was always stipulated as *yavu* – 'foundation' or 'base' – usually 50c for men and young men and 30c for women and young women, this being decided upon by all those present at the weekly village meeting.

On the evening in question one made one's way to the village hall along with a small group of one's peers, entered, sat down on the mat in a position appropriate to one's sex and status in the community relative to those already present, passed one's *yavu* across to the village treasurer, who noted the sum down against one's name in a big book and then set oneself to join in the fun, using the small store of cash one had brought in addition to one's *yavu* to promote good feeling and lots of enjoyment. *Gunu sede* is often uproarious, full of high good humour and ridiculous jokes all derived from the way one spends one's money in buying drinks for other people but *never* for oneself.[14] Several young men walk around among the assembled people holding containers in which to receive the money. They act as criers, retailing one's wishes as to who is to benefit from one's contribution and the hall resounds with announcements like this: '10c given that the mother of Pita may drink, paid for by grandfather Taniela', '20c given that those young men may drink who are looking after the *yaqona*; paid for by Jone', '40c that the gentlemen sitting above may drink; paid for by Adi Varanisese', '5c that Sosi may drink; paid for by Seru', and frequently those who have been pledged will call out in response, asking the crier to come to them: 'Here' (offering some money) 'another one for him' (or her, or whomever the donor might be).

One can, by judicious pledging of drinks set up a mock flirtation that amuses everyone, e.g. a young man and a much older married woman who are cross-cousins might exchange drink after drink in this way; or several girls might get together and one after another pledge drinks in fast succession to one shy and as yet unmarried man in order to tease him by bringing him reluctantly into the social limelight and forcing him to drink great quantities of *yaqona*. Similarly a competitive exchange can take place where a woman for instance, having pledged a bowl to a male cross-cousin who refuses it by paying to have it given back to her, then adds a further increment to the money given so that she may herself refuse to drink and have the bowl sent back again to him. The competition goes on, each adding 10c or so to the money they have pledged each time they continue to refuse to drink. One of them is bound to accept the bowl in the end – *yaqona* can never be returned to the *tanoa*. Once the sum has risen to $1 or $1.50, or even more if both parties are really flush, one of them signifies surrender by, perhaps, slapping a hand down on the mat in a highly exaggerated version of the clapping of cupped hands that always precedes one's acceptance of a bowl of *yaqona*. So a single bowl may wind up fetching $2 to $3 since each party is bound to pay out to the crier the final sum that he or she has named. There is much joking and plotting and giggling and loud laughter, with spontaneous clapping and expressions of thanks from all the onlookers when someone brings off a particularly good joke, or at the culmination of competitive payment to force the acceptance of a single bowl.

After three hours or so, everyone having spent the money they brought, the last few cents remaining to people are collected and *gunu sede* comes to an end. The names of all who contributed their *yavu* are read out together with the sum given, and the money collected from the drinking is totalled and read out. Any expenses incurred, e.g. the cost of buying the *yaqona* root from the village store, are set against the sum total raised and the final total is announced and everyone claps and thanks each other for coming, for drinking and for spending money and the evening of fun is over.

What is interesting sociologically about *gunu sede* is the way that it is acknowledged in the naming to be very different from *gunu yaqona* – one is 'drinking cash' not 'drinking *yaqona*' – and at the same time explicitly allied to it, made analogous to that central ritual of Fijian social life that, on any occasion, offers an image of an ordered and stratified society in which the participant both finds his or her own place and is confirmed in it. It will be recalled that to drink *yaqona* alone would be to lay oneself open to an accusation of witchcraft; drinking alone cannot be countenanced because the act of drinking *yaqona* is above all a social act. It follows from the centrality of the *yaqona* ceremony for the symbolising of social relations that, in the village, one can never, under any circumstances, buy oneself a bowl of *yaqona*. To buy oneself a bowl of the ready-prepared brew would be to threaten the powerful symbolism of *yaqona*-drinking with the ideal neutrality of the commodity transaction. Any act that effectively asserts neutral relations cannot be allowed to impinge on a context that demands acknowledgement of specific ranked kin relations, for it would undermine the very notion of social order. By 'drinking cash' rather than 'drinking *yaqona*', money and the exchange of money is made identical with *yaqona* and the exchange of *yaqona*. Money is not allowed to escape the kinship nexus. *Gunu sede* is an historically recent phenomenon, but it is seen as part of 'the Fijian way' and so comes within the ambit of 'tradition'.[15] In this context, to buy a bowl for oneself would constitute a symbolic severing of one's social ties in a self-referential act that denies connection to kin and community.

In *gunu sede* virtually all drinks are bought for affines and potential affines, i.e. they are bought for cross-cousins. This behaviour is inherent in the situation since it is only with one's cross-cousins that, both within and across sex, one has complete freedom of behaviour in social relations. All other relatives have to be accorded varying degrees of respect and avoidance, with avoidance being strongest between true and classificatory *veiganeni* (brothers and sisters) and true and classificatory *veivugoni* (children-in-law and parents-in-law, i.e. mother's brother, father's sister). Drinks are bought for persons classified as members of other kinship categories, but only within sex, i.e. a woman for her 'sister' and a man for his 'brother', and only rarely by comparison with buying for cross-cousins. Thus in *gunu sede* exchanges of money are made to express the bonds between affines. So money is seen to be susceptible of the same kind of treatment as any other object of exchange between them.

It might possibly be said that money is implicitly incorporated into the exchange relations between affines that are enshrined in the *vasu* relation that obtains between a person and his or her mother's brother's lineage, mother's brother being a matrilateral 'father-in-law'.[16] The junior relative or *vasu* is said to be able to take anything from the mother's brother's lineage without asking for it and without comment being made or ill-feeling aroused. When I asked if money was included here I was told that yes, it was but, as one informant remarked, 'money is not usually visible; it is usually hidden away'. The important thing to note here is that the *vasu* can take from mother's brother's lineage but cannot, because of the avoidance rule, directly ask things of his or her mother's brother. In any case, given the high degree of village exogamy, the *vasu* relation often obtains between ego and a lineage in another village, so the visibility of money in exchange between affines and potential affines could be said to be a matter of some importance. That is to say, it is not perhaps immediately apparent that money can be an exchange object as such and should be used in accordance with the conventions that govern the exchange of other objects between affines.

I concentrate here on exchange of money between affines since its circulation within the group of one's close kin is taken for granted in that one routinely benefits from money available in the domestic group or in the *tokatoka* (the smallest kinship unit beyond the domestic group) in the form of day-to-day requirements such as store-bought food etc. Again, one's obligations to the community, to one's kin at large, incorporate the giving of money in donations to the church, to community building projects and so on. Indeed a recognition of the necessity for this kind of giving – where there is no direct exchange – is made in *gunu sede* in the form of the *yavu* (base) of 30c or 50c. This term is the same as that used for the earth foundation of a house, the height of which traditionally signified the rank of the house owners, and is the root of *yavusa*, meaning 'clan'.[17] Thus the *yavu* in *gunu sede* has strong associations with very basic notions of hierarchy and kinship and the obligations that kinship entails. The giving of the *yavu* entitles one to join the group that is *gunu sede*, i.e. it is made partly analogous to a *sevusevu*. However, whether one actually drinks or not is, for those below the *tanoa* (whose status is below that of chief or elder), a matter of whether drinks are bought for one. No direct return is made on the *yavu* and so, like all other donations of this kind, it must be placed within an apparently traditional context where giving is obligatory and entails long-term and perhaps intangible returns.

In *gunu sede* money, cash, is made into an object in itself. One drinks money. That money is not literally drunk but is in fact amassed for a community purpose is not however obscured by the way *gunu sede* is organised. In 'drinking cash' a twofold recognition is made of the peculiarities of money. Firstly, that it is a store of value, has a use value and an exchange value that will translate directly from one context to another, from the kinship context of personal relations into the market context of impersonal relations; so the money raised in *gunu sede* buys tickets on the boat and covers the expenses of young people and their chaperones in Suva. Secondly, because of these qualities money has to be recognised as a viable object of gift exchange and forced into the nexus of direct exchanges between kin and, more particularly, between affines. Villagers are obliged to use money. So, to confine it to the sphere from which it originated – where brief and limited transactions take place between persons whose kin relation to one another is ideally irrelevant and money is quintessentially private property – would be to undermine kinship relations and the balance of obligations that is fundamental to the gift economy. This means that money has to be symbolically 'laundered' in ceremonial exchange and it is this purification that is achieved in *gunu sede*.

Gift, commodity and affinity

The continuous process of construction of 'the Fijian way' is clear in *gunu sede*. The context is defined as traditional but is at the same time made to contain and symbolically to resolve a number of ambiguities that are inherent in the contrast between 'the Fijian way' and 'the European way', but which are not acknowledged when people are speaking about it.

In *gunu sede* money is made into an object in itself and is exchanged for money through the medium of *yaqona*. Thus, while a twofold recognition is being made of the properties of money, it is also being made of the properties of *yaqona*. *Yaqona* is allowed to move against cash in ritual exchange and in effect this implies recognition of its status as a source of considerable sums in a market context. At the same time it is a valuable ceremonial object that as gift/tribute acknowledges the bonds between kin according to their relative positions in the traditional status quo. So, in *gunu sede* any status one has acquired as a result of holding relatively large amounts of cash is apparently outweighed by the ascribed status given by one's seating position relative to all other persons present. This apparent dominance of traditional hierarchy arises from the fact that virtually all buying is done by and for those who call each other cross-cousin and they are allowed to joke, to compete and effectively to challenge hierarchy under the circumstances of day-to-day *yaqona*-drinking as well as in *gunu sede*.

The point is that the relation between cross-cousins is a relation between equals, whatever the respective position of each party in the hierarchy given by the three-way interaction between rank, seniority and gender. Thus the cross-cousin relationship cuts across hierarchy in the sense that, for instance, a young man may joke boisterously with a woman thirty years his senior or compete in buying drinks with a chief who sits above the *tanoa*, provided he is cross-cousin to each of them. In this way the cross-cousin relationship is made to carry and symbolically to undermine any status that may be attached to control of a large sum of cash. Moreover, in. *gunu sede* traditional chiefs (*turaga ni vanua* or *na malo*), who are sitting above the *tanoa*, are served with bowls of *yaqona* at regular intervals whether or not anyone has pledged drinks for them. The image of the ordered and stratified society, in which each person knows his place and chiefs have properties and privileges that set them apart from others, is maintained. In *gunu sede* money and monetary transactions with their potential for disruption are explicitly subordinated to kinship relations, which subsume the relation between cross-cousins (i.e. between affines), within an existing status quo.

In fact, affinity is the 'hidden' third term that mediates between the contrast posed between kinship relations and market relations, between 'the Fijian way' and 'the European way'.[18] The behaviour appropriate between cross-cousins partakes of both sides of the contrast in that it is at once contained within the notion of kinship but at the same time implicitly threatens the hierarchy of kinship relations with the lack of order implicit in the joking, competitiveness and occasional hostility that is traditionally allowed between them. Again, one's cross-cousins are at once 'insiders' because they are kin and 'outsiders' because they are the only category of kin who are marriageable and because marriage is exogamous to the *mataqali* (lineage) and often to the village or to the island. Indeed, one may not be able to trace any actual kin relation to the person one marries from another island so one's affines may in effect become kin by virtue of the marriage, since by definition any married couple are cross-cousins to one another.[19]

Note that the *vasu* relation between ego and mother's brother's lineage referred to above mediates between the extreme of equality (and potential anarchy) that is allowed in the behaviour between cross-cousins and the varying degrees of respect and avoidance that govern relations between ego and all other kin. The *vasu* can traditionally take anything from mother's brother's lineage i.e., from the father of the matrilateral cross-cousins, but the *vasu*'s rights do not preclude the utmost respect and avoidance of the senior relative nor absolute obedience to his orders.[20]

Here it becomes evident that the symbolic contrast between 'the Fijian way' and 'the European way' is perhaps not so closely allied to the gift/commodity

distinction as it is made to appear. The point is that the construction of hierarchy in the traditional status quo has historically demanded a struggle to
overcome the egalitarian relations between cross-cousins. Their equality is based
in exchange relations of balanced reciprocity – a symbolic antithesis to 'tribute'.
This struggle goes on to this day; it is inherent in 'the way in the manner of
the land'.

Explicit commodity exchanges are seen as morally neutral, provided they are
kept in their place, 'outside'. They are potentially evil only in so far as they might
threaten or confuse traditional relations – hierarchical or equal – both of which
are seen as unquestionably morally correct and good in their proper conduct
within their proper limits. Just as gift exchange is not allowed to be confused with
commodity exchange, so hierarchical relations exemplified by those of chief and
commoner are not allowed to confuse, or be confused by, equal relations between
affines. Cross-cousins may joke outrageously and treat each other to bowls of
yaqona but they do this under the auspices of chiefs and do not violate the
conventions that govern hierarchical seating arrangements around the *tanoa* or
the privileges due to chiefs.

Conclusion

Three different types of social relations have emerged from the above analysis.
First, market relations, in which the transactors are conceptually independent
and equal (because the kin relation between them is ideally irrelevant), engaged
in a short-term transaction that neither confirms, denies nor creates a bond
between them. Second, hierarchical relations, exemplified by chief and
commoner where *yaqona* is given 'raw' as tribute to be disposed of by a chief,
who re-distributes it as drink that can only be accepted; this is the model for all
prestations to chiefs and for their re-distribution. Third, relations between
equals, exemplified by cross-cousins where all exchanges are equally reciprocated
and where this equality is seen both as essential for 'a good time' and as a challenge to the hierarchy that 'contains' it.

The ethnography has revealed that the symbolic contrast between money and
yaqona, the commodity and the gift, 'the European way' and 'the Fijian way'
cannot be entirely explained in terms of a reaction against colonialism and insertion into a world-wide capitalist economy. Rather, both sides of the contrast have
their historical roots in the egalitarian and hierarchical relations that together
constitute 'the way according to kinship'. This is not to say that the symbolism of
commodity and gift was always inherent in Fijian economic processes but rather
that the contemporary contrast is in part a transformation of a continuing
struggle to contain the notion of balanced reciprocity within that of tribute to
chiefs and thus to make affinity subordinate to hierarchical kinship.

So in *gunu sede* the relation between cross-cousins is made to mediate between
the positive and the negative poles of an opposition that is operated by the material symbols given by *yaqona* and money. In the process money is divested of

moral neutrality, purified of any potentially threatening associations with the market and, by being made an object of ceremonial exchange, is seen to be amenable to incorporation into what is understood to be the traditional politico-economy, such that 'the Fijian way' is seen to emerge intact from a confrontation with 'the European way' or 'the way in the manner of money'.

2

MAKING THE PRESENT, REVEALING THE PAST

The mutability and continuity of tradition as process

This article concerns the mutability of tradition. In the act of constructing the present, people may also be constructing a past with which it is continuous and in whose terms it is explicable. The question is whether this process necessarily does violence to either the present or the past. Here I argue that it need not, for what constitutes a living tradition may reveal an extra dimension to the past – one whose validity is not a matter of 'what happened' but of how it may be understood. I argue my case via an analysis of the Fijian appropriation of Leonardo da Vinci's 'The Last Supper' as a material manifestation of 'the Fijian way'. Here the apparent paradox is that images evoked by 'The Last Supper' at once bespeak the continuity of Fijian tradition and transform it. This paradox can, I argue, be resolved if we accept that the Fijian notion of tradition differs from our own.

The Fijian term for tradition and ritual as generic terms is 'acting in the manner of the land' (*cakacaka vakavanua*); it refers to a way of living and behaving that is culturally appropriate. By contrast, our normative understanding makes tradition inhere not in action but in objectified structures; it explicitly distinguishes immutable 'tradition' from processual 'history'. Recent works by Hobsbawm and Ranger (1983), Sahlins (1985) and Borofsky (1987) have brought this crude dichotomy into question. The Fijian data suggest another perspective on it: that culture-specific notions of tradition govern responses to historical change. This finding has specific implications for anthropological understanding of tradition as a historical object. I return to these matters after the analysis below.

A ubiquitous image

'Christ is the head of this household, he eats with us and overhears us.' This is a literal translation of a plaque displayed in many houses on the island of Gau, Central Fiji, where I did fieldwork in 1981–1983. Beside this plaque, on a backing of *masi* (barkcloth) hung photographs of kin and British royalty, fine *tabua* (whale's teeth) and a variety of holy pictures. By far the most popular of these was a reproduction of Leonardo da Vinci's 'The Last Supper' – usually a small version of the much larger tapestry which hung in the village church. There are sixteen Wesleyan churches on Gau – one in each village – and in each of the nine churches I visited there was a tapestry of 'The Last Supper'.

Most of the household plaques had apparently been hung many years before. The tapestries were of more recent origin. Each had been brought home from Lebanon by young men who served in the Fijian Army force in UNIFIL (United Nations Interim Forces in Lebanon) from 1978 onwards and presented as a gift to the church congregation in a soldier's natal village (i.e. to his kin at large) or to his parents or other kin.

Unfortunately I did not question the extraordinary popularity of reproductions of' 'The Last Supper' during my eighteen months in Gau. The plaque made a specifically 'Fijian' statement, but the tapestries seemed simply to testify to a devout adherence to Christianity and so I did not ask my hosts why they valued them or why they were apparently the first choice of gift by a returning soldier. Only after I returned from Fiji did the significance of the 'The Last Supper' for Fijians become problematic to me.

Fijian appropriation of 'The Last Supper' has, I argue, a special significance. Like the plaque that denotes Christ as the head of the house, it enters into construction of 'the Fijian way', of a religion 'in the manner of the land'. However, its more subtle resonance has to do with the contemporary construction of the past. The received history of conversion is of a shift from *qaravi tevoro* (devil worship, lit. facing the devil) to Christianity; it describes a radical break with the past. Against this history, the Fijian notion of tradition as 'acting in the manner of the land' makes the present flow smoothly out of the past; from this perspective 'the coming of the light' did not violate indigenous cultural practice but revealed the inherent Christianity of the Fijian people. This process of constructing the past neither denies nor distorts it. Rather it reveals a dimension to the past that historians and anthropologists have overlooked.

The argument in this article rests on an analysis of the way that images in 'The Last Supper' resonate in Fijian culture. This may seem an inappropriate means by which to illustrate the process of constructing the past. The process is not, however, and cannot be, explicit; it is manifest only obliquely in contemporary cultural practice. The form of 'The Last Supper' is an important element in this process: as a material image it gains much of its peculiar power from the fact that it does not require that anything be said.

In Leonardo's fresco, Jesus Christ faces the viewer. His calm demeanour, his centrality and the light through the window that frames his head, mark his spiritual ascendancy over his disciples who are ranged along the board on each side of him. Christ has just announced that one of them will betray him and their various attitudes express a questioning dismay. This revelation will be followed by a ritual meal at which Christ will offer his own body and blood for consumption in the form of bread and wine. (See figure 2.1.)

Figure 2.1   Tapestry reproduction of 'The Last Supper'

I show below that a series of powerful connexions can be made between 'The Last Supper' and aspects of Fijian meals; and between Christ's dispensation of the bread and wine and a Fijian chief's dispensation of kava (*yaqona*, a mildly intoxicating but non-alcoholic drink made from ground roots of *piper methysticum*). The relationship between God and Christ as his son, 'the word made flesh', may be likened to that between the ancestor gods (*kalou vu*, lit. root gods) and the paramount chief of a country (*vanua*). Here, the process by which Fijian hierarchy is ratified by transcendent power is crucial. Most important of all is the composition of 'The Last Supper'. The disposition in space of Christ and the apostles makes da Vinci's work peculiarly evocative in the Fijian context and underlies its appropriation as an ideal image of the chiefs who are the guardians of 'the Fijian way'.

Connexions of this kind may, or may not, be consciously made by the young soldiers who brought back to Fiji from Lebanon so many tapestries of 'The Last Supper'. It seems probable, for reasons I give later, that Fijians would be as likely to deny these connexions as blasphemous, as to accept them as having informed their choice of religious representation.

I begin by outlining the relevant features of Fijian history and social organisation. This entails a description of how social relations are inscribed in certain spatial constructs, and made manifest in the everyday activities of the meal at home and the communal drinking of kava. Finally I shall discuss 'The Last Supper' as an objectification of the Fijian notion of tradition.

Some historical details

Fiji was colonised in the early nineteenth century. Missionary activity, especially by Wesleyans, was extensive from 1835 onwards (Henderson 1931: 142; Clammer 1976: 12). They found a highly developed culture, for some material features of which they had high praise (e.g. Williams 1858, 1982: 60–89), but were appalled by such traditions as widespread cannibalism and the strangulation of wives to accompany a dead chief to the other world. Missionary success was conspicuous – a fact that Clammer (1976: 56–70) has attributed to their policy of establishing widespread literacy via the use of religious texts. When Cakobau, the paramount chief of Bau, was converted in 1854 missionary success was assured. His conversion came only at the point where this became politically expedient (Routledge 1985: 82–7) and led to mass conversions by his subjects. The missionary, Calvert, claimed 54,000 conversions to Wesleyanism by 1856 – i.e. one third of the population (1858: 401).

At the period of European colonisation Fiji was made up of some large confederations and a number of small chiefdoms. Consolidation of large and complex political hierarchies had long pre-dated regular contact with Europeans (Sayes 1984) and the known history of Fiji up to the 1850s was one of alternating diplomacy and warfare – each of the larger confederations striving for a paramount position (Derrick 1974: 53–6). Internecine warfare decreased in the late 1850's and after some vicissitudes contingent upon the claims of rival colonists and sporadic warfare against them and the missionaries, Fiji was ceded to Britain in 1874. The political influence of the chiefs of large confederations continued under Britain's policy of indirect rule. Today many of their descendants hold positions of power in central government, or in the Council of Chiefs which advises government on traditional matters. When Fiji gained independence in 1970, the indigenous hierarchy was intact; at the time of my fieldwork it was articulated with a democratic system based on the Westminster model.

The data below refer to the island of Gau and primarily to the village of Sawaieke – the chiefly village of the eight villages that make up the 'country' of Sawaieke (see note 1 of chapter 1). Gau is part of Lomaiviti (central Fiji) and continuities in social organisation and cultural practice are such that my analysis is also likely to apply to much of central and eastern Fiji and parts of the northern region.

An ambiguity in Fijian Wesleyanism

Wesleyanism (i.e. Methodism) is still the religion of the overwhelming majority of Fijians. Church organisation, the form of services, the formal tenets of the religion and its striving for community involvement are all very much the same as they would be in Wesleyan churches in England or Australia, but this similarity stops with formal structure. The 'flavour' of Fijian Wesleyanism is undoubtedly different from that found elsewhere.

Wesleyanism posits egalitarianism of the soul – we are all the same in the sight of Wesley's God. This is accepted and approved by Sawaieke villagers, even while their actual practice asserts hierarchy. The status and earthly tasks of chiefs, as of all other persons, are divinely ordained. In the myth of origin of Sawaieke it is 'the coming of the light' that brings 'true kinship' and true kinship posits hierarchy as the proper social order (see below). The superiority of God's power to that of the ancestors is at once created and confirmed in people's attendance upon him in the many church services and in the prayer that precedes every meal, every meeting of every village committee and every community undertaking. Thus the name of God figures in every ceremony 'in the manner of the land' from the everyday *sevusevu* (ritual presentation of kava) to the installation of a chief.

The power of the ancestors in their benign aspect is similarly constituted in the mention of their names: all ceremonial speeches to chiefs begin by naming the dwelling places of their ancestors, the *yavu tabu* or 'sacred *yavu*'. These are the still-existing house foundations of the original ancestors, situated on clan or lineage gardening land; their names form the honorific titles of clan and lineage chiefs. In their benign aspect the ancestors are under the sway of the Christian God: he and his holy dwelling place are first in the hierarchy of chiefs and places. In their malign aspect as 'devils' the ancestors are still much to be feared. 'No one attends on them anymore', i.e. makes them sacrificial offerings of kava

49

or human flesh, but if that attendance is reinstated their fearful power can be unleashed. The ancestors are implicitly invoked in every ceremonial act 'in the manner of the land' but so long as this invocation is under the aegis of the Christian God, ancestral power is for the good and one can still justly begin a prayer to God with the words, 'To Heaven, to the holy dwelling place. You the true God, you the God whom alone is served ... ' So the Christian God is the peak of Fijian hierarchy and is followed by the ancestors and then by the people in their due order.

As we shall see below, Fijian hierarchy is at once expressed, and in part constituted, by the orientation of people to one another inside any building and the orientation of buildings to one another in the layout of the village.

Kinship and social organisation

The Fijian term for kin (*weka*) may be extended to include all Fijians and kinship terms are routinely used in reference and address (see note 6 of chapter 1). With only one exception, all relations between kin are hierarchical. The exception is for kin who are possible marriage partners or siblings-in-law, i.e. cross-cousins. Cross-cousins are equals outside marriage. Marriage transforms this equality into hierarchy: it is axiomatic that a man has authority over his wife. This relation of authority is the pivot on which hierarchical relations turn within and, by extension across, domestic groups.

At the peak of its developmental cycle the domestic group may span three generations. Relative status is given by an interaction between seniority and gender. So a girl's authority as 'the eldest' is limited because she will one day marry out (residence is virilocal) and the relative seniority of girls within a set of siblings is often ignored. Even so, as the eldest a woman must be respected by her younger brothers, over whom she has formal authority. An unmarried woman is subject to her father and elder brothers; on marriage she accepts the authority of her husband and parents-in-law. But a woman's relation with her male cross-cousins outside marriage is, by definition, one between equals.

Equality is evident in that a woman can joke with her cross-cousin, make demands on him, tease him, defy him and so on.[1] All other relations are hierarchical and demand varying degrees of respect and avoidance, most saliently for those who call each other brother and sister (*veiganeni*) – this being the focal relationship for the incest taboo – and for those who call each other parent-in-law and child-in-law across sex. Relations of respect ultimately turn on the hierarchical relation between husband and wife; so the equal relationship between cross-cousins across sex has to change on marriage. This change begins in betrothal and marriage ceremonies where the woman becomes an object of exchange.[2] The ritual transformation of the equality of cross-cousins into the hierarchy of marriage may be confirmed by violence: a man is most likely to beat his wife during the first years of marriage.

Both marriage ritual and violence are a corollary of the fact that a wife's formal subjection to her husband is crucial for his status among men. This is not to say that a wife is 'powerless'; she may have great influence with her husband, may hold and disburse money and other goods. However, it is among married men as 'leaders' of domestic groups that status across domestic groups is reckoned. The hierarchical relation that places a man quite plainly 'above' his wife is inscribed in the space of the house.

All horizontal spaces inside buildings and certain contexts out of doors can be mapped onto a spatial axis whose poles are given by the terms 'above' (*i cake*) and 'below' (*i ra*). Inside a building, people of high social status 'sit above' and those of lower social status 'below'. However, this distinction refers to a single plane and so no-one is seated literally above anyone else. Hierarchy in day-to-day village life finds its clearest physical manifestation in people's relation to one another on this spatial axis and is most evident in the context of meals, kava-drinking and worship.

Meals and hierarchy within the domestic group

Fijian hierarchy is fundamentally constructed within the domestic group – itself primarily defined by the fact that its members routinely eat together. So the plaque that proclaims Christ as 'head of household', as one who 'eats with us', sanctions with his divine authority the relations within that group.

Meals in a Fijian household are always ritualised. The cloth is laid to conform with the above/below axis of the house space, and household members take their places according to their status: the senior man sits at the pole 'above', others are 'below' him, males in general being above females. The senior man's wife is below, nearest the common entrance; her eldest son's wife, or her eldest daughter (if her sons are unmarried) sits opposite her. Every meal is preceded by prayer. The best and largest portions of food are placed on the cloth above, so that one not only sits, but eats, according to one's status. Women and older girls delay their meal to wait upon the males of the family.[3] The seating arrangements and the conduct of the meal are a concrete realisation of hierarchical relations within the domestic group (see figure 2.2).

The actual provision and cooking of food constitute one aspect of the relations between husband and wife. Men provide true food (*kakana dina*) i.e. taro, cassava and yams. By definition there is no meal unless one of these foods is present. Men also raise the pigs which, with 'true food', form the ritual 'feast'. Women provide fish, but this is a 'relish' (*i coi*) and women's catches are not part of ritual presentations. For everyday meals women cook (*vakasaqa*, lit. boil), but on special occasions men use the earth oven to cook (*vavi*, lit. bake). Men's cooking is said to be the tastiest and always forms a major part of the main meal on Sunday, of meals that accompany life-cycle ceremonies and so on.

It is only in respect of food provision that women's labour is devalued by comparison with men's, both within the household on an everyday basis and in the ritual presentation of foods.[4] Thus, in the activity of the meal, a reciprocal

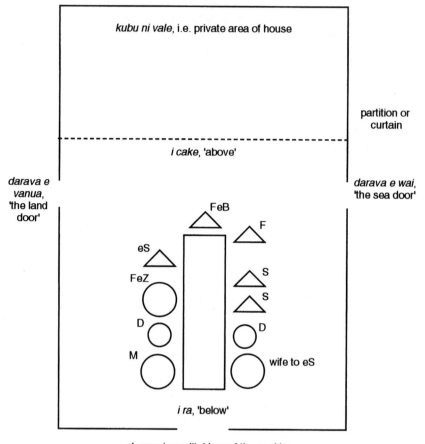

Figure 2.2 Typical seating pattern at family meal
Note: I include FeB (father's elder brother) and FeZ (father's elder sister) as 'guests' at this meal, so as to indicate what their positions would be relative to F (father) and M (mother).

and balanced exchange of labour between husband and wife is transformed into a hierarchical exchange. A wife appears to give less than she receives and to deserve her place 'below' her husband in the space of the house.

Ambiguity in hierarchy beyond the domestic group

In the wider community, beyond the domestic group, hierarchical relations are given by the interaction of three highly salient moral notions: those of rank (i.e. as a member of the chiefly or one of the commoner clans), of seniority (i.e. relative age), and of gender. 'In the manner of the land', the chiefs of ranked patrilineal clans (*yavusa*) hold sway over their own clan; however, an installed paramount chief's authority extends much further.[5]

The term 'chiefs' (*turaga*) may refer politely to married men, to all members of the chiefly clan or to the heads of all the clans considered as a group. The paramount chief (*turaga levu*, lit. big chief) of Sawaieke 'country' is chosen from the chiefly clan. The four other clans in Sawaieke village are ranked in terms of their traditional obligations to the chiefly clan. Clan ranking is given by the inter-action of two opposing constructs: one places chiefs 'above' commoners, the other aligns chiefs with other clans who are 'sea people' in opposition to clans who are 'land people'. The sea/land construct denotes balanced reciprocity in exchange, not hierarchy.[6] The ambiguity in the interaction is in part constituted by the actual layout of Sawaieke village.

As in all Fijian villages, houses are built around an open space, on one side of which stands the church and on another the village hall; the orientation is that of *veiqaravi* (lit. facing each other). Here *veiqaravi* refers to reciprocal obligations between clans to exchange goods and perform services (e.g. burial rites or the installation of a chief). In Sawaieke village, the houses of each clan tend to be grouped together; those of the chiefly clan lie on its central axis. This clan is associated with the sea, other clans with either 'sea' or 'land'. So groups of houses are roughly aligned: land houses are beside sea houses, beside land houses, beside sea houses. Moreover, the long sides of each house in general face one other, so that 'the sea door' of one house – used only by the owners and honoured guests – faces onto 'the land door' (also tabooed) of the next house.

The orientation of the houses stresses balanced reciprocity in exchange rela-tions between clans – and thus a notional equality – rather than hierarchy.[7] Some chiefly houses, however, are still built on an earth foundation (*yavu*), whose height denotes the rank of its owners. Thus relative status is still evident to some extent in the relative height of the remaining mounds.

So, in the space of the village the term *veiqaravi* (facing each other) is rendered ambiguous; it can also evoke its other meaning – that of attendance on others in ritual, e.g. the worship of God or attendance on a chief. I argue below that unambiguous hierarchy – i.e. the assertion of hierarchy as *the* principle of social organisation – depends on the transformation of *veiqaravi*. In other words, the balanced reciprocity inherent in the notion of *veiqaravi*, 'facing each other', has to be transformed into the hierarchy of *qaravi turaga*, 'attendance upon chiefs' (lit. facing the chiefs). This transformation occurs in kava-drinking.

Kava-drinking and hierarchy across domestic groups

The kava ceremony and the *sevusevu* (the presentation of the plant) are the central rituals of Fijian social life. They are performed on all occasions from installation ceremony to informal gathering.

The significance of kava is as follows. First, drinking a bowl of kava in the proper ritual context installs a chief: a chief who is 'made to drink' by the chief of the 'chief-making' clan becomes fully *mana* (lit. effective) and thus paramount; a paramount chief of Sawaieke has 'at his back all the ancestor gods of Gau'. Second, it is as tribute to chiefs that kava roots are offered in *sevusevu*. This rite allows one to join in the drinking, to claim aid from kin etc., but whatever the ostensible reason for its presentation, kava is always an offering to chiefs. Third, 'drinking kava alone' is an idiom for witchcraft. It implies the pouring of libations to the ancestors for some evil purpose. By contrast, kava may be drunk publicly to cure witchcraft-induced illnesses. Fourth, the preparation, serving, acceptance and drinking of a bowl of kava is always 'in the manner of the land'; one should not leave a kava group until the large central bowl is 'dry'. Kava is the drink of chiefs: they receive the root as tribute and re-distribute it as drink that must be accepted; this is acknowledged whether any chief is present or not. Finally, kava-drinking is virtually obligatory; a refusal to drink effectively constitutes a denial of society and a rejection of the status quo.

Kava-drinking is always in some way *mana*, i.e. 'effective' in a transcendent sense.[8] In the nineteenth century, *mana* was ultimately derived from the ancestor gods. In kava-drinking, the top central position of the high chief exemplifies the pole that is 'above' on the axis of social space and, on the scale of human effectiveness, an installed paramount is said to be the most *mana*. In this sense his *mana* is akin to that of the ancestors. In myth this *mana* makes him the focus of what is 'above' in social space. The ancestors are 'above' the paramount but he is the channel for the *mana* they dispense 'downwards' from ancestor to chief to commoner.[9]

Today a chief no longer has powers of life and death over his people; nor can he easily exploit their labour or resources. Each village is run by an elected council on formally democratic lines and so a chief's political influence depends on whether he has been properly installed (for his *mana* can then exact automatic retribution for disobedience) and on the respect in which he is seen to be held by the community at large.

In this context of a marked diminution in the actual politico-economic power of chiefs, kava-drinking has become crucial for 'the way in the manner of the land'. The current mode of drinking is understood to be eminently Fijian, even though people know that in the past women were excluded from kava-drinking while young men (i.e. unmarried men) were allowed only to prepare and serve the drink to their elders. Frequency of drinking is also said to have increased greatly over the past sixty years or so. Thus kava-drinking stresses a hierarchy whose politico-economic and spiritual bases have been subject to radical historical change and at the same time effectively subverts the awareness that change has occurred.

Today, chiefly status and prerogatives are given by the power of the Christian god; the salience of ancestral power is reduced in the face of Wesleyanism. The authority of a high chief still lies in *mana*, but it is ultimately derived from 'the strength of Jehovah, the high God' and is ratified by association with his divine nature. So the prayers of a church minister are an important aspect of any installation and a high chief's chair in church is in a pre-eminent position 'above'.

Kava-drinking is associated with ancestral *mana* and the power of God; it is always hedged about by ceremony. However informal the occasion, the highest status persons present must sit 'above' the central serving bowl (*tanoa*) so that it may 'face the chiefs' (see figure 2.3). Those who sit 'below' the *tanoa* are of lower status. On the axis of social space, one is always 'above' or 'below' others, according to one's position relative to the top, central position. If only men are drinking, young men are at the pole below; if both sexes are present then women take this place.[10] So relative status across households is made apparent on the above/below axis and confirmed by the order in which kava is served, beginning with the highest status person present. The image of an ordered and stratified society exemplified in people's positions relative to one another around the kava bowl is one encountered virtually everyday in the village of Sawaieke.

The transformation of reciprocity into tribute

The young men who look after the kava are *qaravi yaqona*, lit. facing kava or *qaravi turaga*, lit. facing the chiefs and indeed, all those below the central kava bowl literally do 'face the chiefs'. Here 'facing each other' (*veiqaravi*) ceases to denote balanced reciprocity in exchange between clans and is transformed into a hierarchical construct whereby the clan chiefs, and especially the·paramount, receive tribute.

This transformation is mediated by the structural position of cross-cousins who are equal partners to a relationship that typically obtains across domestic groups; by contrast, relations inside the domestic group are always hierarchical. The relation between cross-cousins as equals underlies the notional equality of 'facing each other' that is inscribed in the layout of the village. Marriage, however, transforms the equality of a given man and woman as cross-cousins into the hierarchy of husband and wife. Thus the relation between men as equals and as affines (brothers-in-law) is at once contained by hierarchy and subordinated to it in principle.

In kava-drinking this means that 'ladies' (married women) are seated below married men with young men in an ambiguous position which is either above or on a level with women. Thus, whatever the case for young men, women are always at the pole below. This is because the highest status woman present takes up this position with respect to her own husband just as she does for meals at home. Even a high chief's wife must, when he is present, be seen to be unambiguously 'below'. By virtue of having excluded their wives from the reckoning, married men take their places in terms of their own status *vis-à-vis* one another, according to an interaction between rank (i.e. clan and lineage affiliation) and the relative seniority given by age and kinship relation.

In kava-drinking balanced exchange across groups is transformed into tribute to chiefs. Kava is presented to them as tribute and under their auspices is

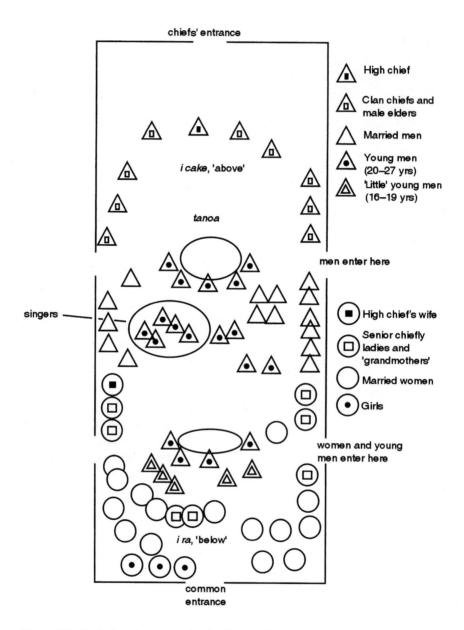

chiefs' entrance

High chief

Clan chiefs and male elders

Married men

Young men (20–27 yrs)

'Little' young men (16–19 yrs)

i cake, 'above'

tanoa

men enter here

singers

High chief's wife

Senior chiefly ladies and 'grandmothers'

Married women

Girls

women and young men enter here

i ra, 'below'

common entrance

Figure 2.3   Typical seating pattern inside village hall when people are gathered to drink *yaqona*

transformed into drink and re-distributed. At meals the balanced exchange of labour between a husband and wife is similarly transformed into a hierarchical exchange: a man both provides and re-distributes 'true food' and his wife merely attends to it in her attendance upon him. In speeches and sermons an explicit analogy is often made between a 'chief' and 'a household head'; thus 'every man is a chief in his own house'. In contexts across domestic groups the terms of the analogy are inverted. Thus, the imagery of kava-drinking evokes the notion of one vast domestic group where the high chief is 'provider' and 'father of his people' and hierarchical ranking can be taken for granted.

'The Last Supper' as an objectification of 'facing each other' (*veiqaravi*)

It is the orientation and activity of Christ and his disciples that makes 'The Last Supper' highly evocative in the Fijian context. Here eating together defines the domestic group and drinking together defines the 'universe' of kin, i.e. the community at large; in other words eating and drinking together in part constitute the actual nature of hierarchical relations between kin.

Da Vinci's fresco shows only men; this is fitting since women in Fiji must be largely excluded from the reckoning if a man is to be accorded his proper status among men. Christ manifests God on earth, the disciples are his chosen executives. Their disposition at the table evokes that of men 'above' the central serving bowl (*tanoa*) in kava-drinking. It is also analogous to the positions of clan chiefs in church: they are seated 'above' and face 'down' the church towards the congregation 'below'. So they are seen to be chiefs in the eyes of both minister and congregation; their position is ratified by association with the divine. In kava-drinking the status of chiefs is similarly ratified by association with the *mana* of the ancestors and with the power of God which, as is apparent in the kava presentation speech, confirms a chief in his place.[11]

When both sexes are drinking kava, women do not sit above the *tanoa*; nor do they sit above in the space of the church. This assertion of their ritual insignificance is mirrored in their exclusion from 'The Last Supper'. However, the seating position of women 'below' in the body of the church shows that, here at least, they may be equal to their husbands. In the body of the church wives and husbands are seated on the same level, with women occupying one side of the church and men the other. This has been, and still is, highly significant for the status of Fijian women.

Colonisation brought radical changes for women. Selective female infanticide, the strangling of chiefs' widows, the giving of women as tribute, and forced marriages were all outlawed.[12] But this had little effect on women's status. However, the notion of females as inferior does seem to have been – and to continue to be – the object of historical transformation. This transformation may have at its source the position of women in the Christian church.

In pre-Christian Fiji, women were barred from the temples of the gods, from the consumption of human sacrifices and from kava-drinking; so they had access to the *mana* of the ancestors only through their menfolk (father, brother or husband). During the past century, however, with the conversion of all Fijians to Christianity, women have been admitted to significant positions in the hierarchy of at least some Christian sects. And all women, including the young and unmarried, are now able to drink kava.

Women's inclusion in kava-drinking apparently lagged a good eighty years behind conversion to Christianity.[13] Both kava-drinking and the church are presided over by 'the chiefs', whose authority rests mainly on their pre-eminence in these contexts. Women have penetrated these domains and are seen to have their place there, even if that place be described as below.

The point is that men cannot allow their wives a full equality of relationship; if they were to do so their own positions *vis-à-vis* other men would become equivocal. Men maintain a general superiority over women and a right to command them that women do not normally question. However, seniority relations between kin mean that formally at least a man can command only women who are junior to him; he should consult his elder sister on important matters. So women pose a special problem for the construction of hierarchy amongst men and most ambiguities turn on the relations between elder sisters and younger brothers and between potential spouses, i.e. on relations across sex and within generation. The fact that women marry out appears to resolve this problem by separating elder sisters from their potential sphere of influence in their natal domestic group. In pre-colonial days this separation may also have effected their exclusion from key ritual contexts.

A man's axiomatic superiority to his wife depends on the fact that women cannot achieve full jural adulthood on the same basis as men. One is adult by virtue of marriage and parenthood, but lineage exogamy and virilocal residence mean that women become adult in a context where they are not 'owners' i.e. holders and users of patrilineally inherited land rights.

Traditionally the man's status as an 'owner' of land and his transformation of that land to produce acceptable offerings were the basis of his right to access the power of his ancestors. A woman given as 'object' in marriage was separated from her own ancestors' land; after marriage she ate the food provided by her husband's ancestors since it was they who made the land fertile. Marilyn Strathern (1984) has shown how the 'objectification' of women in marriage rituals in societies with 'gift economies' cannot be equated with the subject–object relation between people and things in commodity economies. Thus, because objects in Fijian exchange always have 'people' qualities – i.e. are gifts not commodities – a woman retains her subjectivity in marriage. So her rights in her natal lineage were not entirely alienated from her. These rights made her children *vasu* – able 'to take what they want without asking' from men of their mother's lineage. But in marrying out a woman effectively abjured her own ancestors and became adult in a context where the 'true food' she ate was provided by the power of her husband's ancestors. So on marriage she was separated from her land and her ancestors. Ancestral *mana* was dispensed downwards via the high chief of a country and appropriate only for adult 'owners' (*i taukei*) by virtue of their rights in the land whose ultimate owners were their founding patrilineal ancestors. Thus, even as adults, women could be excluded from kava-drinking and the consumption of sacrifices on the grounds that they had no natal right to *mana* from ancestors whom they had 'denied' by marriage, nor to that from their husbands' ancestors who were not their own. They had only an indirect access to *mana*: through men.

These are speculations on my part. I have no direct evidence to support them. However, my conjectures fit with historical data on women's relation to land, and with the exchange between 'the man's side' and 'the woman's side' that establishes children's rights as *vasu*. My historical speculations also help to explain how high-ranking women can be below when chiefly birth is said to be a crucial factor for relative status. Where adult women are most salient for men as jurally inferior in-marrying wives rather than as sisters, where marriage converts into hierarchy a relationship that was previously one of equality, it is easy to come to see women in general as subject to the authority of men.

Furthermore, if women were the more easily excluded from certain ritual contexts because it was not appropriate for them to approach either ancestors whom they had abjured or who were not their own, their admission to kava-drinking may have been effected by their inclusion in Christian ritual on the same general basis as men. Through prayer and church services women have direct access to the Christian God who is the ultimate source of transcendent power; so they can no longer be properly excluded from rituals that connect with lesser ancestral powers. The same reasoning also takes in the inclusion in kava-drinking of young, unmarried men and women. In Christian ideology, however, a child's duty is to his or her parents and a woman's to her husband – precepts constantly reiterated in sermons and informal religious talks. So, since women as in-marrying wives are salient to adult men, it is hardly surprising that when women entered into kava-drinking they took up a place below the young men who in former times would have only prepared but not drunk the kava, but whose position below the *tanoa* was a marker of the most junior of male statuses. That women may still be rightfully excluded from any claim to full equality is apparently confirmed by their exclusion from 'The Last Supper'.

The disciples' orientation in 'The Last Supper' is that of 'facing each other' (*veiqaravi*). They face Christ through their heads being turned towards him and the viewer in that they do not present their backs to us. The group to the far left of Christ do not face towards him, but their attitudes show him to be the object of their concern. The composition irresistibly evokes the image of a group of clan chiefs with the paramount at their centre. Moreover, the orientation of a Fijian viewer of 'The Last Supper' is that of 'facing the chiefs' – the same position as when drinking kava or sitting in the body of the church. To worship God is to face God, to attend upon a chief is to face the chief, and to look after the kava is, literally, to face kava. So the orientation of the viewer and of figures in

'The Last Supper' confirms the transformation of the balanced reciprocity of *veiqaravi* inscribed in the space of the village, into the unambiguous hierarchy of 'attendance on chiefs' – inscribed in the space of the house on the axis of 'above' and 'below'. The clan chiefs themselves, like the disciples, may be considered as relative equals in their closeness to the divine, but 'the people' are unambiguously inferior to them.

'The Last Supper' represents a ritual meal where food and drink are transformed by divine power. The disciples, at Christ's order, provide the Passover meal. His power as the Son of God effects the transformation of the bread and wine into his own body and blood. What is then re-presented to the disciples cannot be further transformed, but only ingested. Thus Christ confirms their discipleship and his authority. This act prefigures the time when, having risen from the dead, Christ will appear again to the disciples and breathe upon them so that they receive the Holy Spirit into themselves. In his analysis of Fijian cannibalism Sahlins (1983) argues that its mythical origin is also the origin of culture and that, as provider of the cannibal feast, the Fijian chief was at once the feeder of the people and their food. He also notes the link with Christian ritual.[14] The historical fact of cannibalism is still highly salient to Fijians even while it is rejected by them as an aspect of 'devil worship' – i.e. attendance upon the ancestors in their most fearful and least respectable guise – and is associated with the dangerous powers of great chiefs in earlier times. However, the explicit parallel drawn here may be rejected by Fijians as both invalid and blasphemous.

Less controversially, Christ's presentation of the wine and bread to his disciples evokes the drinking of kava under the aegis of chiefs. The hierarchical relations exemplified in those of chief and commoner are manifest in the form taken by the *sevusevu*, where kava is given 'raw' as tribute to be disposed of by a chief who re-distributes it as drink that must be accepted.

In one Fijian version of the origin of kava, quoted in the *Native Gazette* in 1913, the first plant is said to have sprung from the grave of a dead chief, who was taken suddenly by the ancestor gods 'when his sun was at the zenith' (i.e. as a sacrifice). This dead chief appeared to his mourning kin to tell them this and to instruct them about the kava, he said:

> That kava plant will be grown to a great height. Let it then be pulled up and its roots chewed and watered, and then be drunk, but its internodes shall be planted again to keep you in remembrance of me.
>
> (quoted in Hocart 1952: 127)

The echo of Christ's words at the Last Supper suggests that, for some Fijians, the analogy between it and kava-drinking is obvious. Historically it was in human sacrifice and kava-drinking that men attended on the gods, and in the ceremonial ingestion of this sacred food and drink, the *mana* a chief had from the gods was dispensed downwards to elders and male adults (i.e. married men).

In a more fugitive sense the story of the Last Supper evokes the ritual installation of a chief as paramount. Here the analogy becomes more complex for, unlike a potential paramount, Christ embodies power that is at once potential and fully realised. By contrast, if a Fijian chief is to become paramount his personal *mana* must be augmented. In myth, the first high chief of a country (*vanua*) and founder of the chiefly clan is always a 'foreigner' – one who came over the sea; in this sense he is 'different in kind (*e dua tani*) from the chief who installs him. He becomes paramount when he is 'made to drink' by the leading 'land chief' who thus confers on him the *mana* or 'effectiveness' of the ancestors of all the landspeople. Christ too was different in kind, the son of God, but he was also a man and a commoner (*tamata ga*, lit. just a person). So he is analogous at once to the paramount and to the land chief whose *mana* 'makes' (*buli*) a paramount. The conscious act of the land chief effects the process that evokes Christ's sacrifice and resurrection:

> Having taken the sacred cup, the chief is in the state of intoxication Fijians know as ... 'dead from kava' (*mate ni yaqona*), to recover from which is specifically 'to live' (*bula*) ... [after these rites] ... The song these warriors sing as the chief passes between their lines is the same they intone over the body of a cannibal victim.
>
> (Sahlins 1983: 87)

The making of a paramount is the supreme act of *mana* that is possible for a land chief, but the realisation of his *mana* is also its defeat. Augmenting another man's efficacy, the land chief creates his own ritual subordination. By contrast, Christ's power admits of no increment. The Last Supper prefigures his crucifixion and transubstantiation as a manifestation of his own will, which is at once the will of man and of God. He installs himself.

Fijian knowledge of the Bible and Christian lore is extensive and highly detailed; most adults are likely to know that Christ's symbol is a fish, and that Peter, the chief of the apostles is 'the rock' – an opposition that evokes the relation between the chiefly clan and the commoner landspeople. In Fijian terms, however, Christ is at one with both sea and land. As a carpenter (in traditional Fiji one of the landspeople) he should be 'afraid of the sea', but he can calm its waves and walk upon its waters. It is only by virtue of his installation that a paramount chief can, like Christ, contain opposition and thus embody divine authority. By birth he is associated with the *mana* of the sea whose emblems are the whale's tooth, the turtle and the chiefly fish, *saqa*. With the installation kava he also gains access to the *mana* of the land, whose chiefs become his commoner executives and thus analogous to the disciples who have from the Holy Spirit the power to establish Christ's church. Finally, a paramount is benign provider, 'the father of our land' (*tama i noda vanua*) and disinterested vehicle of divine justice; he does not will punishment, but his *mana* causes illness to those who disobey him; so Christ is a mild father to his flock, 'the good shepherd', but in his divine manifestation brings punishment on those who wilfully abjure him.

The copies of 'The Last Supper' that are so popular in Fiji are tapestries not prints (though these are also displayed). This is significant because locally produced decorations for both house and church are often pieces of barkcloth, beautifully printed with geometrical designs in earth pigments. Traditional chiefs are often referred to as *ko ira na malo*, lit. the cloths. *Malo* is the paper mulberry tree from which barkcloth is made – a piece of which is tied on a chief's arm during his installation. In the nineteenth century a chief's barkcloth train denoted his high rank. Hocart (1952: 35) tends to use the term *malo* for lesser chiefs, however in Sawaieke its reference denoted all traditional chiefs, including the paramount. Here the following remarks by Hocart are relevant:

> The whole *raison d'être* of a chief is the same as of a god of the land, abundance.... It is the same function as that of a god of the land who receives offerings that the land may flourish. In Ndreketi they appoint a 'cloth' (*malo*), a receiver of feasts, if food is scarce ... it is the worship of the king that brings abundance, and at his consecration they pray that the princes may continue in life, that the fish may keep coming land-wards etc.
>
> (1952: 19)

Today these notions are less explicit, but it is still said that the well-being of people and land requires chiefs, and 'a good chief' is still one who brings prosperity. So it is important that tribute be paid to chiefs in *sevusevu* and in presentations of first fruits; for only when the installed paramount (*na sau*) is receiving and re-distributing the tribute paid to him can a condition of peace and plenty (*sautu*, lit. established *sau*) prevail in the land. The 'cloths' that represent 'The Last Supper' are thus a material manifestation of the ideal chiefs, not only in the images that are represented on them, but in the very nature of the cloth itself.

Making the present, revealing the past

'The Last Supper' can be viewed as an image of Fijian hierarchy, but its popularity in Fiji suggests that its peculiar power may go beyond the way its associations resonate in Fijian culture. If the quintessentially Christian 'Last Supper' can represent Fijian chiefship – which itself exemplifies 'the way in the manner of the land' – then it can also imply that Fijian chiefs were always inherently Christian; that even long ago 'in the time of the devils', before 'the coming of the light', the chiefs embodied a fundamental Christianity – one that was obscured by the practices forced upon them by the ancestors in their malign aspect. The light made them see that human sacrifice and cannibalism, war and wife capture, widow strangulation and polygamy were sins imposed on them by their ignorance of the Christian God. But they had only to strip away these practices to stand revealed as true Christians, as people whose very tradition was at base Christian.

I noted at the beginning of this article that I neglected to ask Sawaieke villagers why they valued their reproductions of 'The Last Supper'. If my analysis is valid, its appropriation can be understood as an instance of *cakacaka vakavanua* ('working, acting, doing in the manner of the land'). This notion of tradition as culturally appropriate action makes it possible for Fijians at once to transform their culture and affirm its dynamic integrity. The Fijian equivalent for ritual as a generic term is also *cakacaka vakavanua*. Thus, in Fiji, ritual is doing something in a Fijian way; its meaning arises from *how* things are done, as well as from *what* is done. Moreover, if one does something in a Fijian way then the doing of it becomes Fijian. This is a processual notion and so it can incorporate change. People in Sawaieke held their practice to be 'in the manner of the land'; they also routinely pointed out that changes had occurred. They seemed to find no difficulty in asserting their indigenous ritual to be at once Christian (*vakalotu*, lit. in the manner of the church) and traditional (*vakavanua*).

Christian ritual itself is not usually said to be 'in the manner of the land'. However, I would argue that it can be seen to be so. Fijian churches are largely European in appearance and the content of Wesleyan services is set down in the Hymn Book and followed to the letter, but these factors do not preclude a distinctively Fijian Christian practice. Services are transformed not in their explicit content, but in respect of such factors as the seating arrangements in church and the prerogative of speech.

These data suggest a somewhat different perspective from that proposed by Bloch (1986a: 184–186) on the interaction between ritual and historical contingency. Fijian ritual is effective not because it denies the passage of time and the changes time brings (as Bloch suggests for Malagasy ritual) but because it incorporates change under the rubric of appropriate action. So history and myth are implicit in Fijian ritual and collapsed into one another: provided they remain implicit, both can be made to manifest the present or to reveal the past. In this sense Fijian ritual posits a transcendent timelessness that defies historical change but does not deny it.

The articulation of history with tradition is also addressed in the works by Sahlins, Hobsbawm and Borofsky referred to at the outset of this article. Hobsbawm distinguishes between genuine and invented traditions: 'where the old ways are alive, traditions need be neither revived nor invented' (Hobsbawm and Ranger 1983: 8). For Sahlins the immutable past impresses itself on the present via 'the cultural scheme' which is received readymade, only to be 'risked in action' and thus transformed (Sahlins 1985: 149–50). Borofsky's subtle account of tradition as process shows that their 'ways of knowing' make Pukapukans able to conceive of their cultural practice as at once dynamic and traditional. He contrasts their perspective with that of anthropologists who may, paradoxically, alter tradition by representing it as uniform and static. Nevertheless, he asserts that 'in preserving past traditions by making them come alive again, Pukapukans were really altering them' (Borofsky 1987: 142) – and thus implies that there was, once, an immutable tradition.

For us ritual and tradition denote fixity. From this point of view, it is difficult to understand ritual or tradition as a historical process. The introduction of new practices becomes a matter of 'invented tradition' as distinct from flexible 'custom' which is allowed to be 'adaptable' (Hobsbawm and Ranger 1983: 2). In Fijian terms tradition, ritual and custom cannot be distinguished from one another and they are all allowed to be processual. Thus Fijian cultural categories are not received readymade as Sahlins would have it, nor are they 'risked' in action; rather they are constituted and made manifest in action and there they find their continuity. The notion of fixity is reserved for history.

The Fijian term for myth and/or history (*i tukutuku*) denotes what is and has been told. As a form of action, speech fixes the past by making it explicit. Speech is the prerogative of those in authority, so 'listening' (*vakarorogo*) denotes allegiance and related myth and history cannot be easily challenged. When it is written, the absolute stability of the past makes it potentially dangerous, so the general histories (*i tukutuku raraba*) that detail landholdings and chiefly statuses at the turn of the century are held by central government and normally released only to those with paramount authority over an area. Here history is not so much a series of transformative events as an immutable past that must justify the present. The history of conversion has been told and written. It justifies the Christian present, but it cannot easily justify that present as essentially and unambiguously 'Fijian'.

Comment on 'the time of the devils' often reflects the received history of Fijian conversion as a sharp break with the past:

> In the old days, men would steal women and carry them off to their own village, and because of this there was also a great deal of murder. The church was not here then and it was because of this perhaps that they sinned.

Stories of the past that attempt reconciliation with the present are inevitably ambiguous. For instance one may be told that great magical knowledge was lost because, with the coming of the light, the chiefs ordered that the book of that knowledge be burnt. Here chiefly authority institutes radical change by rejecting a magic that was 'very effective' (*mana vakalevu*). Nevertheless, it was 'the light' (*rarama*) that instigated the change. Similarly, the myth of origin of Sawaieke village begins by stressing a lack of kinship 'in the time of the devils' and then suggests that traditional obligations between the named chiefs of four clans pre-existed Christianity and that the chiefs took it upon themselves to gather together in one village and to build the church which was 'the beginning of true kinship'.

Fijians take their Christianity to be as much a part of their own way of life as those practices that an outsider recognises without difficulty as 'Fijian'. At the same time they have to reconcile their awareness of conversion as at least a partial denial of what had been 'the way in the manner of the land', with their representation of themselves as having held onto that way.

The ubiquitous presence of reproductions of 'The Last Supper' shows that reconciliation is better achieved in action than in words. In related or written history and myth the disjunction between past and present is explicit and thus unchangeable. By contrast, if tradition is appropriate action, then the notion of transformation is contained within that of continuity. Given that appropriate action is played out in terms of relational spatial constructs (i.e. 'facing each other' and 'above/below') 'The Last Supper' is able to manifest tradition and thus to make continuity obvious and concrete. Christ and the apostles can be seen to have positioned themselves in the same way as Fijian chiefs; since chiefs are seen to be chiefs in their position in social space, so chiefship by visual definition becomes Christian. Pictures of members of the British royal family were also displayed in nearly all Sawaieke houses and I was often told that, at least in respect of its monarchy and aristocracy, the Fijian way was 'the same' as the English way. At cession the British monarch was recognised as the paramount of all Fiji and, during my fieldwork, Queen Elizabeth was said to be 'next to God' and 'just like a little Fijian'.

The power of visual imagery rests at once on its potential for evocation and on the fact that what may be evoked does not have to be made explicit; neither is the potential for evocation limited by what may be said about the image. A concrete image fixes representation, but it does not explicitly describe itself. Thus it is – as a 'humble' object – able to mediate between unchangeable history and mutable tradition (cf. Miller 1987: 98–108).

I have concentrated here on the role that 'The Last Supper' may play in the contemporary construction of Fijian hierarchy. But this hierarchy is itself the outcome of a continual struggle against a fundamental equality, i.e. the struggle to make tribute outweigh balanced reciprocity in exchange relations. So it seems likely that in a discussion about the equality of persons in the eyes of God, villagers could point to 'The Last Supper' for evidence of this. Here one might stress the balanced reciprocity between 'land' and 'sea' that underlies relations between clan chiefs and find its confirmation in the alignment of Christ and the apostles. To arrive at this interpretation one would have only to deny that any more extensive evocation was justified.

It may be objected that in making this point I have invalidated my own analysis. I would argue that, on the contrary, Fijian appropriation of 'The Last Supper' can only be explained if the associations it evokes can contain the opposing values of balanced reciprocity and tribute that are contained by kava ritual. Moreover, 'The Last Supper' mediates between an unchangeable history and a transformed and transforming tradition. According to the wishes and intentions of any given speaker, the values and beliefs it evokes may be taken to be entirely new or a mere transformation of the past, an aspect of 'devil worship' or of Christianity, part of 'the Fijian way' or 'the European way'.

Thus emerges the subtle and profound articulation between the imagery of kava ritual and Christian ritual – a process that may serve to explain the ubiquity of a Catholic image of 'The Last Supper' in Wesleyan churches where communion is rarely, if ever, performed. Once Christian ritual 'belonged' to the colonising power and its legitimating authority, the church. Today Fijians have made it their own – an achievement which would seem to rest in the transforming potential given by 'the manner of the land'.

3

SEEING THE ANCESTRAL SITES
Transformations in Fijian notions of the land

Remarking places and events

Where I lived in Fiji, in the chiefly village of Sawaieke on the island of Gau, people routinely remark on the most ordinary events. So, when the truck that twice a day makes a circuit of the villages is sighted in the distance or its horn heard someone is bound to say, *Lori!* Or it might be the doctor's van, or the drum for church, or women returning from fishing, and all of us present can see or hear whatever it is, but even so someone always remarks 'Doctor!' or, 'There beats the drum!' or, 'Here come the women from fishing!' And any walk with others elicits similar remarks as the group passes a landmark: '*Ia*, the old village!' or '*Ia*, Crabshit Pool!' or '*Ia*, the school!'

One might indeed wish to go to meet the truck or attend the church service, or stop at the place named, but this is rarely the point of the utterance. Rather it seems to be the very fact that the happening is expected or the place known that renders remark on it proper and even satisfying.

What is implicitly remarked on is the passing of time, often in terms of places and landmarks that function as reference points for the succession of events. Historical time too can be marked by the succession of places. The Lands Commission of 1916 recorded histories of the social divisions on Gau and their claims to land: these name various apical ancestors, but more important is the recital of the succession of places where they had made villages.[1] This made it clear that the social division called the *yavusa* was constituted as much by the land to which people belonged as by the people to whom that land belonged. The remarking of places and routine events by contemporary villagers likewise has implicit in it their sense of belonging to those places and that round of events. In this sense of belonging, space and time are experientially dimensions of one another: the self is always placed in time, whether 'here now' or 'here then'.[2]

This awareness of 'time emplaced' informs the process through which Fijian villagers constitute their identities, their sense of themselves, as rooted in their natal land. This chapter addresses their conceptions of the land in so far as these can be gathered from historical records, from accounts of the ancestors, and from what people say and do in everyday life in the *vanua* (country, land, or place) of Sawaieke (see note 1 of chapter 1). The focus is on the land as it is experienced or lived in terms of people's active engagement with it. For Fijian villagers, the idea of the person as rooted in his or her natal place is powerfully real; one is virtually a material manifestation of that place. The corollary of this is that the passing of time, and personal experience of the changes time brings, are made manifest in the land itself.

Moreover, the transformational potential inherent in the awareness of 'time emplaced' renders the ancestral past not as a frozen, timeless, mythical domain, but as historical and dynamic. And even as this dynamic past continues to inform the dynamic present, the changes wrought in the present are made integral to the land, and the present comes to overlap, becomes as it were continuous with, that ancestral past.

Vanua may refer to a part of the world, to a part of Fiji, to a confederation of villages (*vanua ko Sawaieke*, the eight villages of Sawaieke country), to the people who occupy it, to a subset of those people who are classified as landspeople, to a certain spot, or to a place on one's body. Fijian villagers are holders and users (*i taukei*, lit. owners) of land, but because this birthright is grounded in an idea of people as materially belonging to the land, being an owner does not allow one to alienate it. The people are *lewe ni vanua* – *lewe* being given in Capell's (1941) dictionary as 'the flesh or inner part of a person or thing'; in other words, people are the land's very substance.

The phenomenological world of villagers is one where the power immanent in land and sea, and manifest in exchange relations and ritual, materially informs their identity as particular Fijian persons. Their ideas rest in part on verbal representations of the land, but are as much visceral as intellectual; in their daily lives, villagers emphasise embodied sensuous experience: that which seems experientially to be unmediated, directly derived from seeing, hearing, touching, and smelling the land and consuming its products.[3]

Historically more recent ideas about Christianity, 'development' and commoditisation of the economy, also inform villagers' conceptions of the power immanent in the land; so they inform too their conceptions of themselves as persons and their relations with one another. That these conceptions remain peculiarly Fijian is a function of the inherently transformative nature of cognitive processes: in taking on ideas introduced over the past 150 years, Fijians have transformed not only their indigenous ideas and practice, but also those introduced by missionaries and colonisers.

Given their centrality for identity, Fijian conceptions of the land have profound politico-economic implications. In ritual, balanced reciprocity in exchange across groups is transformed into tribute to chiefs, and in day-to-day life villagers routinely appeal to traditions of chiefship. Chiefly ritual appears able to contain equally salient practices of equality, so villagers come to conceive of hierarchy as a given dimension of social relations. But what the analyst finds is a struggle to make hierarchy contain relations of equality, and a recognition that the very continuity of this hierarchy depends on the dynamic of those equal relations, which cannot ultimately be contained by ritual, but only by raw power – by superior physical force. So, in daily village life, hierarchy and equality are set one against the other and each is made at once to reference and to subvert the other.

This historical (and continuing) tension between tribute and balanced reciprocity, between hierarchy and equality, is inscribed in the very features of the land and is evident in people's conceptions of it. But as I show below, the 'meaning' of these features has been and continues to be transformed.

Ancestral places

The term *yavusa* is derived from *yavu* – the earth foundation of a house in which, in pre-colonial days, the bodies of the dead were buried.[4] The names of house foundations are conceived of as eternal so they were given to new *yavu* when people deserted old villages and established new ones; people were (and still are) understood to belong to the *yavusa*, or group of related houses, that was founded by their ancestors.[5]

The existence of old gardens can be inferred from levelled land and the nature of secondary growth, old village sites from the remains of the deserted *yavu*. The height of the *yavu* varied with the status of its owners: a chief's house might be 1.5 metres or more above ground level. So the higher the *yavu* the more powerful its owner, and tributary relations were inscribed in the topography of the land. But equality was implicit here too for houses were built 'facing each other' (*veiqaravi*) with the 'land' side of one house facing the 'sea' side of the next, this referenced balanced reciprocity in exchange relations across households.

The term for kin (*weka*) may be extended to include all ethnic Fijians and kin terms are routinely used in reference and address. With only one exception, all kin relations are hierarchical and require varying degrees of respect and avoidance. The exception is for kin who are possible spouses or siblings-in-law, i.e. cross-cousins (see note 6 of chapter 1). Cross-cousins are equals, but across sex they are equals only outside marriage; any husband is axiomatically above his wife so 'every man is a chief in his own house'. Even so, equal and hierarchical relations are predicated on one another, because marriage depends on relations of equality between cross-cousins across exogamous clans (*mataqali*), both across and within sex.

So, in any village, the varying height of the *yavu* and the disposition of houses evinces an antithesis between hierarchy and equality, between non-marriageable kin (where the paradigmatic reference is to the hierarchical household and clan) and marriageable kin (who as cross-cousins are equals across households, clans, and *yavusa*).

Yavu tabu or 'forbidden *yavu*' are distinguished from old village sites and from the *yavu* of the present village; they are usually situated on garden land belonging to a *yavusa* or to a clan, whose honorific titles are derived from the names of their forbidden *yavu*. Adults say one should not tread on such a place, but one young man told me that children today do not care – if they see a coconut fallen there they go and take it; when he was a child one did not do so. If one wants a thing from a *yavu tabu* one should ask its owners to fetch it.

> Only the owner of the *yavu* can be bold enough to fetch something from the top of his *yavu*. ... If you tread or lay a hand on the top of a *yavu tabu* or one of those dangerous places – places where the ancestors had their gardens – then you will fall ill. If you tread on it, your feet will swell ... until you can't walk at all.

Old village sites belong to their long-dead owners, as do the abandoned gardens inland and the ruins of the fortified hilltop villages; one visits such places only with good reason and in company, for who knows what one might find there? So too, if one is coming home from or visiting another village at night, one goes in a group and talks and laughs loudly to scare away any devils that might be lurking in the bush that borders the road. But some men walk alone at night between villages, and two told me they do not believe in *tevoro* (lit. devils – the ancestors, *kalou vu*, in their malign aspect).

A *vu* or ancestor is one who died before the coming of the Christian church, and most adults maintain that while they continue to exist, they are no longer so effective (*mana*) as once they were. This is because the *mana* (lit. efficacy) of an ancestor, like that of a chief, of the old gods, and of the Christian God is said to be augmented, if not brought into being, by the attendance of people upon them.[6]

Methodist missionary success in Fiji was assured when Cakobau, the most powerful of high chiefs, converted in 1854. Today virtually all ethnic Fijians are Christians, the vast majority still being Methodists and assiduous churchgoers.[7] Services take the form laid down in the Prayer Book, but they differ from those held in Methodist churches elsewhere: the layout and use of church seating evinces hierarchy in the relations between *yavusa* chiefs and the congregation, whose own seating is differentiated in terms of an interaction between rank and seniority (see Toren 1990: 119–137).

People attend on (*qarava*, lit. face) the Christian God, who is above all. The old gods and ancestors still exist but their power has waned for they are no longer the object of the people's sacrifices., so the Christian God is invoked not as 'the only god' but as 'the only god who is served'. But the ancestors resent any meddling with their own places. When the Gau secondary school was built in the late 1970s, a full *yaqona* (kava) ceremony was performed on the site with libations of the drink being poured to placate the ancestral owner. But later he took revenge by attacking at night some teenage boarders at the school who woke to find this devil on their chests trying to choke the life out of them. More ceremonies had to be performed. Older people with orthodox Christian views may deny these occurrences, but most people I know give credit to them.

Villagers in Sawaieke country attend up to four or so church services a week; they also assert ideas of immanent ancestral power and the continued existence of old gods such as Degei (the snake creator god) and Daucina (see below). In their benign aspect under the sway of the Christian God, the ancestors bless their descendants, while misfortune may be their punishment for wrongdoing. But they may be empowered too by those who, ignoring the true God, offer them sacrifices and so unleash their malign powers – a matter I return to below. So the ancestors have still to be feared and their dwelling-places treated with circumspection, for their intentions towards the living seem always to be equivocal.

Besides the obvious *yavu* one may also see great mounds of earth or stones like Naivinivini (Heaped-up). Its present owner, a member of the former priestly clan, told me it was the house foundation of a founding ancestor and the biggest in Fiji. The (edited) story of this *yavu* is given below in the words of an elderly man of chiefly birth (not the owner):

Once there was a founding ancestor [*vu*] in this country of Sawaieke [There's-water-here] called Ravuravu [Killer-with-a-club]. His *yavu* is over there at Nagaga [Drinking-hole] a beach on the way to Somosomo village [Mangrove-mud]. The people used to go there to serve him. But for firewood this chief required trees like the *dawa*, mango and chestnut – tall and heavy trees; it took who knows how many people to drag a tree trunk all the way there.

One day a war happened between Sawaieke and Nukuloa [Black-sand]. Nukuloa was weakening so they searched Fiji for a powerful person to help them. The message went to Dama in Bua [Frangipani-tree], to a chief called Radikedike [Fire-fly]. You can see his *yavu* at one side of this village; this [was the beginning of this] *yavu*.

The Nukuloa chief and Radikedike agreed to become allies. Radikedike was told to come through the reef at Nagali [The-solitary-one] opposite Nukuloa. But he came through at Sawaieke. The Nukuloa chief had said 'You will see a *tavola* tree on the hilltop; it marks where I live.' But at Ravuravu's place there also stood a big *tavola*. Radikedike saw it and came ashore at Vatoaleka [Short-blessing]. If you go there you will see his footprint on top of a stone. This is proof that he came to Gau.

But when he arrived, no one took any notice of him and he realised his coming here was a mistake. He was carrying a hundred huge chest-nuts that hung from his arm – so what about the size of this victorious chief? He wanted to roast his chestnuts, so he climbed up to Ravuravu's house. 'What do you want?' 'I want firewood to roast some chestnuts for me to eat.' Ravuravu said, 'The only firewood is that beside you. If you can carry it, fine.' Radikedike took one of these firewoods, stripped off its leaves, and went outside. Ravuravu was astonished. What a strong man! It took fifty Sawaieke people to drag such a tree so far as here, but this was only one man. 'I am getting old, I shall hand the country over to him and let him lead it.' So these two changed over at that time ...

Now Radikedike always wanted women. The ladies then used to go net-fishing at Muana [Its-tip] – just as you do. On their way back they used to sing until they reached Naivinivini. He built his mound [his *yavu*] there where the women ceased to sing. Near Denimana [Crabshit Pool] you will see the [deserted *yavu* of the] old village, which was situated there when Radikedike took over.

That this story is taken to be a valid account of the past was evident in the teller's insistent linking of its details to the present; moreover, it was prefaced by observations on the ritual duties of *yavusa*, on the remarkable physical size and powers of the chiefs of former times, and a comparison between their strategies in war and the teller's experience of war in Malaya. But for both the teller and his audience (myself and half a dozen children), the continuing power of such a story lies in its references to known landmarks, whose salience is presumed to be of the same order for the hearers as for their forebears. The past referred to is distant and radically different from the present, but the story emphasises material and manifest continuity between the present and that past.

It explains that Naivinivini is the house foundation of an ancestor god and, given that the height of chiefly *yavu* inscribes hierarchy in the land itself, suggests that its size reflects glory on Sawaieke people whose ancestor was so great as to merit it. The storyline is a common one: a founding ancestor arrives as a stranger, shows himself to be *mana*, and is given power by an ageing but still powerful local god. That this warlike chief has to be warmed by fires made of the trunks of fruit-bearing trees denotes his waning powers, that those powers are still great is given by the size of the trees thus consumed. Ravuravu must be overcome if the rebellious tributary village of Nukuloa is to triumph over Sawaieke. His name denotes war, so the heat (*katakata*) he absorbs will make him *yalo katakata*, hot-spirited or angry. A tall *tavola* tree marks the dwelling of Ravuravu – its wood is used for making the great slit drums on which, in pre- and early colonial times, one group challenged another to war and beat out the rhythms of its success in killing and eating the enemy (Seeman 1862: 363; Clunie 1977: 25, 27). Given that a boy's umbilical cord is buried and a tree planted on top of it, tree and man are identified; the war-drums and Ravuravu manifest the land's immanent power converted into material form via consumption of its sacrificed products. Ravuravu's power derives from the burning of fruit-bearing trees, a form of consumption here analogous to explicit sacrifice: to killing and eating subject people and to drinking *yaqona*.

In telling how Sawaieke village emerged victorious and how peace came to Sawaieke country, the story explains and justifies Sawaieke's precedence as the chiefly village and the paramount position of its *yavusa* chiefs. The very presumption of Nukuloa, in seeking to escape from its tributary relation to Sawaieke, makes Radikedike mistake his entry through the reef. He leaves his footprint on a stone as he comes ashore and climbs the hill where he takes firewood, not to spend its fruitfulness in generating in himself a warlike heat, but to roast chestnuts to eat. The huge chestnuts denote his own fruitfulness and strength, and his eating of them gives him another form of the heat that is proper to men, the heat that makes a man desire women. The leadership of Radikedike and the attendance of the Sawaieke people upon him is implicit in their allowing him to build his great *yavu* at the spot where the women returning from fishing ceased to sing; it also implies that he had many wives and fathered many children.

Radikedike may be identified with gods of other areas, e.g. Daucina, the Lamp-Bearer, famous all over Fiji (Hocart 1929: 191). In the form of a handsome stranger or a desirable cross-cousin, Daucina haunts coastlines and streams and seduces any woman foolish enough to bathe alone at night. In Gau, Radikedike is not identified with Daucina; the latter is a *tevoro* (devil) whereas Radikedike by contrast is considered a local ancestor – one whereby Gau people have the same founder god, *veitauvu*, as people from Vanua Levu, the island from which Radikedike originated. Those who are *veitauvu* are 'owners' in each other's country: this joking relationship references the equality between cross-cousins, and I return to it below.

Today the *yavu* of Radikedike stands in a grove of trees at one side of Sawaieke village; and, like the deserted *yavu* of the old village and the forbidden *yavu* in the bush, is respectfully avoided. Young people seem not to know that the dead were once buried in the *yavu* of houses, but children do not play in such places, nor does anyone walk there. The villages of Sawaieke country, including Nukuloa, continue annually to make formal tribute to Sawaieke chiefs; though as the Lands Commission records show, Nukuloa chiefs were attempting to assert their independence as late as 1916. The *tauvu* relation between Gau and Vanua Levu is still observed and their joking is unremitting; a visitor from Vanua Levu is an honoured guest for whom no attention is too much and to whom nothing can be refused. Likewise, young women continue to be vulnerable to the attentions of Daucina. Eating and *yaqona*-drinking are also, at least implicitly, still forms of sacrifice: a prayer is said before every meal (even morning or afternoon tea), every *yaqona*-drinking helps constitute the position of chiefs *i cake* – above – and the drinking of the installation *yaqona* makes the paramount chief one who has 'all the ancestors in Gau at his back'. Older wooden houses in Sawaieke are built on *yavu* of varying height, but many of the new houses of concrete breeze-blocks are not; their layout within any village is still that of *veiqaravi* (lit. facing each other). And at three different times on Sunday and three or four times during the week a great drum made of the wood of the *tavola* tree calls people to church, which stands at the centre of the village on one side of the *rara*, village green.

Ancestral powers in land and sea

In prayers and sermons in church one is regularly told that the Christian God made the world and everything in it. But many of the stories told to children in school or that one hears when people are gathered to drink *yaqona* or to work together stretching pandanus for making mats, suggest that it was the original ancestors who formed the land in distinctive ways. The water of Waiboteigau, 'Water-broken-from-the-middle', the stream that rises in Gau's inland hills, was stolen from two powerful ancestresses whom the Sawaieke chiefs claim as theirs.[8] The water was carried away by the first of ten brothers in a leaf of a plant called *salasalaqato* – so fine-textured, said the teller, one would not believe water could be carried in it. When the first brother – Radua – arrived at the top of a hill he saw that his nine brothers had set sail without him; in anger he threw the leaf full of water to the ground and the course taken by the water that flowed from it retraced that marked by the water which had dripped from the leaf as he had made his way from the ancestresses' house to the top of the hill. Radua slipped and fell on the hillside and there he left his handprint in a stone near the source of the stream.

Besides these features – the *yavu* of the old villages, the deserted gardens, the occasional mound or cairn of stones, the foot- and handprints of the ancestors – there are the graves of forebears. Villagers in general hold that the material substance of the dead should become one with the land from which, in life, they obtained their food by virtue of the fertile powers of its first owners their founding ancestors. So the bodies of those who die elsewhere are sent home to their native village to be buried in the land of the clan or the *yavusa* to which they belong.[9] And once a year young men are ordered to make 'clean' (*savasava*), that is, to weed, all graves in preparation for the holiday and ritual season that is Christmas and New Year. Thus all the dead, including the pre-Christian ancestors, continue to be respected.[10]

In the days when the *tabu* (prohibition) still had force, a chief might forbid any taking of fruit or fishing of streams. The place would be marked with a pattern of crossed sticks or somesuch and one who offended against the *tabu* would fall sick and even die. These kinds of *tabu* were called *vakatalele* (lit. 'something hung up'). The powers that inhabit the land still protect themselves and their products – their efficacy being manifest through the imposition of a *tabu* by one who has the ancestral right to impose it and who does so under proper circumstances.[11] During my first fieldwork a married man in his 40s told me that even today 'the *tabu* according to the land is still effective'. He had tested this himself. Some years before, on the death of a person of high chiefly rank, he had laid a *tabu* on the salt water from Sawaieke to Navukailagi, fishing could take place only right out near the reef. One night he and his wife were coming back from such a trip and were close to Sawaieke when they saw a large crab and he speared it. His wife was angry with him for breaking the *tabu* he himself had instituted but he told her it did not matter. 'I wanted to know, Christina, I wanted to see for myself if the *tabu* according to the land was still *mana*.' When the hundred nights were over and the *tabu* was formally lifted and everyone went net-fishing, he was there, swimming along to join the others, when suddenly a fish with a sharp snout came leaping towards him, in and out of the water, making straight for him very fast and it struck his face with a glancing blow to the cheek, cutting it there. 'And then, mother of Manuel, I realised the *mana* of the *tabu* according to the land. I saw it. I had proved thereby the *mana* of that *tabu*.'[12]

All parts of the country are owned and inhabited – even if one does not always know by whom. Indeed many references to old gods and ancestors are oblique; so I was often told by young people in their late teens that 'something' (*e dua na ka*) was there, or likely to be there, in spots we passed on those occasions when I went to the gardens – in a large and beautiful bamboo grove, in a stand of *ivi* trees on a hillside and, always, in any spot where the remains of old *yavu* were to be seen. The knowledge of all these places and landmarks as formed, held, owned, guarded, used, inhabited, by human or ancestral beings, enters into villagers' conceptions of what the land is and who they are themselves.

Implicit in much Fijian cultural practice is the idea that land and sea literally empower those who belong to them (at once their 'substance' and their 'owners') by providing for their material needs – the hardwoods and softwoods, the bamboos and vines for house building; the paper mulberry for barkcloth; pandanus for mats; the coconut for food, oil, string, baskets, bowls, and other things; and the many tubers, fruit trees, fish, shellfish, seaweeds, and so on that form the basis of the subsistence economy. People need money for clothes, kerosene, certain foods, and consumer goods, for secondary-school fees for their children, for weekly donations to church funds and, intermittently, to community projects such as new school buildings; but land and sea still provide the necessities when money fails – a common occurrence in a mixed subsistence and cash-cropping economy.

This potency of land and sea is transformed into equal relations between people via the balanced exchange of goods and services across households and *yavusa*, and into hierarchy in tributary prestations of *yaqona* roots to chiefs, under whose aegis it is transformed into drink and re-distributed to the people. Chiefs reciprocate tribute with *tabua* (whale's teeth).[13]

Throughout central Fiji, with respect to ethnically Fijian people, everyone is either 'land' or 'sea' in relation to others. Within Sawaieke village, members of *yavusa* Sawaieke are 'land', members of the chiefly *yavusa* Nadawa are 'sea'; in relation to the island of Batiki, Sawaieke country (all eight villages) is 'land' and Batiki is 'sea'; so even though one is born into a given classification, one may be 'sea' *vis-à-vis* certain people even while one is 'land' *vis-à-vis* others.

Chiefly *yavusa* are 'sea', but this does not mean that 'sea' is above 'land', for the exchange relation between them is one of strictly balanced reciprocity. So, when eating in each other's company, people classified as 'sea' do not eat fish and those who are 'land' do not eat pork; each makes available to the other the products of their labour.[14] That one is by birth either 'land' or 'sea' can explain personal behaviour or dispositions, for example, one is no good at fishing or gets seasick because one is 'land', or skilled at fishing because one is 'sea'.

Men as gardeners who provide 'true food' (*kakana dina*, root vegetables essential to any proper meal) are associated with land, and women, who provide fish, with sea (see note 4 of chapter 2). A baby girl's umbilical cord is placed under a stone in a stream or on the reef so she may become skilled at fishing; a boy's is buried at the base of a newly planted tree so he may become a good gardener. A tree may prompt the remark, 'I planted this for so-and-so' or 'That is my tree'; and if such a tree does not flourish a boy's elders may express worries about his health.

These formalisations of the way land and sea enter into identity are aspects of the material but still implicit senses through which one knows oneself to be attached to a place and a very product of it – knowledge that is rendered explicit in the responsibilities one bears in relation to others.

In Sawaieke, people do not make much of what were once important associations between certain fish, trees, birds, and each *yavusa*. They talk more of the privileges they have in other countries (*vanua*) as a function of ancestral links to them, or describe the forms which their own *sevusevu* (tributary offering usually of *yaqona*) takes in these different places, or how the style of their *yaqona*-drinking ritual is distinguished from others. These identifying distinctions are linked to land and sea and to conceptions of oneself as a product of one's native place – but they are made between countries, as much as within them. Links between countries rest in the relation between their ancestors; those who are *veitauvu* (lit. of the same root) have the same ancestor god or *vu* while those who are *veitabani* (lit. mutually branching) have ancestors who were cross-cousins to one another. These joking relationships denote balanced reciprocity between people of two countries.

Households, *yavusa*, villages and countries are linked by *sala ni veiwekani*, paths of kinship created by marriage; so relations between *veitauvu* and *veitabani* denote chiefly kinship and reference ancestral marriages. These paths are affirmed and in part constituted in the many life-cycle rituals and in everyday *yaqona*-drinking; they are the route too for the connections between village churches within a country. Marriage takes place between groups whose relative status differs, but it does not itself create hierarchy because the exchange relations are reciprocal and balanced over time. The hierarchical relation created by marriage is that between husband and wife; it is the basis of hierarchical kinship within the household.

In all journeyings about their country, people traverse the paths of kinship created through marriage, and the equality of cross-cousins (and of those who are *veitauvu* and *veitabani* across countries) makes these paths ideally level. But the paths connect households within which hierarchy is axiomatic. Chiefly ritual projects on to the community at large an image of the hierarchical household and references the height of chiefly *yavu*. So inside any given house, village hall or church, hierarchy appears to become dominant because one has inevitably to find one's appropriate place on the above/below axis that describes the internal space of all buildings. In certain villages one may be above others and the object of their deference and respect; in others one may be below and have oneself to defer. However, in all villages one may find too one's cross-cousins, with whom one may sit as an equal.

Women are embodied paths of kinship because they 'carry the blood of posterity' (*kauta na dra ni kawa*); a woman goes to a man as his equal, his cross-cousin, but as a wife in her husband's house she is never an owner (*i taukei*); on his death she is likely to return to her own village where her brothers are bound to provide her with the staple vegetables. Married women eat 'true food' from land belonging to their husbands' ancestors; once married, even the fish a woman catches are implicitly provided by the same ancestral source, for if she is pregnant and does not yet know it, she ruins the fishing for all the women present. Because one of their number has yet to recognise that she will bear a child who will belong to her husband's house, his ancestors withhold from her, and from all the other wives present, that which their own labours must provide.[15] Thus a lack of success in fishing implicitly reminds the women that they are not owners in their husbands' houses. Women's low status as wives, by contrast to their status as sisters, is historically dependent on their material relation to land, which rendered them unable to attend on and be empowered by their own ancestors; this low status is being transformed by Christian practice whereby a woman can approach God directly without the mediation of a man (see Toren 1988).

The ancestors' benign power from the Christian God makes the land fertile and enables a man to fulfil his obligations to produce 'true food' for consumption and exchange and *yaqona* for tribute to chiefs. But invocations of the ancestors are usually only implicit, for example in the names of the forbidden *yavu* that form the honorific titles of *yavusa* and clan. Even so, in accepting an offering of *yaqona*, one highly respected man of chiefly birth called not only on the Christian God, but on 'the ancestors of the land [*na vu ni vanua*, lit. the roots of the land] that they might also bless our living in the manner of kinship'. Explicit references to fertile power tend more often to invoke the Christian God; so one young man told me that he began each day's work in his garden with a prayer that his work would be fruitful.

God and commodity exchange as sources of material power

In prayer and other formal expressions of belief, villagers assert the Christian idea that humans are 'the highest' of God's creation. Thus in a prayer offered at a meeting of the island-wide council, the Sawaieke preacher prayed extempore: 'To Heaven, to the holy dwelling place. You the true God, you the God whom alone is served ... you created the heavens and you created the earth too that we people might inhabit it. We the people know that we are the most excellent of the creation in your hands ...'

The Christian God and his holy dwelling place come first in any recital of names and places, and Christian practice continues to transform the land; so the landmarks of power today include those wrought by 'development' (*veivakatoro-caketaki*, lit. moving upwards together). In 1981 some unused *yavu* in Sawaieke were levelled in the cause of development, making one old man weep and rail impotently at the bulldozer: 'Now our *yavu* are lost, those that belonged to our ancestors.' Some old people sympathised, but most people I spoke to did not; 'it is good that the village be made clean', they said.

That villagers associate development and Christianity is clear in a sermon I heard in 1983 in which the preacher – a Sawaieke villager aged about 43 – talked about the kingdom of heaven and urged us all to change our ways so that we might be worthy of it. He made development (e.g. the opening up of new roads), and by implication the congregation's involvement in development projects, identical with the progress of Christianity and personal enlightenment. The church and our sincere membership of it are, he told us, the very foundation (*yavu*) of all that is good about life in Fiji.

In another sermon, primarily directed towards children, a man in his 50s, an occasional preacher, said: 'The most important thing for you is your gardening land (*qele*, lit. earth, soil). We can't obtain what Indian people can. No. Therefore we must look after the soil that is ours. The soil is ours, it does not belong to the Indians. The soil is ours, it is yours.' He prefaced this statement with the story of an industrious man who every day worked hard on his land and who, when about to die, told his two sons, 'Look, you have your soil, in that soil is hidden a pot of gold; one day it will become visible to you.' Then he died. The sons looked hard for the gold, turning over every patch of earth and incidentally planting crops. These they sold, and because they never ceased to work their land they prospered, and at last the meaning of what their father had said became clear. 'This was their pot of gold; they already had it, it was just their own soil.'

Here is a version of the Protestant ethic, for this tale is not about producing crops for consumption, exchange, and tribute so as to fulfil one's duty to kin and chiefs; it is about producing commodities for sale. The preacher emphasised that land is the material source of well-being for Fijians and does not belong to (and so cannot empower) Fiji Indians who, in other contexts, are often said to have 'no kinship' and to be fully conversant with 'the path of money', which itself implies that commodity exchange might be antithetical to kinship. However, the telling of this tale in church suggests that the diligent production of commodities is desired and blessed by the Christian God and thus implies that it is not antithetical to 'the way according to the land', which is itself held to be at once Fijian and essentially Christian (see Toren 1988). But kinship is in part constituted in gift exchange, so at least some of the profits from the sale of produce must be fed back into exchanges between kin.

One cannot alienate land, but one can alienate its products and thus one might get rich (*vutuniyau*, have plenty of valuables) and gain lots of money. The term for money, *i lavo*, was derived from that for the fruit of the *walai*, a vine that is used for lashing together the parts of temporary houses which, by implication, have no proper *yavu*, foundation. Today, by contrast, money derived from producing commodities is made an explicit foundation for prosperity. So the story suggests that to get rich by selling the land's products is entirely legitimate;

but during my 1981–1983 fieldwork, no adults ever suggested that one could actually get rich through hard work, though clearly one might use the idea to encourage good practice in the young. Then I was told that a villager could become rich only by attending on the ancestors in their devilish guise, i.e. by witchcraft. One could 'drink *yaqona* on one's own', pour libations to an ancestor and name one of one's close kin – who was thus offered as sacrifice – and so empower the ancestor and oneself, so that riches simply came to one. Here personal riches resulted from a selfish, evil act that was antithetical both to kinship and chiefly authority.[16]

However, by 1990, *yaqona* had become a lucrative cash crop and one could indeed become relatively rich by dint of hard work. So on my second field-trip I heard people respond to the sight of a garden well filled with mature *yaqona* plants with estimates of how many thousands of Fijian dollars the crop would raise. Money gained by cash-cropping *yaqona* had conspicuously enriched those families with many sons who had remained in the village and had raised their status too, for it enabled them not only to build new houses of concrete blocks, to buy videos and boats, but also to contribute substantially to village projects; in one case where riches had not, at least in part, been re-distributed, people suggested that they were ill-gotten gains, obtained by embezzling certain public funds.

So commodity transactions have not precipitated a sharp break with tradition, for money and commodities are not allowed to escape the kinship nexus.[17] Illegitimate riches – by definition those one keeps to oneself – are associated with tradition in the form of an appeal to the ancestors in their malign guise and with 'the path of money' in respect of immoral behaviour. Legitimate riches are those one is prepared to give away and in so doing at once demonstrate and constitute kinship, they are associated with tradition in so far as they are obtained through exploitation of the land, whose ultimate owners are one's own ancestral gods, and with development and Christian practice in so far as the latter are seen to augment the power of chiefs and increase the well-being of the community at large. So villagers' ideas of a transformed and transforming tradition – *cakacaka vakavanua* (lit. working, acting, doing in the manner of the land) – allow for a notion of themselves as truly products of a land that has assimilated market exchanges and Christianity (in the case of Gau people a thorough-going Methodism) to itself.

Transforming the emplaced past in the present

Fijian villagers emphasise direct embodied experience of the land: seeing, touching, hearing, and smelling. In old *meke* songs that accompany narrative dances and songs that are more lately authored and sung to guitar music, they regularly celebrate their villages and countries by name, the song of the birds that live there and the smell of flowering trees and plants that grow there. The smell of a place can be a mark of certain ancestors: this is true of the vanilla-like scent of the sand at a beach near Sawaieke, while an inexplicable bad smell in the house alerts one to the potentially malign presence of 'the two ladies' (*ko i rau na marama*). Smell is a feature of personal attractiveness, so the flowers that women wear to community celebrations (and later usually present to male guests) are selected as much for their scent as for their appearance, and when a man comments on a garland he is likely to suggest that its smell is seductive: 'The scent of your garland is wafting my way' (*E boi vinaka mai na nomu isalusalu*). Here the act of smelling is implicitly a form of consumption and may be allied to the idiom for sexual intercourse, whereby the man 'eats' and the woman is consumed.

Consumption by smell is powerfully evoked in mortuary ceremonies or *reguregu* (lit. sniff-kissing). The corpse is laid out on the floor of a house in the honoured place above, and just before the coffin is closed and removed for burial, the close kin of the dead come one by one, press their noses against the cheek or forehead of the corpse and sniff deeply, taking into themselves its sweet, rotting smell. This ceremony implies that, in the past, death as a radical conversion of substance was pivotal to the cycles of consumption and exchange between the people and the land. The intangible substance of the dead was consumed by their living kin and their tangible substance became part of the foundation of houses to constitute immanent ancestral efficacy (*mana*).

This immanent *mana* was made material in the fertility of land and people and, crucially, in the person of the paramount chief. The people were the land's substance; they gardened and fished, consumed the products of their labour, and exchanged them in terms of a balanced reciprocity between land and sea. At the same time they rendered certain relations hierarchical through the transformation in ritual of balanced reciprocal exchange into tribute and thus constituted husbands as heads of houses and certain heads of houses as chiefs.[18] The sacrifice of death broke the cycle of exchange and tribute between people, and between people and the land, for the dead were removed from those exchanges between kin to become objects of consumption. But just as consumption of the food products of the land fuelled the living and created the heat of sexual desire that produced children, so the land's eventual consumption of the material substance of the dead constituted the ancestral *mana* that drove the entire process. His installation made a chief at once the object of sacrifice and the sacrifice itself; in drinking the installation *yaqona* he died as a man to be reborn as a living god (Sahlins 1983). His sacrifice rendered the *yaqona* root he received as tribute a medium for the conversion of immanent and dangerous ancestral *mana* into a material form whose effects could be known by the lesser chiefs (i.e. married men) who drank after him.

A paramount chief also received tribute in the form of people taken captive in war; they were sacrificed on such occasions as the building of his house where they were buried upright at the base of its corner posts, or their bodies might form the rollers over which his outrigger canoe was launched. Such prisoners were also regularly eaten; thus 'the flesh of the land' – but of land that was not one's own, for one did not eat close kin – was directly consumed by the high chief, to at once express and constitute his *mana*, which was dispensed to other men who ate after him. In his own person he converted immanent ancestral power into a manifest efficacy in war and into fertility and so came to embody his country's prosperity, while his talking chief or herald was literally its face or eye (*matanivanua*).[19]

Today death can be a sacrifice only to the Christian God and villagers are likely to deny that any other ideas are implicit in mortuary and installation rites and in day-to-day *yaqona*-drinking. But the transformations of earlier ideas evinced in what is said ·and done by contemporary villagers continue to bind their identities to the land itself. And even as the land has been and continues to be transformed by human action, so villagers transform their conceptions of the land and the past in which it was formed.

Historically these conceptual transformations were rendered more radical by the move from war villages in the hills to more peaceful confederations of villages on the coast – villages that nevertheless were sometimes at war, then with the 'coming of the light' (*ni lako mai na rarama*) and mass conversions to Christianity in the wake of conversion by powerful chiefs, the coastal villages became settled once and for all. Under British rule the land claims of all were written and mapped; graphic and written representations of the land began to enter into people's consciousness of themselves in relation to land and tied their ideas more closely to genealogy than is likely to have been the case in the past. Today one cannot be deprived of one's land rights because one does not use them, but neither can one formally give land to others; that land rights were written (even though these records are open only to chiefs) rendered the giving of land and the gaining of it by force of use, largely impossible.

The ancestors inhabit the land they formed and through the cycles of production, consumption, exchange, tribute, and sacrifice of which the land is an integral part, they continue to impress historically constituted relations on their descendants. So the tension between competitive equality and hierarchy, between balanced reciprocity and tribute, that is evident in the topography of the land still informs tussles for higher status and chiefly rivalry, both of which are today manifest in a competition to contribute larger sums of money to community projects than others can do. But the actions of the ancestors are not immutable, because the land itself has been and continues to be transformed – the *yavu* levelled, roads built, buildings erected. And in any village, beside the green and adjacent to one another, stand the church and the village hall, where community-wide meetings are held and committees formed to oversee day-to-day village affairs. So relations between people may be 'in the way of the church' (*vakalotu*) and 'the way of central government' (*vakamatanitu*) even while they continue to be 'in the way of kinship' (*vakaveiwekani*), 'the way of chiefs' (*vakaturaga*), and 'the way of the land' (*vakavanua*).

This chapter rests on adult conceptions, but in writing it I have had in mind contemporary village children who, in constituting their own personal identities as

Fijians, are inevitably coming to understand the material world (and thus their relations to one another) differently from their elders. So when, for example, adults remark on banal occurrences and the places one has reached on one's way, these utterances and the uttering of them willy-nilly become part of what it is to be a Fijian agent in language. In this sense the kind of thing that is said by adults today was said by their parents and their parents' parents before them, and will be said again by future adults, but what has changed and will continue to change is the significance of the utterance – i.e. that to which it refers in a material sense external to the person and that to which it refers conceptually in terms of the manifold associations that any given utterance may carry in its train.

Thus a future ethnographer will collect data that may at once seem very similar to my own and significantly different – not only because each person's experience is always unique, but also because the tenor of village life is changing even while it remains the same. During my 1981–1983 fieldwork young children engaged in commodity transactions only on behalf of their elders, but in 1990 they were doing so on their own behalf – for example, selling their labour and the products of their labour to get the money for admission to a house where the owner of a video shows tapes of films and sporting events. These children are also engaged in relations which, in impressing upon them the obligations of kinship and chiefship as constituted in giving and tribute, render purely market transactions as potentially threatening to 'the way according to the land'. In the course of all their complex relations with others, to household and kin, to land and sea, to the Christian God and the ancestors, they are cognitively constituting their identity as particular persons who are at once products and producers of a specifically Fijian history.

Like their forebears, these children are experientially placed in time, in a continuing and transforming present in which the transformed and transforming past continues to inhere. They themselves experience how this past continues into the present through the sights, sounds and smells of the land and through fishing and gardening; but like their elders before them, their conceptions of that past are mediated by their relations with their own contemporaries as well as with adults and so must inevitably differ from the conceptions held by adults. This process of cognitive construction in particular persons, mediated by their relations with others, underpins the continuity of culturally specific concepts even while it transforms them, and allows for the appearance of fixedness in a situation of radical change. In this specific, Fijian, case it makes the ancestral past continue into the present even while, for any given person, it effects transformations in the meanings of that past and thus in the meanings that 'the land' can have for present and future generations.

Part II

THE MATERIAL BASIS OF MEANING

Sawaieke children's understandings of the world they live have been central to my work as an anthropologist. My interest in children, however, has had little to do with any idea that their voices were not heard in the ethnographic record and that this injustice had to be redressed. In my view children should be included in ethnographic research on the same basis as adults – that is, as informants, because only children can give the researcher access to what they know as children about the peopled world. And, as the papers in this part reveal, what children know is of real value for ethnographic analysis.

As an undergraduate in psychology I was fascinated by psycholinguistics and cognition, but I wanted to know how people come to hold ideas like God or 'race', to be certain that democracy is the only proper form of government, or that one's astrological sign is the key to character. In this connection, the methods of experimental psychology seemed to make little sense, in large part because they depend on reducing complexity to a manageable number of variables, which is very good for certain purposes, but not for explaining how people constitute over time the ideas they assert to govern their lives. By contrast, the test of ethnography as explanation is how much complexity it can take in while still remaining coherent and without sacrificing any of the data – some of which may appear at first sight to be contradictory or irrelevant or just plain wrong. The point here is that virtually any aspect of people's lives that comes under study is bound to be manifested in manifold forms of social relations, and the material logic of these relations, even while it is lived by the people with whom one works, is by no means obvious to would-be analysts, who cannot help but assimilate what they see and hear to what they already know. It is convenient for us as anthropologists loosely to classify these relations in terms of domains such as religion, politics, economics, law, kinship and so on, but the challenge that anthropological research presents to us is that of rendering analytical the terms used by the people with whom we work.

However good one's pre-fieldwork training, one goes into the field a novice because participant observation is a skill learned only by practice and it resides as much (perhaps more) in the obsessional writing of fieldnotes as it does in the participating and observing; in other words, one's early fieldnotes tend to be more or less useless, but one has to have written those in order to produce the later, useful material. The discipline of writing fieldnotes makes one a better observer, and the better one becomes at observing, the richer and more nuanced one's fieldnotes ... and so on; moreover, it's in the course of endlessly describing all the mundane details of daily life that one discovers what the interesting questions might be.

I went into the field with the idea that I should work on the domain of what was then called 'the symbolic' and how, in respect of some specific instance, a knowledge of the symbolic is constituted; ritual was clearly crucial to this process, in large part because of its apparently coercive and unchallengeable quality – a point well-made by Maurice Bloch. During the course of my field-work I did all the usual things that anthropologists do and without which there could be no sound ethnography: learning the language, mapping the village, a household survey, finding out about the political economy of the area and the obligations that obtained across clans and between chiefs and the people, collecting genealogies and information on household economy, attending village meetings, church services, festivities, life-cycle ceremonies and so on and so on. And in the course of all this I filled up a goodly number of big books of field-notes, but I didn't know until around twelve months or so after I'd begun, what should be the focus of my work with children – that is, until it dawned on me that my notebooks were filled with diagrams of the seating arrangements that obtained whenever people gathered inside houses, churches, village halls and temporary shelters, to eat, worship, discuss village affairs, welcome an important visitor, or observe a life-cycle ceremony. These diagrams constituted a record, as it were, of a form of day-to-day, taken-for-granted ritualised behaviour that Sawaieke villagers hold to be a necessary expression of hierarchy, itself taken to be a principle of social relations. So I decided that my systematic work with children should focus, among other things, on their ideas about the spatial distinctions in whose terms Sawaieke adults differentiate status.

There is little point in working with children unless one gathers data in a systematic way; this means obtaining cross-sectional data from all age groups up to at least 12 or 13 years old. In my own case I have little systematic data from children under 5 in large part because pre-school village children are not, for instance, much used to drawing and not really amenable to entering into easy conversation with adults. But because I was kindly allowed to carry out my work in the local primary school I was able to include all the children who attended – i.e. all the local children from two villages of the Sawaieke *vanua* who were aged up to 13 or so. I worked in the school for three months and sat in with and taught in all classes; I took English reading classes for instance and helped children with their pronunciation, but I never occupied the position of authority that goes with being 'a teacher'. I never told children off, I overlooked actions that other adults would have censured, I encouraged children to chatter to me and laugh with me and 'tell stories' (*veitalanoa*, i.e. chat or talk about this and that) and the tasks I set for them were always a novelty and, as such, more fun than schoolwork. They walked me to and from school and often enough we enjoyed one another's company outside the village at one of the swimming holes in the bush or beside a stream; at home in the village they were likely to be shooed out of my house by some adult who disapproved of their being there or called to do an errand. Moreover, during the first year of my fieldwork my son Manuel, then aged 7 (he turned 8 during his year in the village) had himself attended the school and taken part in all its learning activities and sports, including the school concert at Christmas and so on. Given that we lived in a house with three children aged between 5 and 10 in the centre of the village and were, by virtue of our peculiarity, highly visible, it must have been the case that the children (like their parents) had observed this particular relation between mother and child and formed their own views about it and, in the children's case, had decided that my apparently *laissez-faire* attitude meant I could be regarded as at once trust-worthy (i.e. I wouldn't tell tales on them) and approachable.

I did not attempt to analyse the children's data until I returned to London and I found it a most difficult task – in large part because one is analysing these kinds of data for regularities and does not know at the outset what they will be and where they are going to emerge. For example, the children's drawings of *yaqona*-drinking threw up such apparent oddities that I analysed the whole set of drawings twice before it seemed that a pattern was emerging, and then took all the figures and graphs into one of my former teachers in University College (Professor Jonckheere) whose expert eye detected a possible conflation of what might be two variables and suggested I look at that particular group again – which I did, and of course he was right, which meant a further re-analysis of the entire set. Then came the problem of coming to grips with what the analysis seemed to suggest and this was where I really had to start thinking hard, for apart from the fact that every one of the 67 children with whom I worked had a unique take on what was going on in *yaqona*-drinking, the regularities that emerged also seemed to suggest that the views of certain children were directly opposed to those of adults. For the reader who might be inclined to think otherwise, I should point out at once that this was not anything like rebellion; these were well-behaved little children aged between just under 10 and 12 years-old or so whose ideas happened to contradict their parents'.

As should become plain in the three essays in this part, these kinds of data – for all that initially they may throw one into a panic – are a godsend to the anthropologist. Their systematic nature means they can't be ignored or conveniently forgotten and also, in coming to grips with them, one is likely to be forced out of one's own taken-for-granted into a much closer and more subtle understanding of the people with whom one works, and thus into a better general understanding of how people constitute their knowledge of the world they live – knowledge in whose terms they describe themselves and their own lives.

The essays in this part are all, in one way or another, concerned with the way that the material conditions of people's lives – from the layout of the village and the houses where they live to the cloth at which they sit for meals and the very food they eat – are concrete instantiations of social relations and as such structure the conditions in which children constitute their own understandings of the categories in whose terms adults talk about the peopled world. But the material conditions of people's lives do not declare their own meaning to the anthropologist. Rather their meaning has to be found out and here children as informants become crucial to the anthropological endeavour.

Children have to live the world and in the course of doing so they find out the meanings that adults give to its manifold aspects. It follows that finding out what children know gives the anthropologist a privileged access to what one might characterise as the puzzles the world poses to children and the processes in and through which they make sense of them. As will become plain to the reader of these essays, finding out what puzzles the world poses to children may help us solve theoretical puzzles in anthropology – e.g. the source of what anthropologists have long recognized as 'the power of ritual'.

The three essays in this part, while they focus on the same set of data, make use of them for rather different purposes; moreover, as will become plain, the theoretical development from one paper to the next was facilitated by my reading of Matrurana and Varela and of Merleau-Ponty (whose *Phenomenology of Perception* was brought to my attention by Jadran Mimica). Here I should remind the reader of the theoretical synthesis proposed in the introduction: *mind is a function of the whole person that is constituted over time in inter-subjective relations with others in the environing world.* So wherever throughout this book I use the term 'construction' I am always referring to the process Piaget called 'genetic epistemology' – i.e. the cognitive construction of knowledge over time, and *not to* so-called social or cultural construction – a usage I find misleading if not useless. The making of meaning is certainly a social process but, as I showed in my introduction, it is also a function of the autonomy of human being.

A final word – the essays in this part are, so far as I know, still unique in the way they make use of what children know either to criticize fundamental aspects of anthropological theory or to elaborate certain of its key propositions. The astute reader who feels the want of a fuller, more phenomenologically based account of what it is to be a Fijian child is, however, referred to various forthcoming papers on how Fijian village children come to embody an understanding of shame, how they constitute kinship as intentionality, how their sense of themselves as Fijians is embedded in what it is to be Christian, and how a particular understanding of space–time enters into their ideas of self and other (Toren, forthcoming, a, b, c, d).

4

SIGN INTO SYMBOL, SYMBOL AS SIGN

Cognitive aspects of a social process

This essay challenges a common anthropological assumption that we can demarcate a domain of 'the symbolic', that this domain is self-evident, located 'out there', its paradigm being given by ritual. This assumption itself rests on the conventional anthropological distinction between sign and symbol, where the sign is propositional or simply referential and the symbol is evocative of meaning beyond itself, and thus on the notion that the sign too is obvious. Here I argue that we should cease to make an *a priori* distinction between sign and symbol and that we should give up the lingering notion that to understand ritual is to analyse its meaning as a relation between metaphors. At best, such an analysis can be only the first step towards understanding the peculiar power of ritual.

I argue below that the notion that any given ritual act is 'symbolic', that is, that it 'stands for' something other than itself, is the product of a process of cognitive construction in persons over time. In other words, for young children ritual is *not* symbolic in the conventional anthropological sense. Rather, young children take ritualised behaviour for granted as part of the day-to-day material reality of their existence. So, in the Fijian case discussed here, the ritualised drinking of kava is, for children, merely what people do when drinking kava. The activity is of the same material and cognitive order as, say, house-building. By contrast, an adult understanding of kava-drinking entails the conscious awareness that the activity is not merely an end in itself, but rather that it expresses certain intangible meanings which themselves make the ritual performance obligatory. This chapter charts the process by which Fijian village children come to understand ritualised behaviour as expressive of certain otherwise intangible truths. My data show that it is only with respect to older children and adults that the analyst is justified in interpreting ritualised behaviour as symbolic.

To some readers this may seem perhaps an obvious and unremarkable observation. However, it is only when we understand the process through which 'the symbolic' is cognitively constructed that we can also understand the coercive power of ritual. As I show below, young children may have a fairly thorough grasp of the explicit rules of ritualised behaviour, but it is the process of constructing over time the meanings of that behaviour that makes them, as adults, convinced of the extrinsic necessity of those explicit rules. Moreover, in so far as one can show how this process occurs, one can also explain certain aspects of how people come to be at once products and producers of a specific, and inherently dynamic, cultural history.

The data described below were obtained during my fieldwork in the village and district of Sawaieke, on the island of Gau, central Fiji, from June 1981 to March 1983 (see note 1 of chapter 1). The data address the Fijian concern with status differentiation in terms of people's disposition in space. I begin with a very brief description of the ritualised behaviour in which this concern is manifest; there follows an account of the way that Fijian children construct their notions of differential status with reference to the spatial axis described by the terms *i cake* 'above' and *i ra* 'below'. As we shall see, this psychological process has to be described as constructive in its nature, but *it does not give rise to a cognitive structure whereby the meaning of above/below can be fixed.* Taken together, these data illustrate something of the way that culturally prescriptive acts at the level of the group enter into cognitive processes in particular persons. I end with some suggestions as to the implications of my analysis for our understanding of ritual.

Manifesting hierarchy

In Fiji, hierarchical relations are typically made manifest in people's relative position on the above/below axis that describes the space inside buildings, usually with reference to a single plane. This hierarchical construct is the spatial corollary of the exchange relation by which chiefs receive tribute and re-distribute it to the people. By contrast, the term, *veiqaravi* ('attendance', lit. 'facing each other') refers to exchange relations of balanced reciprocity that ideally obtain between clans (*yavusa*) and is inscribed in the orientation of buildings to one another in the space of the village. However, the term *veiqaravi* also refers to attendance on chiefs in kava-drinking where people's disposition in space connotes hierarchy across households. I have shown elsewhere how hierarchical above/below is itself a transformation of the ambiguous notion of *veiqaravi*, and is thus simultaneously a transformation of balanced reciprocity into the hierarchical exchange relation of tribute and re-distribution (Toren 1988). Across households this transformation is effected in the ritual of kava-drinking.

In kava ritual the root of the plant is presented to chiefs in its 'raw' form and under their aegis is transformed into drink and re-distributed 'cooked' to the people (the root of the plant is pounded and infused in water). The ceremony of presentation or *sevusevu* is an obligatory form of tribute to chiefs, no occasion 'in the manner of the land' can take place without it; it is at once an everyday matter and the key ritual act of tribute to chiefs. So a chief becomes paramount and fully *mana* (effective) when he drinks the bowl of kava that is prepared and served under the aegis of the commoner chief who is head of that clan that 'makes the chief'. The commoner chief's own *mana* is at once realised and compromised in the act of installation, for in conferring upon another man a privileged access to the 'gods of the land' he thus creates his own ritual subordination. The chief who 'makes' a high chief accords to himself the status of one who 'listens to' and 'attends on' the other, like a young man to an elder or a woman to her husband. His act projects an image of the hierarchy of the household onto relations across households: the high chief becomes 'father of the people', who thus seem to stand to one another as ranked siblings. Nevertheless,. the installing chief retains his status as chief and the reciprocal and balanced relations between clans remain intact, contained, but not denied by, the hierarchy that is given by seating positions in kava ritual and the order of the drinking.

On an everyday basis kava ritual transforms balanced exchanges across clans into 'tribute to chiefs'. In other contexts (e.g. marriage ritual) exchange is competitive, but balanced over time, the various clans 'face' or 'attend on' each other. In kava-drinking people are also said to be *veiqaravi* ('facing each other') but they do so in a space which is hierarchically valued where a small group of chiefs faces 'down' towards the people from whom they receive tribute and the people face 'up' towards the chiefs, whose *mana* from the ancestors and ultimately from God is the source of all prosperity. If men and women are drinking together, a small group of male chiefs is above the *tanoa*, the large circular bowl in which kava is prepared; a group of three to five or so young (unmarried) men sit behind and at the sides of the *tanoa* 'facing the chiefs', preparing and serving the kava; beside the young men and taking up the middle space around them are married men in their due order according to age and rank; below them sit young men not involved in kava preparation, and women. Women in general pay somewhat less attention to status distinctions among themselves than do men, though it is true that elderly women of chiefly rank are usually accorded a seating position that is above that of other women. Given that the form of kava-drinking itself works to constitute the above/below axis of the space where it takes place, one is always in a certain status position *vis-à-vis* all others present, and this status is confirmed by the order in which the drink is served, beginning with the highest-status person present.

The Fijian term for chief may denote any married man or, much more exclusively, the group of clan chiefs (including the high chief). It also refers to all persons (irrespective of sex) who are members by birth of the clan from which a paramount chief is chosen. Rank distinctions supposedly operate such that chiefs are above commoners; within sex, rank predominates over relative age where the rank difference is understood to be the marked term, for example, a named clan chief sits above other clan members even if he is somewhat younger than they are. However, for statuses below that of named chief, relative age is the deciding factor. So, within sex, the interaction between rank and seniority poses little difficulty for status differentiation on the above/below axis.

Gender is another matter. Male status varies as a function of age and rank. Female status is always ambiguous. Where a woman is the eldest of a set of siblings she is owed the respect of her brothers who should defer to her wishes in any matters of ritual importance in her natal household. Thus she has a superior say, for instance, in the marriages of her brothers' children. However, as an in-marrying wife, this same woman owes respect and obedience to her husband, that is, to a man who is her brothers' equal.

The term *veiwekani* (kin) at its widest extension takes in all Fijians; in the behaviour prescribed for interaction between the various categories of kin, hier-archical relations are made to contain, and so prevail over, important egalitarian relations. These egalitarian relations are at once constituted and expressed in balanced exchange between cross-cousins both within and across sex; this rela-tion typically obtains across households. By contrast, all other kin relations are hierarchical and require varying degrees of respect and avoidance; within the household hierarchical relations are at once constituted and expressed in exchange relations that are made to appear unbalanced. This appearance is constituted ritually in the course of every meal where a wife's contribution appears to take the form of tribute to her husband, and her inferior position is manifest in her seating place at the cloth at the pole below. This ritual transfor-mation of the wife's contribution (in terms of both the foods obtained and the labour of preparing them) makes concrete the Fijian axiom that 'Every man is a chief in his own house'. The fundamentally balanced exchange relations between men and women at the level of the group are transformed in marriage into a hierarchical relation between particular husbands and wives.

This transformation begins in the betrothal and marriage ritual. Here the bride ceases to be party to a balanced and reciprocal exchange between equals (i.e. between cross-cousins) and is transformed into 'gift'. Marilyn Strathern (1984) has shown how the 'objectification' of women in marriage rituals in soci-eties with gift economies cannot be equated with the subject–object relation between people and things in commodity economies. Thus, because objects in Fijian ceremonial exchange always have 'people' qualities, that is, are gifts not commodities, a woman retains her subjectivity in marriage. Her rights in her natal lineage will devolve on her children who, as *vasu*, may 'take what they want without asking' from men of their mother's lineage. In respect of herself the woman's rights are greatly attenuated and while she has influence over her husband her formal status is rendered inferior to his. This inferior status is reiter-ated on a daily basis when she takes her place at the pole below at every meal in her husband's house.[1]

There is no neutral seating position inside a Fijian house, village hall or church. The internal space of buildings is valued according to the spatial axis given by the terms 'above' and 'below'. When people are seated together in a space, their relative positions on the above/below axis are understood, *by adults*, to be an expression of the status that has accrued to them outside the ritualised contexts in which that status is actually manifest. One sits in a place that is called 'above', because one *is* above others in a hierarchy that is given by an interaction between notions of rank, seniority and gender. For adults this means that older is above younger, chiefs are above commoners and men are above women. The product of this interaction gives rise to an inherent conflict between rank/seniority and gender.

Here I remind the reader that the above/below axis refers to a *single* plane. Thus in houses, village halls, churches, temporary shelters, and also when kava is drunk out of doors, one part of the space is called 'above' and the opposite pole of the space is 'below'. However, no-one is literally above or below anyone else. In kava-drinking the relative status of all persons in the community is manifest in the activity of the meal at home. The cloth is *always* laid on the floor along the given above/below axis of the house space, and household members have their places there in terms of their relative status. The significance of kava-drinking and meals for people's understanding of relative status is the subject of the rest of this chapter.

Children's construction of the significance of 'above/below'

Children's drawings of kava-drinking

The data below were gathered with the help of children who attended Sawaieke primary school and who ranged in age from 5/10 to 14/2. All sixty-seven children (the entire school roll) were asked to draw a picture of people drinking kava in a gathering in the village hall in Sawaieke; they were told that men and women, young men and girls were all present and having lots of fun. These instructions thus distinguished two possible statuses for each sex. After they had drawn their pictures, each child discussed his or her drawing with me and either spontaneously or in response to questioning told me who were the persons depicted and where they were seated. My questions distinguished a third possible status distinction for each sex, that of high chief and chiefly lady.

I have discussed in detail elsewhere the children's own drawings and their commentary on them (Toren 1988, 1990). Here I simply summarise some of the findings. Most important was the conclusion that the significance of above/below (*cake/ra*) is the product of a genuine constructive process. In spite of definite individual differences (i.e. all drawings had idiosyncratic features), reliable group differences emerged with respect to the age and sex of the children. With the exception of the very youngest child (aged 5/10), all had a knowledge of the polar extremes of above/below; both boys (median age 7/5) ,and girls (median age 7/8) accorded the position above to the high chief, but differed with respect to the position below. Boys give this place to females, girls to females and young men.

Age was a factor in children's ability to make fine status distinctions: younger children did not go beyond the three statuses for males suggested by myself and tended to make only one distinction for females, that of *marama* ('married women'); older children used two more distinctions for males and one more for females. For all age groups there was an interaction between the number of status distinctions made and the sex of the child doing the task; thus, at any age, girls made more distinctions for females than did boys while boys made more distinctions for males than did girls. However, for all children, more status distinctions were made for males than for females.

Younger children showed the high chief alone in the place above. By contrast, the oldest children depicted a small *group* of chiefs above; they also tended to make four or five status distinctions for males. However, they accorded the position below to females as a relatively undifferentiated group, even where they had made the maximum number of four status distinctions among them. Thus, they too, like the youngest children, showed females or females and young men below. Again, this choice was highly correlated with the child's own sex: boys showed females below, girls showed females and young men below. The oldest children's response to the matter of who sits below thus appeared to have remained unchanged; however, the data obtained from children in the middle age range of the sample make it plain that this is unlikely to have been the case.

These children produced drawings that showed a push for equality across gender and within status categories. Thus, boys (median age 11/1) and some girls (median age 11/0) showed either the high chief or a small group of chiefs above, with below them men and women seated according to age seniority, and young men and girls together at the pole below. Others, all but one of them girls (median age 11/1), produced an even more radical representation where the high chief or a small group of chiefs were seated alongside their respective wives above. Below them married men sat with their wives or women of their own age and at the pole below young men sat with girls.

These drawings were especially noteworthy since it is only in the most exceptional circumstances that men and women sit on the same level in kava-drinking and certainly women never sit on the same level as their husbands. Thus these children in the middle age range *depicted a situation they can only rarely or never have seen*, one that makes gender largely irrelevant to the ordering of status. Indeed, a majority of the girls appeared to have constructed a principle whereby status is differentiated according to an interaction between rank and seniority alone. The girls whose drawings showed this radical 'push for equality' across gender and within status categories also showed the greatest concern for differentiating between females, making three or four status distinctions. I use the term 'principle' here to express the explicit Fijian adult notion of hierarchy as a kind of moral imperative; perhaps I should emphasise, therefore, that the precise form that the 'hierarchical principle' takes differs across particular persons as well as across groups.

The drawings of the oldest children revealed that they were more aware of the possibility of ambiguity regarding the position of the high chief when compared with other chiefs, that is, they always showed a small group of chiefs together above; but they also reconstituted a definition of 'below' as the place of females, who were treated as a relatively undifferentiated group over against the ranks of men. In other words, these oldest children had grasped both the principle of hierarchy as manifest in a relative ranking on the above/below axis, *and* the way that gender is a complexly interacting factor that assigns the place below to women in general and tends to make status distinctions for them of lesser importance than they are for men.

The 'problem' of gender is given by the fact that the position of all females below conflicts with the notion that people of chiefly birth are above commoners and older people above younger people. This inherent conflict between three apparently separable factors appeared in the drawings of children aged around 11/0. These data, taken together with those from the youngest and the oldest children, show that the children are constructing a principle of status differentiation out of the interaction between rank, seniority and gender. No single factor may be given analytic priority over the others because, as the children's drawings show, being above is about being a chief and an elderly male while being below is about being a young man or a female, rank by birth being largely ignored.

Prepared drawings

In another task, children were asked to look at ten prepared drawings of different situations and to say who were the persons represented and where they were seated. This task was designed primarily to find out to what extent children would make use of the plane of the page to distinguish different status categories and whether there were any differences in response to the different situations. Here I confine myself to discussion of the main findings that emerged from analysis of children's responses to these drawings (see Toren 1990 for the complete data). A total of forty-seven children, ranging in age from 6/6 to 14/2, took part in this task. The drawings used were simple and schematic so that the seated figures could be said to be either male or female, young or old according to my own or the children's wish. The drawings fell into one of three categories: they showed people drinking kava, eating meals or at meetings. Specific instructions were given for the labelling of each drawing but, in general, the children were asked to label the figures so as to distinguish men, young men, women and girls; they might also be asked to label the high chief and his *matanivanua* ('herald', lit. 'face of the land') or asked to decide themselves whether the high chief was present and if so to indicate which figure represented him; they were also asked to indicate the position in which each of the figures was seated.

The responses to these drawings were analysed to discover the extent to which children made use or the plane of the page to distinguish the various status categories from one another and how consistently they did so. The prediction was that for drawings depicting meals and kava-drinking the children would be more likely to make consistent use of the plane of the page to distinguish status categories than they would for drawings depicting meetings. In other words, I expected children to establish an ordering of status on the above/below axis such that, for instance, having chosen a figure at the top or bottom of a page as 'high chief' and therefore 'above' the rest, the children would proceed to rank the other figures in order of descending status using the plane of the page as an implicit guide. The analysis of the response revealed that not only was there, overall, a high level of consistency in children's responses to the drawings, but that they fulfilled the prediction that there would be a greater consistency of response to the drawings depicting meals and kava-drinking than to those depicting meetings.

The merging of spatial and status categories

Analysis of the children's own drawings and of their responses to prepared drawings establishes that hierarchy and the above/below axis are merged, such that children construct their notions of the interaction between rank, seniority and gender by reference to the above/below axis; for example, to say that a man 'sits above' is to say that he is of high status. The merging of hierarchy with the spatial axis was found for children of both sexes as young as 6/3. Given that a partial merging was found for children around 6/0 one may assume that an understanding of above/below in terms of its polar extremes occurs just before school age.

Children's responses to prepared drawings confirmed the merging and produced further interesting findings. Perhaps the most illuminating but perhaps not so very surprising, is that the position of mother below is the anchor for situations within the household. So, for prepared drawings of meals, all children chose the figure below to be mother, and this was the case whether she was taken to be at the top or bottom plane of the page. By contrast, the figure said to be above was either father, father's elder brother, father's father, mother's brother or a 'guest'.

This finding suggests that mother is most salient in the household, and that it is her position at meals that defines the place that is below. Note that the woman who is mother is wife to a particular man. By contrast, children's own drawings of kava-drinking and their responses to prepared drawings of contexts other than meals show that, in the community domain, it is the high chief who is most salient and his seating position that there defines the place above.

But how does this merging of status with spatial categories come about? Piaget has always emphasised that a child's early cognitions are tied to concrete referents, a point also made by Bourdieu (1977). This is as much the case for my own data concerning a so-called 'symbolic' construct as it is for the so-called 'logical' constructs investigated by Piaget and his co-workers. What emerges most forcefully from the children's data is the crucial importance of the spatial axis given by above/below as this is made manifest in concrete form in houses, churches, at meals and in kava-drinking.

Children acknowledged the salience of 'the high chief' above for contexts across households and for 'mother' below at home before they were fully aware that differential status governs one's position on the above/below axis. For these youngest children it appears that status is concrete. In other words, the

94

paramount is above because 'above' is the term that names that part of the room where he sits; similarly, a woman or a young man is below because this term names that part of the room where they sit. The fact that for kava-drinking boys give the position below to females, and girls to young men as well as females, suggests a child's own gender identification is a factor in his or her construction of the significance of above/below. Nevertheless, one can argue that the youngest children are not talking about status in the adult sense of the term when they describe the seating position of the figures in their drawings, but are rather expressing a simple awareness of the two poles of the above/below axis and the people who generally occupy them when adults gather together.

This is confirmed by the way that, when children begin to accommodate what they know about above/below with what they know about differential status, they produce drawings that distort the typical empirical situation in kava-drinking. The data suggest that it is not before age 8/5 at the earliest that children become aware that it is *relative status* that is expressed on the above/below axis. The youngest children merge status and above/below only in the crude sense that they know that the high chief sits above and women, or women and young men, sit below with married men in between. An enlightened merging of the spatial axis with an awareness that status may be derived from contexts independent of it, occurs for many children at around age 11/0, when their drawings reveal a conflict between rank/seniority and gender in status differentiation. They 're-order' the empirically given image of hierarchy in kava-drinking in terms of an interaction between rank and seniority and largely ignore gender as a variable in differential status.

The children's data show that the high salience of above/below as constitutive of differential status is the foundation for complex adult notions of hierarchy with respect to kinship and political relations across clans, villages and chiefdoms (*vanua*, lit. 'countries'). Adult notions include ideas of *mana* (lit. 'effectiveness'), legitimacy, personal achievement, the significance of mythical relations between the ancestors of clans and of certain ritual observances such as the *sevusevu* (presentation of kava), kava-drinking and so on. Thus, adults never say that a man is above because he sits in that part of the room that is routinely described as above. Rather, he is accorded this position because his status makes it appropriate. For adults it is a matter of conscious awareness that social status governs a person's position above or below. For adults, in direct contrast to children, where the high chief sits is above, because the quality of being above is inherent in him as high chief, and where women sit is below 'because they are women who are seated with chiefs'.

However, it seems that the above/below axis is understood to be more constraining in some situations than others. This is clear from children's labelling of prepared drawings of people at meals, drinking kava and at meetings. From my own observation of meetings where there was no kava, people are no more likely to violate there the constraints imposed by above/below than they are when kava is in evidence. But children's responses to prepared drawings showed them to be more concerned with these constraints for the contexts of kava-drinking and meals than for meetings. In labelling drawings of meetings they were significantly less consistent in representing, for example, an elder above a married man, above a young man.

This differential response reveals a heightened salience of spatial constraints in certain contexts, and one is led to ask why it should occur. It cannot be because meals and kava-drinking have a set and regular format, this is also true of meetings. Nor can it be explained by any absence of association with ideas of transcendent power: prayers precede meetings just as they precede all meals and children's knowledge of the association between kava-drinking and *mana* (here meaning a transcendent 'effectiveness') is likely to be rather vague.

I would argue that it is adult notions of meals and kava-drinking as rule-governed activities that produce children's heightened awareness of the spatial constraints imposed by above/below. For adults, ritual practice can be, and is, expressed in terms of explicit rules.[2] These explicit rules mean that the cloth at meals has to be placed along the above/below axis of the house space and that the *tanoa* in kava-drinking must be placed so that it 'faces the chiefs'; the *tanoa* mediates between the two extremes of the above/below axis and marks out the chiefs' positions above it from the positions of those who are seated below. The cloth similarly draws attention to the disposition of people on the above/below axis. Thus the children's heightened awareness must hinge on the fact that certain concrete elements in kava-drinking and meals are always disposed in the same way and it is the disposition of these concrete objects that emphasises the above/below axis.

The significance of meals and kava-drinking is such that differential status is inscribed both in the activities themselves and in the space where they occur. A chief drinks first when kava is served, speaks first in a meeting and (every man being a chief in his own house) eats first at home. What distinguishes meetings from kava-drinking and meals in drawings labelled by children is that, aside from the figures depicted, there are no other concrete elements present, no *tanoa*, no cloth, to draw attention to the necessity for a continued and *consistent* ranking on the above/below axis of all those 'below' the figure chosen to represent 'the high chief'.

I would argue further that the salience of kava-drinking for an adult understanding of local hierarchy comes in time to outweigh that of any other situation where relative status is expressed. The heightened significance of kava-drinking for adults is no doubt connected with the following: though non-alcoholic, it is mildly intoxicating; it is drunk on all ceremonial occasions; the *sevusevu* and the drinking itself are obligatory and imbued with ideas of the transcendent power of the ancestors and the *mana* of chiefs, whose position in life is 'divinely ordained'. Primary-school children must know something of such matters, though their knowledge is probably at best only partial, but they too come to accept kava-drinking as providing the 'correct' image of the nature of local hierarchy. This conclusion is entailed by the finding that, while drawings by children around 11/0 represent a hierarchy where rank and seniority govern differential status and gender is largely irrelevant, those by the oldest children (the majority over 12/6) represent an image of hierarchy that accords with the typical empirical nature of kava-drinking.

However, it is the salience for younger children of material objects, such as the cloth at meals and the *tanoa* in kava ritual, that underlies the mature conception of above/below. The continuity between a child's and an adult's conception of the hierarchy inscribed in people's positions on the above/below axis actually rests on the *material stability* of ritual; that is, on the fact that certain highly salient material elements are always disposed in the same way. So any additional understanding of the 'meaning' of kava-drinking that accrues to adolescent or adult is inevitably articulated to an awareness of status as being more clearly manifest, more concrete, in certain ritual contexts. The very fact that the adult conception of kava-drinking is richer, more complex, more meaningful than the child's is itself dependent upon the initial and continued salience of the *tanoa*.

Thus children learn about the hierarchy manifest on the above/below axis in specific situations such as meals and kava-drinking and come to associate space with hierarchy in these situations. The learning process is one of gradual construction and it is initially tied to certain material objects such as the *tanoa*, the cloth at meals or the house itself, but these material objects are cultural artefacts; they refer not simply to themselves but to relations between people. So the fully developed adult conception of above/below inverts the child's concept: what was initially understood as material and concrete comes to be seen as an *expression* of a deeper and more abstract principle: the principle of hierarchy as derived from an interaction between rank, seniority and gender.

Sign and symbol as a continuum of meaning

The obligatory ritualised behaviours of adults provide the conditions under which children have cognitively to construct the meanings that make sense of adult behaviours. The child's effort is directed towards expressing and elaborating meanings he or she has already perforce constructed as given in a metaphysical (rather than purely material) sense. What is constitutive for children is, for adults, expressive. In other words, above/below for younger children is what is called a 'sign', that is, a 'signifier' whose 'signified' is certain relations between people in space; for adolescents and for adults, above/below has become what is called a 'symbol', one that contains the sign through a process of cognitive construction so that it comes to stand for status differentiation.

It is this finding that leads me to argue that we should drop any *a priori* distinction between sign and symbol in respect of the analysis of ritual. For, where we anthropologists, along with Fijian adults, take above/below in reference to a single plane to be symbolic and so implicitly metaphorical, the youngest Fijian children take it to be propositional. In the simplest possible terms this means that, for children, ritual refers to nothing other than itself: 'kava-drinking is about drinking kava' and 'eating a meal is about eating'. The activities are not symbolic in the conventional anthropological sense (which is not to deny that for any given child they have specific significant associations, etc.).

It is because we, as adults and anthropologists, have privileged our own notions over those of children that we have taken it for granted that for everyone ritual must stand for something other than itself and that this something is carried by the material symbols, the behaviour (including the language used, etc.) that are prescribed for a given ritual act. My data show that the notion of ritual as symbolic in this sense is an artefact of a developmental process whose eventual outcome inevitably conceals the nature of the process itself from those in whom it is instantiated. This is because the process itself entails that any previous awareness of the conflict between rank/seniority and gender is denied at the point where a mature understanding is achieved. It is only thus that each person can come to make an apparently coherent whole out of parts that are inevitably in conflict. And it is only at this point that above/below becomes fully symbolic for older children, whereas it is propositional for younger ones.

If, as I argue, ritual comes to stand for something other than itself as the outcome of a developmental process, this implies that our received anthropological notion of the symbolic inevitably distorts our analysis of 'the meaning' of ritual. For such meaning as is ascribed to any given ritualised behaviour by ourselves and others lies not only in the ritual process itself, but in the very developmental process through which persons make meaning out of ritual. *This is a process that in its nature is always unfinished, for meaning is always capable of further elaboration.*

The data here also suggest that cognitive construction of 'the symbolic' should not, as Bloch (1985) proposes, be distinguished from the construction of so-called logical relations, for example conservation of volume. In childhood, cognition is initially tied to concrete referents but a mature understanding requires that 'appearances' be in some sense disavowed. So, for example, differential status is freed of its connection to properties of the environment that are at once material and symbolic (the house, the *tanoa*), just as the volume of a liquid is disconnected from the shape of the container that holds it. Vygotsky, Bruner and other psychologists have shown that Piaget under-estimated the child's cognitive capabilities; indeed, work on the earliest cognitions of infants suggests that the ability to make certain basic conceptual discriminations is innate. However, the cognitive processes that govern, for example, conservation of volume or quantity or a linear construct of time do seem to be constructed over time. The products of these processes are derived from an interaction between the child's cognitive abilities at any given time and the nature of the experience/information on which those abilities are brought to bear.

A principle of status differentiation given by an interaction between rank, seniority and gender is constituted by children via reference to material factors given by people's disposition in space in relation to the *tanoa* in kava-drinking, the cloth at meals, the space inside houses, churches, etc. These material factors are reproduced by adults as necessary, that is, rule-governed, manifestations of that principle of hierarchy. So certain adult behaviour is rationalised in discourse by reference to this principle: it becomes traditional to arrange the space inside buildings and to make *tanoa* to accord with the proper expression of God-given hierarchical relations between kin. Thus adults can say that the chief sits 'above' the *tanoa* and is 'faced' by his people because this 'shows our respect for the chief', a chief who has all their ancestors 'at his back'.

Here Vygotsky's account of the way language mediates cognitive development is crucial for, as he shows, 'learning to direct one's own mental processes with the aid of words or signs is an integral part of the process of concept formation' (1986: 108). I would argue that the naming of the above/below axis itself forces children ultimately to make 'aboveness' and 'belowness' attributes of persons as a mark of differential status; that is to say, the way that the terms 'above' (*i cake*) and 'below' (*i ra*) are used by their seniors forces children to place a status construction on their growing awareness that the terms cannot merely name spaces or positions in space. The notion of ritual as rule-governed behaviour (Lewis 1980: 21) is important here. It is the interplay between rule and practice, practice and principle that allows above/below simultaneously in part to constitute hierarchy and to express it, and it is in this interplay that ritual takes on its coercive power in its claim to represent another reality, one that is immanent rather than grossly material, accessible only through tropes.

Roy Wagner has described what he calls 'the obviation model of trope expansion' (1986: 96); here 'core symbols' are made, synchronically in a ritual process or over time in an historical process, to play against one another. So, for example, a ritual sequence may take its meaning against the ground provided by kinship, exchange relations, marriage; when it is kinship that is in focus, the relation is reversed and the ritual sequence becomes the ground and kinship the figure whose 'meaning' is posited in ritual terms. This type of 'figure–ground reversal' is central to Wagner's 'obviation', the process by which a core symbol comes to be at once proposition and resolution, to 'stand for itself'. I would argue that, in so far as Wagner has described the process by which people make meaning, this process is itself likely to be predicated on one such as that described in this chapter.

Data from the youngest children can be understood to demonstrate a fusion between 'figure' and 'ground' with respect to the meaning of kava ritual: the material fact of kava-drinking is its own *raison d'être* and a high chief is 'above' because 'above' is where he sits. To find in kava-drinking what adults find there, children have to realise what they see as concrete to be also figurative in a specific way: they have to realise kava-drinking as being 'about' status differentiation as well as 'about' drinking. Further, if they are to arrive at an adult construct in which kava-drinking is, quite explicitly, understood as a core symbol of Fijian culture, they must come to see kava-drinking as an activity in which the figurative, the 'meaning' aspect of kava ritual, is its only valid justification.

This is a type of figure–ground reversal in which the adult notion of ritual as symbolic is the ground against which children are confronted with ritual as intransigent and material fact. Adults insist on children observing the explicit rules of ritualised behaviour because they hold these rules to express a metaphysical principle whereby differential status is given by God. So, to behave appropriately as adults children have to make the material fact of ritual merely the symbol of its significance, rather than its own justification.

Given that my data show that a 'core symbol' has to be constructed by persons out of their experience over time, it follows that neither cognition nor knowledge can, as in Bloch's model, be divided into the ideological and the non-ideological; nor can the meaning of what we often call 'the symbolic' be located, as in Sperber's (1980) model, in the activity of a symbolic mechanism in the mind. The process of coming to understand the 'meaning' of a complex notion such as Fijian above/below is a developmental one and thus distinct from the 'on-line' process by which people derive meaning from novel metaphors. This is not to suggest that metaphor is irrelevant, but rather that it is here a constitutive element in a developmental process. Indeed, I have suggested above that, for example, kava ceremonies become increasingly significant for adults in so far as they assimilate to 'the meaning of kava' all the many subtle suggestions of differentiated power that it can evoke. This raises the question of how notions of the self enter into the cognitive processes of the 'knowing subject', a question I cannot pursue here, though I note in passing Ricoeur's (1978) provocative observation that 'we are assimilated, that is, made similar, to what is seen as similar ... self-assimilation is part of the commitment proper to the "illocutionary" force of the metaphor ... [we] *feel* like what we see like' (1978: 156). In this connection, the child's experience until well after puberty is that he or she is literally below (i.e. smaller than) others to whom obedience and respect are owed, and above (i.e. taller than) yet others who may justifiably be ordered about. In other words, the earliest understanding of above/below is actually inscribed in the child's own body. The inferential projection of this experience onto others is a crucial part of the process by which a mature understanding of hierarchical relations is reached (cf. Johnson 1987).

It follows too from my data that cultural categories are not, as Sahlins (1985: 145) maintains, received 'ready made' and then 'risked in practice'; nor are they, as Bourdieu (1977: 87–8) argues, merely reproduced as 'practice' for which consciousness and discourse are largely irrelevant. Rather, complex features of cultural practice and the discourse that provides for its reproduction are the product of a genuinely constitutive process, a process that suggests that cultural heterodoxy is inevitable and not, as Bourdieu maintains and Sahlins implies, contingent. This constitutive process has its cognitive focus in ritual. Given that, in the specific case discussed in this chapter, a conflict between rank/seniority and gender is inherent in the principle that effects status differentiation, it is predictable that across sex, people will have somewhat different ideas about the nature of that principle (see Toren 1990 for an account of Fijian notions of personhood and gender). So it may be argued that heterodoxy is an inevitable

100

product of the cognitive process by which that principle is constituted. This heterodoxy (to say nothing of more subtle individual differences) further implies firstly, that the conflict will emerge in discourse and secondly, that it will shape the nature of historical transformation.

I have noted elsewhere that the apprehension of meaning is, cognitively speaking, in itself a rational process, whatever its products look like (Toren 1984). Here I suggest further that all cognitions inevitably have a symbolic dimension, if only because, in being brought into being, any given concept is made to reference both predictable and unpredictable aspects of experience by virtue of people's continuing construction of meaning over time, aspects of experience that may or may not be made explicit. Further, where any new elaboration of meaning is made explicit and enters into others' understanding, there we find the process by which meaning may be understood as the product of a specific cultural history. Thus any 'concept', a term I have largely avoided throughout because of its connotations of boundedness, of being finished, has to be described in terms of a continuum of meaning whose dimensions may be made to manifest as either 'sign' or 'symbol' but which, from an analytical point of view, can only be understood as always both.

Meaning can be constrained but it cannot be fixed; thus Volosinov argued as long ago as 1929 that understanding language 'amounts to understanding its novelty and not to recognising its identity' (1986: 68). This observation holds, true, I suggest, for understanding ritual. As the product of human cognitive processes, 'meaning' cannot be located anywhere outside the minds of human subjects, for it is only momentarily instantiated in the product of their interactions. This is not to imply, absurdly, that meaning is so labile as to preclude communication and the continuity of communication, but rather that it is always in the process of 'becoming'. That this is indeed so is, I suggest, borne out by my Fijian data, which show how a diversity of personal notions of the meaning of ritual may yet allow for unanimity in respect of the explicit rules of ritual practice, and so work to fix as apparently unchanging an historically specific form of social order that is nevertheless changing in everyday practice.

5

MAKING HISTORY

The significance of childhood cognition for a comparative anthropology of mind

It is often taken for granted that, at least with respect to cognition, to their grasp of particular concepts, children simply become – with perhaps some minor variations – what their elders already are. So we may study children to find out how they are 'socialised', but our efforts will have little or no bearing on an analysis of relations between adults. Perhaps socialisation theories were never quite as crude as this, but anthropologists tend still to assume that the endpoint of socialisation is known. This assumption is at the root of contemporary anthropologists' general lack of interest in children.

Theories of socialisation, of acquisition, of child development have been – and remain – ahistorical. This is the case even though, especially in the area of child language acquisition, there exist sophisticated studies showing that children do not merely acquire, as it were untransformed, the meanings that adults hold before them.[1] Indeed, the processes through which children constitute themselves as adults are fundamentally open-ended.

All cognitive processes implicate the person's emplacement in the world, the sense of which is mediated by his or her engagement in the complex relations we describe under the rubric of 'kinship', 'religion', 'political economy' and so on. So, to investigate how key concepts in these domains are constituted over time by particular persons is to investigate history in the making. In other words, human cognition is a historical process because it constitutes – and in constituting inevitably transforms – the ideas and practices of which it appears to be the product. In brief, human cognition renders intentionality as inevitably historical.[2] Intentionality is a biological phenomenon attributable to organisms other than humans, but human intentionality is a function of inter-subjectivity as a human biological phenomenon. Human cognition is predicated on our being simultaneously the (explicit) subjects and (implicit) objects of our own actions and words and the loci of the relations with others in and through which we lead our lives.[3] So an account of cognition as a microhistorical process requires that we investigate precisely *how* it is informed by the history of relations in the collectivity.

The feasibility of such studies, however, demands a new theoretical perspective on mind. The prevailing notion of mind in anthropology and psychology entails a 'dialectical synthesis' that rests on, and reproduces, certain taken-for-granted analytical distinctions – between biology and culture, the individual and society, body and mind, etc.

Below I try to show that a model of mind that is anthropologically, biologically and phenomenologically sound has to be based on the recognition that mind is an *embodied* phenomenon. This draws attention to mind as a function of a certain kind of biological organisation; but embodiment refers too to the fact that mind is not exhausted by knowledge processes that are or can be articulated by subjects; these are only 'the tip of the iceberg' as against those unconscious processes we constitute as knowledge in the body – e.g. particular ways of moving. Along with this recognition goes the more radical realisation that as organisms we are informed not by the peopled world of objects 'out there', but by historically structured states of our nervous systems which function to bring forth the world that we inhabit.[4]

From an anthropological point of view, this model of mind demands a focus on children as at once subjects and objects of history, and on the processes in and through which they constitute their knowledge of the world. But this article is emphatically *not* a plea for more ethnographies of children. Rather, it suggests that not only are studies of children's cognitive processes essential if we are to understand what adults are doing and saying, but also that to neglect to study children is to prejudice analyses of the key features of adult life. By the same token, to study children in the absence of a concurrent study of relations between people in the collectivity at large, can result only in an inadequate analysis.

All our acts are social, just as we reveal ourselves as social beings in all our acts, for there is nothing we can do (even in the domain of private pathology) that is not in some way mediated by our relations with others.[5] Moreover, all our acts are constitutive, if only for ourselves, of the notions these same acts might be said to express. However, the way relations with others mediate our constitution of meaning is especially illuminating in those cases where we can see shifts in meaning over time, either within persons in a longitudinal study, or between persons in a study that uses data obtained systematically from people of different ages from infancy onwards. I have shown in detail in my study of Fijian hierarchy how adult notions structure the conditions under which children constitute their own distinctive ideas (Toren 1990). One fascinating aspect of this process is that meanings made by children may be direct inversions of adult meanings.

Below I discuss four such inversions: Fijian children's views of status as conferred from without versus adults' views of status as immanent in the person; Manus children's materialism in the face of their elders' 'animism'; Abelam children's assumption that pictorial representation is possible where Abelam men deny it; and Euro-American children's understanding of 'racial' categories as evaluative versus adults' understanding of them as perceptual.

It makes no sense to dismiss children's ideas as immature, or to argue that they do not understand what is really going on. Children have to live their lives in terms of their understandings, just as adults do; their ideas are grounded in their experience and thus equally valid. The challenge for the anthropologist is to analyse the processes that make it possible for children to lead effective lives in terms of ideas that are an inversion of those held by their parents and other adults.

An examination of this puzzle suggests that an analysis of, say, a politico-economic process, is illuminated by a concurrent analysis of precisely how children constitute cognitively the key concepts that inform that same politico-economic process. To understand this is to understand how people come to be 'enchanted' (as Bourdieu would say) by meanings they themselves have made; how they come to take for granted their own concepts and practices. It is to understand too how this very process, as manifest in the concepts and practices of adults, structures the conditions in and through which children will come to maturity as particular, historically located, persons who will actively constitute a world that is at once the same as, *and different from*, the world their elders know.

Illuminating inversions of meaning

In any gathering in a Fijian village house, church or hall, an above/below axis governs people's disposition *vis-à-vis* one another, usually with reference to a single plane; no-one is literally above or below others. Above/below is the spatial corollary of the tributary relationship that is constituted in kava ritual, where the root of this plant is presented to chiefs, under whose aegis it is made into drink and re-distributed to the assembled people. This ritual transforms balanced reciprocal exchange across households and larger collectivities into tribute.

Children's commentary on their own drawings of kava ritual helped me to show how crucial is the above/below axis for their cognitive construction over time of differential status, in terms of an interaction between apparently separable cognitive constructs of rank, gender and seniority, no one of which could be accorded primacy. This finding led me to challenge the prevailing theory of Fijian hierarchy as founded in a rank distinction between chiefs and people (Toren 1990). I showed too that, while the psychological process of coming to understand above/below is constructive in its nature, it does not produce a cognitive structure whereby the meaning of above/below can be fixed.

From both an analytic and an indigenous adult point of view, the kava ceremony is central to Fijian collective life. However, where adults see it as expressive, as 'standing for' something other than itself, the youngest children in my sample see kava-drinking as kava-drinking – it merely 'is', like other things in the world. Adult notions of kava ritual make its performance obligatory. Their activities are the ground against which children constitute concepts of kava ritual as expressive; so, at around age 9, children begin to show an enlightened awareness that the above/below axis is about differential status. But their concepts are not, *and even when these same children are grown-up never will be*, the same as those of the adults with whom they are in everyday relations.

Where children around 6 to 9 years old understand a person to be above if he or she sits in that part of a space that is called above, adults understand that position to be above because a high-status person is sitting there. So, for children, who know that all spaces inside buildings are categorised in terms of above and below irrespective of whether anyone is there or not, space confers aboveness or belowness on people; for adults, people confer their own status on the space in which they are.

These data made me realise how profoundly important is the routine evaluation of space inside houses and other buildings for the continuity of Fijian hierarchy, and how the spatial axis itself has continually to be constituted anew in routine ritualised behaviour. However, I should not have been able to make these connexions, nor to offer empirical evidence for a new analysis of Fijian hierarchy, had I not had to recognise that the youngest children's understanding of above/below was grounded in sound inductive reasoning from empirical experience: the above/below axis *constitutes* relations between people as hierarchical. Even so, the thorough-going nature of adult ritualised behaviour (e.g. the above/below axis is always manifest in bodily comportment) forces children ultimately to deny their early knowledge and, in coming to understand status differences as expressed in space, to invert the relation between people and the spaces they occupy.

Here it is important to realise that the process of coming to understand ritual as expressive is not the same as that of understanding a novel metaphor, for while metaphor is an integral part of, or encompassed by the symbolic as manifest in ritual, it cannot, of itself, have the coercive power that ritual has for one who constitutes its meaning over time out of day-to-day experience.[6] When I as a foreigner and anthropologist talk of the meaning of kava ritual, I can grasp that meaning *only* as metaphor. What I cannot do, except through some imaginative effort at empathy, is grasp its meaning as an aspect of the complex set of processes by which a Fijian child becomes a Fijian young person, an adult, an old person.

My findings suggest that the meaning of ritual is cognitively coercive in so far as the process by which we come to constitute its meaning is obscure to us.[7] And I would argue further that it is by virtue of an experience that is cognitively similar to that of Fijian children that we all come to have 'the meaning of ritual' inscribed in our very bodies, in our emotional responses, in our confident understanding of the behaviour of those alongside whom we live our own lives. The irony here is that our understanding can only ever be partial, for only rarely and retrospectively can we grasp the significance of the process by which we came to know.

It is interesting to consider the Fijian case alongside some findings of Margaret Mead who, in 1932, showed that Manus Island adults, but not children, spontaneously attributed causal spirit powers to, for example, the operation of the wind chimes she had hung in her house. By contrast, when children were asked why a canoe had slipped its moorings, or why the wind chimes sounded, they said in the first case that it was some known person's fault and in the second that it was the wind. Mead herself attributed these and countless other determinedly material causal statements to the fact that Manus children were not yet participants in ritual life and knew little of the relations their parents carried on with the spirits of the dead. She remarks that when children did attribute power to inanimate objects, they were using some stock phrase heard from their elders or were retailing a bit of current gossip, etc. She did not record these cases. However, in my view they are just as interesting as 'spontaneous attributions', since they suggest that, given that the children were materialists and their parents animists, the children took it for granted that, for instance, their guardian ghosts were bound (when they finally met up with them) to have a properly material form like everything else. Fijian children seem to grant a similar unproblematic literalness to above/below as distinguishing different spaces on the same plane, presumably because the terms can be, and are, used simply to name certain spaces – as one might say, 'give me the bowl, it's next to you above', where above refers to a space on the floor.

Related findings are reported too by Anthony Forge (1970) writing about the *tambaran* – paintings and sculptures produced by Abelam men and understood by them to be a material aspect of the ancestors, brought into being through the sacred and powerful medium of paint. Men explicitly deny that *tambaran* are images *of* anything, and indeed refuse to attribute meaning to representations in general, so they have difficulty in identifying people and objects in photographs and so on, and insist that what they see are flat planes of colour. But Forge also saw children spontaneously draw images of animals, etc., in the dust on a smooth patch of ground, even though they were scolded by adults for doing so, and he reports that children identified objects and persons in photographs without any difficulty. This raises the interesting question – one that Forge himself did not pursue – of precisely how the men's notion of the paintings as a closed system, as having no reference to objects outside themselves, is brought into being in the course of cognitive development. For even in this brief observation of children's behaviour we can see that men's ideas about *tambaran* appear to entail a denial of their own experience as children, when they seem likely to have known that one might unproblematically represent things through the medium of drawing and painting.

One might compare these three cases – of Fijian villagers, Manus Islanders and the Abelam – with one that is, on the face of it, very different. Certain aspects of learning appear to be domain specific; e.g. neonates can distinguish living kinds from non-living kinds and, within the former category, humans from other animals. Lawrence Hirschfeld (1988), using data from psychological studies of Euro-American children's acquisition of 'racial' and 'ethnic' categories, wants to argue further that we are innately predisposed to classify human groups around moral evaluations.[8]

It seems that young children (3.5 to 5 years old) invert the relation adults make between the affective and perceptual dimensions of racial categories; they focus on moral evaluations where adults, by contrast, focus on perceptual attributes.

The children attribute moral values to racial terms before they can use the terms reliably to classify others or themselves; moreover, their negative judgements seem to bear little relation to the stated attitudes of their parents, teachers, etc.

The studies reviewed by Hirschfeld show that young black children are making as many negative evaluations about 'black people' as are white children; what they are not doing is reliably identifying themselves or others as belonging to the category 'black'. But these data cannot show that the children are incapable of constituting categories on the basis of skin colour, eye colour, hair type and so on. Rather, they suggest that children cannot easily reconcile these distinctions with negative moral evaluations, e.g. that they cannot identify themselves or someone they know as 'black' if they have already come to know that 'black is inferior', for this entails that the child must negatively evaluate itself or persons whom he or she knows and/or loves. Children's negative moral judgements are not about difference per se; that they centre on 'out groups' suggests that differential power relations between adults inform the process through which children constitute their own understandings.

Hirschfeld does not address the conjunction between perceptual and affective attributes in respect of 'race' as a historically constituted category; he does not explore 'racial categories' as moral constructs that inevitably imply racism.[9] Irrespective of whether they are black or white, racist or not, adults know about the evaluation of racial categories. But Hirschfeld can argue that racism is innate, because he cannot connect what children know with the knowledge of adults.

A child's ideas are related to, but do not precisely mirror, those of its peers and seniors. Rather, a child's notions properly belong to the child as a function of its age, cognitive abilities and the history of its relations with others in an environment that has a specific cultural history. Given our profoundly racist history, the challenge is to analyse how it is that children reproduce prevailing racist attitudes before they are able to use racial and ethnic labels either for others or themselves.

The affective dimension of concepts tends to be carried in the body itself and what we convey through bodily praxis is for the most part outside our own conscious awareness or control and outside the conscious awareness of those who observe us. Given that affective and evaluative judgements are conveyed as much by these means (and arguably more directly than in speech) it does not seem fanciful to suggest that what we know about racist judgements may be conveyed in our very bodies – and even despite our best intentions. For young children this material 'sub-text' may be more powerful and more salient than spoken attitudes that are concerned to deny it. Indeed, racist notions are so deeply rooted in Western history that it is no more surprising that a child of black activist parents should make negative moral evaluations of 'black people' before he or she fully knows to whom this term may apply, than that the child of parents who are feminists should make negative moral evaluations of 'women'.[10]

Cognitive processes and social mediation

Certain domains of meaning, e.g. 'colour' or 'living kinds', may indeed be a function of specific cognitive processes. From an anthropological standpoint, this is not necessarily problematic; it becomes so only when domain specificity is taken to imply a relative absence of social mediation and thus of historical variation.

Many anthropologists (of whom Hirschfeld is one) and virtually all psychologists use the term 'social' as if it can be applied to only a subset of human knowledge and to only a subset of cognitive processes. But human cognition is inherently social because human intentionality is predicated on inter-subjectivity, so we cannot make meaning in a way that is non-social. That neonates can distinguish humans from other animals is itself evidence that cognition is – from the beginning – bound to be mediated by others.[11]

Mind is the condition of human being in the world. Only if we ignore the fact that the brain and the nervous system of which it is part are literally embodied, can we separate the cognitive from the social. So the human mind cannot be analogous to a set of computer programs – however complexly rendered. That our cognitive processes are constituted through our embodied engagement in the world and predicated on inter-subjectivity makes these processes profoundly different from those programmed into a computer. For humans, living and knowing are the same thing. So, from an analytical perspective, the biological, the cognitive, the affective and the social are aspects of one another rather than separable and dialectically related processes.[12]

Cognition as a biologically microhistorical process

All living organisms are autopoietic unities – i.e. they are autonomous and self-producing, at once products and producers of the biological processes that are proper to them; so the structural organisation of an organism functions to specify those changes of state in the environment that produce changes in the state of the organism. Thus the organisation of the nervous system, in organisms that have one, functions to constitute the world those particular organisms inhabit. I take this view of the biology of cognition from Maturana and Varela (1972; 1988). Discussing his earlier work on colour perception (Maturana *et al.* 1968), Maturana suggests that if the activity of the nervous system is determined by the nervous system itself, and not by the external world, then the external world can 'only have a triggering role in the release of the internally determined activity of the nervous system' (1972: xv).

This view is compatible with the recent theory of the physiology of perception proposed by Freeman who shows that, in rabbits, any single olfactory identification 'depends on the simultaneous, co-operative activity of millions of neurons spread throughout expanses of the cortex' (1991: 34). The contour plots mapping this neuronal activity show that, while a consistent plot can be produced by initial conditioning, it does not remain constant for any given odorant (sawdust for instance), but changes as a function of the animal's experience (conditioning to an additional odorant, say banana). This suggests that one cannot retain a distinction between perception and cognition because 'an act of perception is not the copying of an incoming stimulus. It is a step in a trajectory by which brains grow, reorganise themselves and reach into their environment to change it to their own advantage' (ibid.: 41).[13]

Leaving aside its perhaps questionable evolutionary implications, this statement is most obviously applicable to humans in respect of the processes of formation and continuous transformation of embodied cognitive schemes, over time, from birth to death. As humans, all of us have a certain biology in common and we are all subject to the same general physical conditions of the world and the same physiological processes; but we are biologically social too and this means that the world our structural organisation allows us to 'bring forth' is a world whose particular significance is mediated by particular other humans. Cognitive schemes are 'self-regulating transformational structures', i.e. they are autopoietic but, for any one of us, the continuous formation and transformation of cognitive schemes is inevitably mediated by particular relations with others.[14] It is in respect of our different histories that we differ from one another as particular persons within particular, socio-culturally specifiable collectivities. So, to take perhaps the most fundamental example, social relations enter into the very structuring of attention – in other words, what one attends to is a function of one's history and even novelty is historically constituted.[15]

The world of objects and other people is implacably present to us all, but inevitably we live it as a product of our own minds. This does *not* preclude the making of sound, defensible and well-grounded statements about the peopled world. It simply recognises that all such statements are informed by the speaker's history because, given that humans are biologically social creatures, all our cognitions are mediated by relations with others. Neither does it preclude communication and mutual understanding; rather, it recognises that because we are biologically social beings the very notion of subjectivity presupposes intersubjectivity. So when we talk to others we assume that they mean to mean in the same way as we mean to mean, and indeed in large part we are right because all of us have inevitably to talk through the world, out of the assumed commonality of our physical and physiological experience and by reference to things in the world. However, at the same time that we are communicating through reference to the world, the meanings we make and communicate are mediated by the history of our relations with others; so while we can communicate with others, we inevitably do so from our own perspective, which includes our understanding of the other's perspective on ourselves.[16]

So if it is not the world of objects 'out there' that informs us but historically structured states of our own nervous systems, it seems mistaken to hold to any theory that rests on the binary distinctions that we have been accustomed to take for granted: biology/culture, individual/society, body/mind, perception/

cognition, emotion/rationality, subject/object, universal/relative and so on.[17] For if one accepts that we are informed by states of our nervous systems and that history enters into the formation of these states, then these binary distinctions collapse and the fundamental terms of our theories have to be re-worked. So, for instance, terms such as 'universal' or 'relative' in respect of cognitive theories become irrelevant when confronted with a biology of cognition that simultaneously suggests an all-encompassing universalism and the most extreme relativism.

Moreover, given the inverted relationship between what adults know and what children know with respect to certain key issues, an understanding of precisely how cognitive processes are constituted and what this might tell us about collective relations between people is a proper focus for anthropological endeavour. It also requires a new kind of study – one that complements an analysis of relations between people in terms of 'political economy', 'kinship', 'ritual', etc., with an investigation into how children constitute over time the key ideas that adults use to describe these relations. It is this kind of study that should enable us to understand how these key ideas are historically transformed in the very process of their constitution.

The child in psychology and anthropology

The assumption that one can take for granted analytical distinctions between 'the individual' and 'society', and between 'biology' and 'culture', is central to normative theories of socialisation and cognition in both anthropology and psychology. The child is taken to be biologically an asocial individual who becomes social/cultural by virtue of actions performed upon it by others. Thus the child is made the locus of a split between 'individual' and 'society', between 'biology' and 'culture', and processual relations with others are reified as 'structures' that are outside and beyond the particular persons who are cognitively constituting them as such.[18]

We are so enchanted by the idea of 'the individual in society' that we have been prepared to accept it even in the absence of any field-based ethnography concerning what this phrase might mean to the particular people who are so described. And this is remarkable because since Marx, to say nothing of Durkheim, and more recently Dumont or Strathern, it has been acknowledged that 'the individual', 'society' and 'culture' are analytical abstractions rather than empirical entities.

Any analysis of what is known inevitably requires an analysis of how it comes to be known and this implicates notions of the person. Many recent works talk of 'social construction' or 'cultural construction' – terms that crept unexamined into the anthropological literature some years ago; indeed, 'social constructionism' has recently become a new dogma in social psychology. However, what its proponents see as a radical departure is itself a product of the very theoretical impasse that social constructionism pretends to dismantle.

So, for instance, the contributors to a recent psychology text on 'collective remembering' take the view that what 'individuals' say and do and what they remember can be explained by 'context' which is itself conceived of as 'discourse' (Middleton and Edwards 1990). Note that here 'context' and 'discourse' replace what was referred to as 'society' in earlier social psychology. The 'discourse analytic' approach privileges language as the domain of consciousness, of memory, of social relations, of culture. The various authors ignore the cognitive processual nature of remembering in particular persons and privilege its instantiation in collective processes. But neither do they analyse these collective processes in respect of their politico-economic and other ideological dimensions. Further, in ignoring the cognitive dimension, they fail to address the genuinely constructive processes through which particular forms of sociality are constituted. In short, 'social construction' is a meaningless term, for it implicitly locates constituting processes in some abstract space between people; relations between people in the collectivity are reified into 'discourse' and thus become – yet again – a domain of human experience rather than the very stuff of it.[19]

Any act (remembering, for instance) implicates the embodied cognitive processes that constitute it. In other words, it implicates the whole person; so any act is at once affective, symbolic and material – i.e. intentional. Because the person always acts in and through relations with others, particular forms of intentionality constitute and are constituted by the politico-economic processes that describe collective relations. This is true of intentionality as manifest in walking or eating, in writing a book or reading it, or in crowning the queen – and remembering is critical for all our acts, from the most simple to the most complex.

From birth onwards, each person is the active locus of his or her relations with others. So what is said or done has always to be analysed as a constituted product of the experience of particular persons, i.e. of the history of their responses to what other people have said and done. It is through our embodied experience in a world whose relatively invariant material processes (e.g. gravity, the cycles of day and night and the seasons, and other physical and physiological processes) are historically constituted that we map phonemic distinctions onto the world. Or to put it more simply, as children we learned to speak because around us other people were speaking and we came to apply our classifications with certainty, not only because around us other people did so, but because our embodied experience of relatively invariant material processes, mediated by our relations with others, gave us a reliable basis for being certain.[20]

It has been pointed out that the child is a 'cultural invention' and that 'somehow, whatever it is that is out there in the culture that says "this is what a child is" is being communicated to and constructed by the child himself' (Kessen 1983: 35). This implies not only that other people's notions of what a child is enter into the child's cognitive construction of ideas of self and personhood, but that we have to recognise that our own theories have been, and will always be, produced by persons who are themselves at once products and producers of historically specific notions of what a child is.

This is not to say that our theories are necessarily invalid. Indeed, one may argue that in so far as each theorist's position is derived from what he or she observes and is able to think about these observations as a function of his or her own history, each one of us gets hold of some aspects of particular human realities. However, at this point in our own history it seems important to address the continuing representation of the child as 'other' and its implications for theory in the social sciences.

Take the notion of the child that is constituted in classical psychoanalytic theory. In order to point up its historical specificity, it is useful briefly to address one of its nineteenth-century analogues. Crudely one might characterise the child in Freud's theory as an analogue of another notion prevalent at the time – that of the instinctual savage. The imperialist ideology of the time characterised the savage as requiring the civilising influence of the mission, the market and the law – all of which were thought of as helping to bring savage appetites under control; these appetites were manifest in the stereotype as indiscriminate lust, generalised aggressiveness, cannibalism and other oral desires for items thought of as non-food. By implication the toilet habits of the savage had also to be brought under control since one of the savage's qualities was to be 'dirty'. The child in classical Freudian theory is very like this stereotypical savage – a version perhaps of 'the good savage' who can be made to want what the socialising agents want to impose; this is the child who is tamed and socialised through control over his or her 'drives' (for the savage substitute 'instincts') and particularly through control over his or her sexuality as this is manifest in gender identification, and the notions of conscience and morality. Some colonial administrators, missionaries, etc. characterised the savage as amoral rather than immoral, as one who could be made to learn what was proper. Indeed, for these same more 'well-disposed' persons the adult savage was 'like a child'.

My point here is that, in all its transformations both classical and contemporary, psychoanalytic theory has to be understood as the artefact of historically specific political and economic processes, by virtue of which it has become part of a particular rhetoric of control. Indeed, the impotence of psychoanalysis as explanatory social theory lies in its failure to realise itself as a historical product; this, I would argue, is evident in its projection onto the very body of the child of a struggle for power that can only be waged in the field of adult sexuality.[21]

The child as 'other' in early conditioning theories was also understood to be in a state of nature – as was implicit in the easy generalisations that were made from the behaviour of dogs, rats and pigeons to the behaviour of persons in general, and children in particular, in respect of learning. Perhaps there is little to be wondered at in the fact that the massive elaborations of conditioning theory, from its early Pavlovian roots, took place in the United States with the work of Watson and later of Skinner and other behaviourists. The 'black box' theory of mind that was central to this behaviourism complements rather neatly

American notions of radical individualism in which any given person starts off without any history and makes his or her own, independent of other people. The more sophisticated 'social learning' theory showed children's perception and imitation of others to be crucial to what they learned, but social learning theory too subscribed to a taken-for-granted individualism that was modified by 'society' but was never itself a matter for interrogation.

Of course, the individual as the rational, freely choosing, autonomous actor who enters into contractual relations with others on the basis of rational calculations of advantage, is central to classical economics theory, and to its contemporary forms. However, it seems highly unlikely that any of us in the West, or anywhere else, actually hold ourselves to be individuals in this sense; apart from any more subtle differences between people, class and gender are bound to be important here. So, it is not only the case that one has to throw out 'the individual' as an analytical category – one has to question the extent to which it is actually a prevailing idea (see e.g. Ouroussoff 1988).

Most important for my purposes here is that the notion of the child as an asocial, ahistorical individual is implicit in the various psychological and anthropological theories of cognition, though it takes somewhat different forms in each of them. Thus the child at the centre of Piaget's consciously biological model of cognitive development is a philosopher in the making, one who cannot help but seek a rational grasp of the world – a notion that may be related to Piaget's inheritance as a European intellectual of the projects of the Enlightenment. However, when Piagetian notions are taken up by American psychologists who have elaborated a cognitive stance, for example Case (1984), what one winds up with is the cognitive transformation of the black box – the computer model of mind in which the programs (i.e. the cognitive processes) are conceived of as separable from the hardware (i.e. the brain). The behaviourists refused to speculate at all about what might be the nature of mind, on the grounds that all they had to go on was what was manifest in behaviour. In so far as they refuse to grapple with either sociality or embodiment, cognitive scientists may similarly be said to take a peculiarly narrow view of mind.

Given the mind/computer analogy, it is not surprising that the model of the child that is explicit in psychological studies of 'morality' and/or 'social cognition' is usually that of the child as scientist (see e.g. Ross 1981). Piaget's baby philosopher, uncontaminated by relations with other people, is a disinterested enquirer into the nature of things – this baby cognitively constructs meaning out of his or her experience of the world because it is human nature to do so. By contrast, the baby as intuitive scientist, while similarly uncontaminated, cognitively constructs meaning out of his or her experience of the world in order to be able to control it. Note too that in psychological studies what is referred to as 'social' or 'cultural' is often taken to be a source of 'error' and to stand in the way of judgements that would otherwise be perfectly rational.[22]

Anthropological analyses more often recognise that adults' notions of children and childhood are bound to inform the nature of the development of cognitive processes, and there has recently been some interesting work on notions of the person, on ethnopsychologies and so on (e.g. White and Kirkpatrick 1985). However, when it comes to the study of cognitive processes as such, anthropologists tend to be relatively undiscriminating in their acceptance of psychological models. So, for example, Holland and Quinn (1987) seem to suggest that they can render viable an artificial intelligence model of mind by inserting 'cultural knowledge' into a theory of cognitive 'scripts' which are constructed out of experience of familiar and stereotypical sequences of events. However, even if we accept that mind may be modelled on an information-processing machine, scripts are too highly structured (and thus too rigid) to accommodate the demands that the world makes on human cognition; in brief, this idea of the cognitive scheme as script is not (as is Piaget's scheme) inherently transformational. Moreover, Holland and Quinn also seem to suggest that 'cultural models' are immanent in language and are received, as it were, ready-made – a notion that renders language itself, to say nothing of language acquisition, an ahistorical phenomenon.[23]

Psychological models of mind are ahistorical by virtue of making the social merely a source of extraneous influences on the processes of cognitive construction.[24] Normative anthropological models of cognition, also premissed on distinctions between society and the individual and culture and biology, tend to give equal or even greater weight to the 'social' or 'cultural' side of what is taken to be a dialectical relation between the two terms within each of these dichotomies. However, these anthropological models too remain ahistorical by virtue of their unsophisticated understanding of mind. One might except in part from these strictures the work of Lakoff (1987) and Johnson (1987), both of whom have interesting things to say about how we embody the meaning of concepts embedded in common metaphors.[25] Yet neither of these works analyses the nature of politico-economic relations between people in the collectivity and how these inform cognitive processes in particular persons – in other words, they attempt only a partial analysis of how cognitive processes are constituted over time. Perhaps Jean Lave (1988) comes closest to addressing the complexity of cognitive processes in her analysis of rational problem solving as historically constituted; however, while she identifies many of the problems addressed in this article, she continues to seek their solution in a dialectical relation between 'culture' as an aspect of 'constitutive order' and 'cognition' as located in 'the experiencing of the world and the world experienced through activity, in context' (pp. 178–179). Here 'culture' and 'cognition' are understood to be located at different levels of a 'socio-cultural order'.

This notion of different levels is misconceived for no-one ever confronts 'culture'; rather, the challenge that the world presents to any of us is that of comprehending its complexity as this is mediated by our relations with others. This mediating process means that all our concepts inevitably have a symbolic as well as a material dimension.

Conclusion

Each of the ethnographic instances cited above – Fijian, Manus, Abelam and Euro-American – concerns children's inversions of adult concepts that inform crucial aspects of the political economy of the people concerned. And in each case, if children are to take on the adult point of view, they have to deny their initial, empirically sound understanding. Fijian children have to make status immanent in the person rather than conferred from without; Manus children have to substitute spiritual causation for material causation; Abelam boys have to realise ancestral power through a denial of the possibility of graphic representation; and Euro-American children have to give up their initial understanding of racial categories as moral evaluations and come to see them as merely material.

I have described these as conceptual inversions in order to emphasise that the children's concepts are as valid as those of the adults. In the Fijian case it is adult behaviour that presents children with two contrary, but integrally connected aspects of a single concept, and it seems highly probable that this is true too for the other ethnographic examples. That children constitute the meaning of one aspect of a concept before the other suggests not that it is necessarily the more simple, but that adult behaviour has rendered it the more salient – even when denied. So I would argue that none of these cases can be properly explained as merely a function of a simple developmental shift from concrete to symbolic conceptualisation. In no case can the adults be said to 'know better' than the children, even if they may be said to 'know different' and to 'know more'. Moreover, in each case, what the child knows remains an integral (if implicit or even denied) part of the adult's concept. So adults communicate to children what they know, rather than what they say they know – an observation that suggests that, as anthropologists, we cannot fully understand relations between adults unless we investigate what children know about these relations and how they know it.

Thus a fruitful (and so far largely neglected) method of analysing continuity and change in relations between people is to complement their study with a concurrent study of how, over time, children constitute their understanding of what adults are doing and saying and of the relations between them.

In this article I have argued the case for an anthropological theory of cognition that recognises that humans are biologically structured to be at once products and producers of their own, collective and personal, histories. Such a theory cannot be about 'individuals' who are conceptually separate from 'society' and 'culture', whose 'perceptions' can be distinguished from their 'cognitions', whose 'emotions' are neatly separable from their 'rationality'; it has to be about persons who, as the loci of the social relations in which they engage, are bound to manifest the biology of cognition as historically located subjects. And this model, I suggest, demands a focus on children, and on the processes in and through which they constitute themselves as mature persons who are at once the subjects and objects of history.

115

6

RITUAL, RULE AND COGNITIVE SCHEME

This essay elaborates some of the broader implications of my previous work concerning everyday ritualised behaviour in Fiji and how it informs the process of children's cognitive constitution over time of a concept of differential status between people in the community at large. It concerns the interplay between rule and practice in ritual and ritualised behaviour and, elaborating an idea put forward by Lévi-Strauss, suggests that one can generalise the cognitive product of such behaviour as being 'the idea of the rule', and further, that one can with reason speculate that 'the idea of the rule' is the ultimate *raison d'être* of ritual whose 'meaning' aspect is bound to remain secondary. I begin by summarising the results of earlier work and suggesting how they may be applied more generally (see note 1 of chapter 1).

My study showed that Fijian village children constituted over time a concept of status differentiation (i.e. of hierarchy) in terms of a complex interaction between ideas of rank, seniority and gender.[1] Here 'rank' is broadly a function of one's birth as a member of a chiefly or a commoner clan, 'seniority' is a function of relative age, and 'gender' marks out a woman's relation to a man as wife or sister (see note 6 of chapter 1). By age 11 to 12, children have cognitively constituted a mature hierarchy scheme which allows of the interaction between rank, seniority and gender and is sufficiently subtle and broad to allow of the full range of possible discriminations between adults.

But how do Fijian village children come to constitute cognitively this particular idea of hierarchy? My data suggest that they do so by making meaning out of certain routine behaviours that are performed by adults and enjoined by them too on the children themselves. These routine behaviours are especially noticeable at meals, *yaqona*-drinking, church services and village meetings and concern bodily comportment and people's disposition relative to one another inside any village building. In house, church, village hall and temporary shelter the internal floor-space can be, and is, described in terms of an above/below axis: usually the area near the common entrance to a building is below, and the area farthest from it is above – the reference being usually to a single plane. So, when people are seated on the floor in these spaces, they are always and inevitably positioned relative to one another: above, below, or on the same level; one takes up one's position in any space according to one's status relative to other persons present.[2] So, whenever one eats, drinks *yaqona*, worships, or discusses village affairs, one's status relative to others present is always manifest on the above/below axis that describes the space in which people are gathered.

From their earliest years children observe and have to accommodate to this adult concern with people's disposition in space and their relative status. So, for instance, while a toddler may, on informal occasions, move relatively freely among a group of seated *yaqona*-drinkers, its movements are restricted if it ventures too close to the *tanoa* (the central wooden bowl in which the drink is mixed and from which it is served) or if it seems about to violate the space where chiefs are sitting. In such a situation it will be stopped and set down on the mat with the injunction, 'sit down, be quiet' or 'it's forbidden to go up there [where the chiefs are]' or 'don't touch the *tanoa*, it's forbidden'. A 4-year-old is expected not to move about unnecessarily or, if required to pass among seated *yaqona* drinkers or people who are eating, or seated together inside a house, to adopt the proper body posture and walk *lolou* (incline from the waist or crawl on hands and knees).[3] A child of 4 or 5 whose behaviour violates conventional body posture in such a situation is likely to be punished. Thus, the child's earliest accommodation to adult concerns is a function in part of imitation and in part of sanctioned obedience.[4]

According to my data, Fijian village children between the ages of 6 and 9 or so are assimilating their knowledge of these required behaviours to the valuation of the spaces in which people congregate.[5] That is to say, they are aware that the high chief sits above others, that to sit at the pole below is to be low in status and that, as children, they are themselves below everyone who is senior to them.[6] However this is a still a relatively 'raw' understanding – one that is compounded of their knowledge that the space inside all houses, the village hall, and the church has one pole called 'above' and another called 'below' and their knowledge of who habitually sits above and below when people are gathered together. So, for these 6- to 9-year-olds, a chief is above because above names the place where he sits; while women (according to boys) or women and young men (according to girls) are below because below names the place where *they* sit. That gender is already a factor here is evident in the difference between boys' and girls' views of who sits where; however it is not an *explicit* factor in that it is still tied to the concrete spaces in which people gather. However, by age 9, children are beginning to take on the adult view that differential status is independent of the spaces in which it is made manifest. This is evident in the way many children between 9 and 11 or so make differential status by and large the product of an interaction between rank and seniority and ignore the significance of gender.[7] A mature grasp of status differentiation as the outcome of an interaction between rank, seniority and gender is arrived at by 11- to 12-year-olds.

Thus, children learn about the hierarchy manifest on the above/below axis in situations where specific behaviours are mandatory – situations such as meals, *yaqona*-drinking, and church services. In other words, children come to associate spatial distinctions with status distinctions in situations where certain behaviours are *always* prescribed, though they may be more or less constrained in accordance with the formality of a particular occasion. These prescriptions have to do not only with where one sits, but with the placing of salient material objects and with how one comports oneself. For example, the position of the *tanoa* – a wooden vessel in which *yaqona* is mixed and from which it is served – marks out 'the chiefs' who sit above it from 'the people' who sit below, and the cloth for meals is always laid on the floor along the above/below axis such that people may take their places according to their relative status. With respect to bodily comportment, one must, for example, walk *lolou* when passing among seated others; enter or leave a building only through those doors whose use is appropriate to one's status; 'sit properly' with crossed legs; clap politely with cupped hands before accepting a bowl of *yaqona*; take food only from dishes directly in front of or below one at the cloth; bow one's head and close one's eyes while praying, etc.[8] And, of course, one must always attend to the necessity of seating oneself in a proper position relative to others present.

The idea of the rule

Like ourselves, Fijian adults are likely to assert that their behaviour in certain respects is governed by rules – that is to say, that they do a thing in a certain way because that is the way it *should* be done. However, the idea that behaviour is (and should be) rule-governed appears most often in explicit prescriptive injunctions – especially to children – concerning what to do, how to do it and what *not* to do. From around age 3, Fijian toddlers are regularly told that some activity in which they are engaged is forbidden and that they must sit down and be quiet; indeed, when adults speak to young children it is virtually always to tell them to do or not to do a certain thing. One might compare this Fijian experience with that of, say, upper-middle-class and upper-class English children who are likely to be on the receiving end of injunctions like the following: 'eat with your mouth shut', 'don't make any noise while you're eating', 'take your elbows off the table', 'don't run in the house', 'stand up straight', 'say excuse me', 'it's rude to interrupt', 'shake hands with your aunt', 'stand up when a visitor enters the room', 'say thank you', 'say please', and many others of the same kind.

What is striking about these injunctions by adults to children – in both the Fijian and the English case – is that from the child's point of view these rules when stated have no transparent purpose outside the simple doing of them; that is to say, they have no intrinsic instrumental end. Rather, they are learned as something one does, apparently for its own sake, under certain circumstances. It should be noted, too, how pervasive these behaviours are. In the examples I have used, the prescriptive injunctions by adults to children concern greeting behaviour, physical deportment, and eating and drinking. The rules rendered explicit in these injunctions constitute the ritualised aspect of these behaviours.

In anthropological texts, 'ritual' refers usually to discrete ceremonies. I use 'ritualised behaviour' here to refer more widely to behaviours that are pervasive in daily life, so taken for granted that their ritual quality is rarely recognised. My point here is that most if not all, behaviours have a ritualised aspect – that is to say, an aspect that can be rendered explicit as 'a rule'.[9]

Adults are usually capable of ascribing a meaning to ritualised behaviours, but from the child's point of view that meaning cannot be obvious; it does not declare itself. For the child, the significance of the behaviour may be simply that 'this is how you do X'. So, for example, when you eat you keep your mouth closed, don't make a noise, and keep your elbows off the table. Or its significance may be that your father or mother or school teacher told you to do the thing that particular way. But otherwise the behaviour carries no extra meaning. In other words, there is no notion for the child that these arbitrary acts are symbolic of something else, that they have meaning beyond themselves. Of course, prescriptive injunctions from parents, people a child loves or fears, or those in authority, have a significant emotional dimension (which no doubt informs too the infant's and young child's voluntary imitation of others), but the crucial thing here is that the symbolic meaning of the prescribed or imitated behaviour is not intrinsic to it. Rather, what the child comes to know is that there is usually 'a right way' to do things, that it is considered proper or correct to observe this or that mode of behaviour, which may itself be rendered explicit in the form of 'a rule'.

The idea that behaviour is and should be meaningful is important here; indeed, this idea is itself necessary if the child is to render ritualised behaviour meaningful. That the child should come to seek out a meaning for a prescribed behaviour makes phenomenological sense in that he or she already has extensive experience of the gestural or paralinguistic dimension of communication. Here I suggest that the following steps might be general in the cognitive developmental process of rendering ritualised behaviours meaningful. First, the child performs a behaviour for its own sake – either because it has been told to or because it identifies with those others whom it sees performing that same behaviour. This performance is usually described as 'imitation' and is prevalent in children up to age 6 or 7, informing their play as well as the other activities of daily life. Second, where the behaviour is prescribed by injunctions, its prescriptive quality forces the child over time (roughly, age 6 to 9) to become aware that this particular behaviour has a meaning beyond itself, that it is symbolic of something else. Third, at around age 9, the child begins to work out what it is that the behaviour is symbolic of, to constitute its deeper significance, e.g., to understand that a particular style of table manners goes along with a particular style of physical deportment and that both may be meaningful in a particular way, that they may, for instance, differentiate 'people like us' from 'people not like us'. Finally, around age 11, the child arrives at an understanding that behaviour that it first understood as having no extra significance, as being merely 'the way you do X', is actually principled – that is to say necessary. So, for instance, the upper-middle-class and upper-class English child may come to understand that table manners, greeting behaviour and general deportment may evince 'good breeding', an idea that seems still to be prevalent in Britain, still to be accorded a kind of mysterious efficacy, and still crucial to class consciousness.[10] It is at this point, at the point where a behaviour has been rendered meaningful, that it becomes intrinsically coercive: the behaviour can be rendered explicit as 'a rule' *because* its meaning aspect has come to be understood as its *raison d'être*.

Further, I would argue that the nature of ritual and ritualised behaviour is such that it demands that we seek out its deeper meaning; that is, if one *must* behave in a certain way, this implies that the behaviour itself has significance, that there is a meaning there to be found. However, it is important to note here that many if not most of these ritualised behaviours become automatic, are embodied by the child, well before the symbolic meanings of the behaviours are constituted. The embodiment of a behaviour is crucial to the process by which its 'meaning' is cognitively constituted over time, and it is this process itself that renders the behaviour mandatory, a rule. So, Piaget notes that '[cognitive] structures – *in being constructed* – give rise to that necessity which a priorist theories have always thought it necessary to posit at the outset. Necessity, instead of being the prior *condition* for learning, is its *outcome*.[11]

Indeed, one can argue not only that ritual is best defined as 'behaviour understood to be governed by explicit rules', but also that the very idea of 'the rule' is the ultimate product of ritual and ritualised behaviour.

Rule and practice

People may rationalise their behaviour by reference to rules; they may say that they do a thing in a certain way because it *must* be done in that way because it is the proper way of doing it. But this appeal to the rule as justifying behaviour does not mean that the behaviour can be objectively *explained* as rule-governed. However rigid may be the ritual prescriptions describing, for example, a particular form of *yaqona* ceremony, when one looks at the performance of a particular behaviour by the same person on different occasions, or its performance by different people on the same occasion, it is quite clear that the behaviour itself may differ over time and across persons. In the Fijian case, adults are not only aware of but routinely comment on historical changes in ritualised behaviours – for example, that women are now admitted to *yaqona*-drinking from which they were still excluded a generation ago, or that it is now considered proper for a woman to sit with crossed legs (i.e. 'like a man') where once she was required to sit with her legs drawn back under her and to one side – a posture still adopted by Sawaieke women on very formal occasions.

Moreover with respect to a description or explanation of a particular ritualised behaviour, no one gives exactly the same gloss on it; and this is so even when, as in the case of Fijian children's understandings of who is above and who below in *yaqona*-drinking, a definite pattern of understanding is discernible as a function of age shifts and of gender.[12] So, in the case of Fijian children's understanding of the ritualised use of space, one can chart the general course of the process in and through which they constitute an idea of status as inherent to the person – a cognitive scheme that makes hierarchy intrinsic to day-to-day relations between people and given in the nature of things.

Cognitive schemes and 'the idea of the rule'

My use of 'cognitive scheme' here is derived from Piaget; it is useful because it makes possible a theoretical description of psychological phenomena; moreover, its inherent 'transformativity' makes it possible to conceive of cognitive structures as continually emergent rather than as fixed. In other words, a Piagetian cognitive scheme may have as its product 'the idea of the rule' but cannot itself be described as 'a rule' or as 'rule-governed'. For Piaget (who always strove for biological validity in his descriptions of psychological phenomena), structure and process are inextricable aspects of a single phenomenon. In his formulation, cognitive structures are 'self-regulating transformational systems'; they are autopoietic – self-producing or self-organising.[13]

Autopoiesis is as much a psychological as a biological phenomenon, and so it can be applied as appropriately to the creation of meaning as it can to the process through which, for example, the human foetus is a product of the complex processes of epigenesis that describe the interaction between the zygote (the ovum fertilised by sperm) and the environment that nourishes it (the woman in whose womb it comes to maturity). Humans are biologically social organisms, and it is through their sociality that their autopoietic psychologies are realised. In other words, for humans, the creation of meaning is always mediated by specific social relations. So the processes through which any human neonate, infant, child, young person, adult, makes meaning entails that he or she accommodates to the meanings that others have already made and are making. We act always in and through relations with others, and in the course of our daily lives in acting on the world we make meaning in response to the meanings that others present us with.

It follows that cognitive processes are inherently transformational; they cannot *not* be at once transformed in the process of production and transforming of the conceptual objects on which they act. So mind may be understood as the fundamental historical phenomenon; in the course of its autopoiesis, its self-production, it produces the ideas of which it seems to be the product. I have argued above that one of these ideas is the idea of 'the rule', an idea that is ubiquitous in so far as it is a product of the cognitive developmental process by which we make meaning out of ritualised behaviours – behaviours that are at once routine and always unique because they are peculiar to specific historical circumstances.

Epistemological anxiety and 'the idea of the rule'

Here it is interesting to speculate, in light of some observations by Lévi-Strauss (1981) [1971], that the idea of the rule is a powerful (and general) antidote to the epistemological anxiety that is, so far as we can tell, a function of the human condition.

In the closing chapters of *The Naked Man*, Lévi-Strauss discusses the distinction between myth and ritual. On the basis of his comprehensive investigations of the mythology of the Americas, he argues that myth as discourse addresses contradictions and fundamental existential problems given in the human condition. Myth, he says, attempts to obliterate the reality of change and decay by referring contemporary day-to-day problems to primal originary conditions. But myth is a phenomenon in language and as such it inevitably resides in or creates distinctions and discontinuities; it carves up the world and comments on it.

Ritual is of a different order. Lévi-Strauss argues that ritual is always an attempt to assert continuity in the face of the epistemological anxieties created by mythological speculation. Its qualities of repetitiveness, order and obsession with the details, with the 'what' and the 'how' of behaviour, makes ritual work to efface speculation. It re-asserts the continuity of experience, obliterates discursive disorder and the unpredictability that is given in speculation.

Thus, as both Lévi-Strauss and Bloch (1974, 1986) have shown, ritualised behaviour is not properly made analogous to language; it is not a way of 'saying something' in a non-verbal form that might just as well be conveyed in speech or writing.[14] Moreover, Bloch's work suggests that ritualised behaviour (for all that the rules can change) is by and large remarkably stable over time precisely because ritual in its nature coerces compliance from participants. Thus, while one can argue *in* and *with* language, ritual precludes argument on the part of these who are participants in it.[15] However, while I agree with the arguments of both Lévi-Strauss and Bloch here, I want to push their observations somewhat further and to argue, in line with the first part of this essay, that its manifestation as 'rule' is the fundamental *raison d'être* of ritual and that *for this reason* its meaning aspect is bound to be always and inevitably secondary. I would argue further that the validity of this observation is evident developmentally as well as analytically: for young children 'a rule is a rule is a rule', whereas for older children and adults a rule can only be an artefact of its deeper meaning.

Here it is important to realise that ritual and the routine performance of day-to-day ritualised behaviours create an appearance of consensus. In other words, when one's behaviour appears to be objectively the same as other people's, one tends to assume that other people hold the same ideas about the 'meaning' of that behaviour as one does oneself. My study suggests that there are as many interpretations about the 'meaning' of Fijian use of space as there are Fijians, but distinctively different concepts (such as those held by boys and girls concerning who, precisely, sits below) are never likely to be made explicit. People may argue about 'the rules' that prescribe a particular ritual performance (i.e., about how to do it), but they do not usually interrogate one another about what the rules 'mean'. And on those rare occasions that they do so, because the meaning of a ritualised behaviour is not intrinsic to it, its 'definition' is usually the prerogative of differential power.[16]

Bourdieu (1977) argues rightly that the 'rule' cannot properly be appealed to as an explanation of behaviour; however the fact that the concept of the rule is ubiquitous surely requires some explanation. Note, however, that in reference to ritual and ritualised behaviour, the idea of the rule itself references a continuum of meaning: at one end, it may be understood that certain prescribed behaviours have to be followed rigidly, in a particular order and under particular conditions (e.g., a Roman Catholic mass); at the other end, that it is important that behaviours not be precisely prescribed, but that there is 'a right way' of doing something which remains to be found out on each occasion (e.g. certain shamanic rites). Thus the rule may be that 'what is proper' remains to be revealed, as in certain charismatic religious ceremonies where inspiration is the order of the day.

Moreover, while for adults the 'meaning' of ritualised behaviours may provide a rationalisation for their performance, that meaning does not necessarily have to be elaborated or even known. Thus, people may refuse to attribute a particular meaning to a ritualised behaviour; they may say that they do not know its meaning, that they do such-and-such because their ancestors, their parents, or their teachers did so, or just because it is the right thing to do. That is, the 'meaning' of ritualised behaviour may reside solely in its being performed, or having been performed, by highly valued or authoritative others. However, it seems possible too that adults are consciously aware that ritual and ritualised behaviours create order and predictability and that this is at once their *raison d'être* and their meaning. So it becomes necessary to enjoin their performance on children.

I noted above that Fijians often comment on changes that have occurred over time in their ritual and ritualised behaviours; sometimes these comments are disapproving, but they are more often merely observations. The Fijian term for ritual and tradition as generic terms is *cakacaka vakavanua* – 'working, acting, doing in the manner of the land'; it refers to a way of behaving that is culturally appropriate. Thus, ritual is doing something in a Fijian way; its meaning arises from *how* things are done as well as from *what* is done. Moreover, if one does something in a Fijian way, then the doing of it becomes Fijian. This is a processual notion and so it can be made, without difficulty, to incorporate change even while it asserts that there is a proper, a Fijian, way of doing things.

Here 'the rules' that prescribe ritualised behaviours are defined not by their rigidity across time, but by their appropriateness for changing circumstances. In other words, the idea of the rule does not require that one hold the notion that rules may not be changed or cannot become obsolete. But the idea of the rule, as manifest in ritual and ritualised behaviour, does carry in its train the orchestration of collective action or (to use Paul Wohlmuth's term) the attunement of any given person's behaviour to the behaviour of those alongside whom he or she lives. But ritual and ritualised behaviours cannot be regarded as 'texts' precisely because their meaning aspect is necessarily secondary to their performance. As I have shown above, this is not to say that their meaning aspect is unimportant but rather that it is the product of a process of cognitive construction over time. It is this ontogenetic process itself that makes continuity and transformation aspects of the same phenomenon; in other words, it allows at once for the stability of ritual and ritualised behaviours over time and for historical shifts in their performance.

And because inter-subjectivity inevitably mediates processes of cognitive construction in particular persons, these processes are bound to be informed by politico-economic relations that describe the character of the collectivity. Inter-subjectivity makes each one of us the locus of manifold relations with others that inform the endogenous constitution of cognitive schemes; so each one of us constitutes cognitively the social relations of which we are the transforming product.

Part III

LIVING HISTORY, MATERIAL MIND AND THE STUFF OF THE WORLD

The reader who is sufficiently patient or fascinated to read every essay in this volume, should find in this last part a vindication of the model of mind and human being proposed at the outset. The introduction was written especially for this volume and so it represents the latest development of the ideas that underlie and inform the three essays below. In each case I was concerned to suggest how the governing ideas of Fijian dualism are maintained over time and, in the self-same process, transformed. In other words, as I showed in the introduction to this volume, transformation is not a function of external pressures, but an intrinsic aspect of the process through which each of us makes meaning out of meanings that others have already made and are making – a process that makes us *living embodiments* of the history of our relations with others.

Nevertheless, what people make of the historical contingencies that impinge on them is a profoundly interesting aspect of the process of constituting knowledge: in general it may be said that what we do is to assimilate such contingencies to our existing understandings of the world and in so doing transform them to a greater or lesser degree; indeed we cannot do otherwise. But this very assimilation has a reciprocal effect on the knowledge that is its object – Christianity for instance, or democracy; the knowledge that is denoted by these categories is itself inevitably transformed. I suggested as much in 'Making the present', the second essay in this volume, and the same goes for all the essays in this final part; it is to be hoped, however, that they constitute an advance on my previous understanding and analysis of the taken-for-granted of daily life in Sawaieke. Thus each of the first two essays attempts, as does 'Seeing the ancestral sites' in Part I, to render analytical villagers' insights on their own lives and thus to make the ethnography deliver up its significance without recourse to the usual technical vocabulary of anthropology; in effect this means that these particular papers could be translated easily into Fijian without the use of English 'loan words'. More important perhaps, from my own perspective, is that this proceeding led me by degrees to the new analysis of Fijian dualism that is represented by the final chapter.

My book, *Making Sense of Hierarchy*, like most of the papers in this volume, in effect concentrates on the hierarchical aspect of social relations. And this is the case even though, like the papers, it recognises the high salience of equal relations between cross-cousins and the significance of balanced reciprocal exchange between them and between collectivities: houses, clans, *yavusa* (groups of clans), villages and countries. Indeed from the beginning my analysis of *yaqona*-drinking showed how in effect it transforms balanced reciprocal exchanges between collectivities into tribute to chiefs and in the process brings into being the relation of chiefs above *vis-à-vis* the people below. But because hierarchical relations are instantiated in the design and use of the *internal* space of all buildings, and because a great deal of day-to-day life takes place indoors and virtually all ceremonies (whether indoors or outdoors) come within the spatial confines that are prescribed for *yaqona*-drinking (though see Toren 1994b for an interesting counter-example), it is easy to take on the idea that relations inside houses dominate over relations between houses, even when one knows that this is not the case. One has to contend, too, with all those other analysts from Hocart to Sahlins whose own predilections make tribute outweigh balanced reciprocity and allow chiefs to encompass the people. Thus a good deal of what I wrote in effect seemed to suggest that I took hierarchy to be the dominant value in Fijian social life. That is, until I took a closer look at how villagers talk about the relations between the sexes that inform sexuality and marriage and at how what they say throws light on the developmental cycle of marriage as this appears to an outside observer – a proceeding that provoked the insight that allowed me to change my analytical language.

'Transforming love' suggests that the compassion of kinship and the passion of sexual desire can only properly be understood as aspects of one another. This insight was, as the reader will see, prompted by what villagers had to say, and because desire often precipitates marriage and marriage is crucial to the process of constituting hierarchy in Fiji, it made me realise not only (and yet again) that equal and hierarchical relations are of equal significance for Fijians, but how I could demonstrate this argument in my analysis. 'Cosmogonic aspects of desire and compassion' was written in response to an invitation from Daniel de Coppet and Andre Itéanu to whom I am grateful not only because their one-week workshop on society and cosmology in Oceania was remarkably interesting and enjoyable, but because their own use in analysis of Dumont's idea of the encompassment of contradiction and a hierarchy of values, compelling though it is, made me realise why Fijian social relations cannot be properly described in these terms. So, in 'All things go in pairs or the sharks will bite' (which was written after the previous essay though published before it) I was able at last to make sense of this wonderfully suggestive and mysterious saying by one of Hocart's informants – it sounds like a saying, though it does not appear in any of the collections of Fijian proverbs with which I am familiar.

'All things go in pairs ' – like the other two essays in this part – ventures an analysis of Fijian social relations that calls established views into question. It follows through the implications of giving *equal weight* to balanced reciprocal exchange and tribute as they inform day-to-day life in the village and *vanua* of Sawaieke and, in the process, is able to make sense not only of what Hocart's informant had to say to him some time around 1911, but also of certain observations that he considered evidence of social degeneration, and of what was reported to the Lands Commission in 1916 about the paramount chiefship of Sawaieke – how it came into being and the vicissitudes of succession. In so doing it is able to reconcile a number of outstanding issues in Fijian ethnography, such as what it is that entitles 'the sister's child' to 'take without asking' from mother's brother and how this relationship informs chiefly succession; it also demonstrates in passing how appropriate is Lévi-Strauss's idea of the house to the analysis of Fijian social relations. The reader who looks at this last essay in the light of the model of human being proposed in the Introduction will see too why Lévi-Strauss's structural analyses of mythological transformation continue to make sense, despite their being predicated on an inadequate model of mind.

Mind is a material phenomenon because it is the artefact of the way we humans embody the history of the relations with others that we have lived. We speak and act out of that history and so it is we who bring the past into the present and project our understanding of the way things are into the very stuff of the world – into all its manifold objects and all its people. So, for example, a contemporary Sawaieke villager whose new breeze-block house has three or four rooms, rather than the more usual one, still uses the largest room in accordance with the necessity for status differentiation in space and thus still has one door give onto the space below and another – called the honoured door – that takes the high status visitor straight into a place above.

Thus what is most fascinating and wonderful to me in all this is how the material in each of these essays demonstrates that history (or what some call culture) inheres in the present as a function of what we generally call 'living' – an insight I have to attribute to the impact that Sawaieke villagers' understandings of the world had on my own. Which is proper – because as I have been at pains to show, that's the way mind works.

7

TRANSFORMING LOVE
Representing Fijian hierarchy

The following story – a Fijian man's account of how he came to fall in love with his wife – was told me during the wedding celebrations for a young couple in Sawaieke, the village on the island of Gau in Fiji where I spent eighteen months, from July 1981 to February 1983 (see note 1 of chapter 1). The man who told me this story was in his early forties – gentle and humorous, a thoughtful husband and father; his wife was a witty and lively woman, understanding and kind, the mother of many children. Their marriage appeared to be contented and successful; they were clearly fond of one another.

My friend began his tale by saying that as a young man he had desired his wife's sister; she was prettier, he said, and more lively; but one of his classificatory fathers had advised him differently. Look, he had said, at the other one. She would make a good wife; watch her, you will see that she is skilful at women's work, knows how to look after a family. So my friend had changed the focus of his attention and had found that all his father said was true. It didn't matter to him, he said, that she was 'no longer a girl' not a virgin, indeed already a mother – he asked his father to ask for her in marriage. Then they got married and he took her home and at first all went well, though perhaps they were rather shy with each other, not quite at ease. Then one night he stayed out late drinking kava and woke up bad tempered the next morning. He went to breakfast, but it was late, already past ten, the others had eaten and the tea was cold; his wife served it to him cold. He had thrown the tea back at her, right in her face and then he had hit her hard, punched her with his fists and when she fell to the floor he kicked her and then he left the house.

I looked at him dismayed; his voice and expression were amused, fondly reminiscent. This was terrible, I said, how could he have done such a thing? But he lifted his hand, gesturing that he had not yet finished. Wait, he said, you will understand it all soon. Three days had passed and he and his wife did not speak to one another. The first day or two she spent at her mother's house; when she returned each went about the daily duties – his wife with her eyes downcast and a sorrowful face, she cried a lot and would not look at him, and he felt grim and angry. Then on the fourth morning he got up, bathed, brushed his teeth; then he dressed and sat down at the cloth for breakfast. His wife was in her place *i ra*, below, her eyes downcast and her face turned away from him – he mimed the posture for me, the corners of his mouth turned down, his whole person expressive of injury – but as she handed him his glass of hot tea their eyes had met. And at once, he said, they began to laugh. She began to laugh and he began to laugh and they could not stop. They laughed and laughed, recalling details of the previous events, how he had thrown the tea and punched her, how she had screamed and run off to her mother, how they had gone about unspeaking. He looked at me then, smiling, sure that I would understand; *sa qai tekivu na veilomani dina*, he said, 'and thus began true love'.

At the time I did not, as he had said I would, understand this story. This paper is an attempt to do so, to show how in Fijian thought and practice sexual love or desire is constituted in opposition to compassionate or familial love and how compassionate love is wrested violently out of desire, which is thus transformed and apparently contained by the hierarchy thought proper to social order.

From the analyst's point of view, there are no acts that are symbolic of love, for love is constituted out of those acts that are supposed to stand for it. From cradle to grave each one of us is inevitably situated in relation to love via the manifold interactions which love encompasses and in which it is inscribed. This is not to say that everywhere 'love' is made to take the same forms, but rather that, whatever forms it is made to take are constituted in and through social relations, and that because we are each born into and can only become who we are in relations with others, we willy nilly constitute ourselves in relation to love, to its presence or absence, and we submit to the meanings others have made of love and to those meanings we make in response to theirs. So one cannot signify love in any simple way because any dyadic relationship in which love enters (wife–husband, parent–child, sister–sister, brother–sister, lovers, cousins, friends, etc.) inevitably informs the others and so each new relationship in some sense contains those that precede it and/or coincide.[1] So in any person's experience, 'love' undergoes a kind of developmental cycle that itself implies specific power relations both within and across households, domestic groups, families. So it is that for any people, the acts that at once constitute and express love within dyadic relationships are an integral part of the political and economic processes that describe social relations at large.

In this essay I attempt to uncover something of the interacting processes through which certain Fijian villagers come to be at once subjects and objects of love. The analysis of this developmental experience is intended to show how suitable a vehicle is love for the playing out of power relations, how central and fundamental it is to those other social processes with whose nature anthropologists are more usually concerned. My other, less obvious, purpose lies in an attempt at once to preserve the particularity of my own and others' personal experience in so far as this is contained in what I was told and what I saw and heard, and to show how this proceeding itself makes possible a revealing analysis of Fijian social relations. I am not so much concerned with 'reflexivity' as with the analytical insights that emerge from an attempt to preserve the insights of Fijian villagers on their own experience. I begin with some information on the Fijian categories within whose terms 'love' may be spoken of.

The mutual compassionate love that constitutes kinship

Veilomani, the term used by my friend to speak of true love, is the mutual compassionate love that helps to constitute kinship. One's kin in the widest sense are all other Fijians; 'loving each other' is part of what it means to be Fijian. The root *loma* denotes the inside of a thing and in many compounds the mind or the will, e.g. *loma ca*, lit. 'evil-minded' denotes malice; *loma donu*, lit. 'straight-minded' denotes sincerity. The verbal form *lomana* means to love, pity or have mercy on; *kauwaitaka* – to care or to be concerned – was given me as a synonym. The reduplicative form *loloma* translates as love, pity or mercy, while *i loloma* is a gift or a token of love. It is the 'free gift' as distinct from the gift – *i soli* – that manifests obligation and implies exchange. But the gift out of love coerces recognition of the love that gave it and the form taken by this recognition denotes the status relations entailed. For, while the love denoted by *veilomani* is reciprocal, such that the will of each party to the relationship is in harmony with the other, it is also – with the important exception of cross-cousins – a function of unequal relationships. The nature of this inequality varies according to the interaction between rank, gender and seniority that governs any particular hierarchical relation between kin. In marriage, it is axiomatic that the husband holds sway over his wife. This relationship is crucial for the continuity of Fijian hierarchy for it transforms a relation of competitive equality between cross-cousins – by definition one always marries a cross-cousin – into the hierarchical relation between husband and wife. Cross-cousins are kin to one another but the competitive and equal relations between them make them a special kind of kin, as does the potential for sexual relations.

Here I must emphasise that in Fijian village life all one's relations with others are encompassed by *veilomani* – mutual compassionate love – and where these relations are hierarchical are, for people older than 14 or so, characterised by respect and avoidance. With one's cross-cousins one is familiar and asserts equality, both within and across-sex, so in day-to-day friendly relations with them, *veilomani* takes on an aspect of equality.

Elsewhere I have shown how marriage seems to contain and overcome the implicit threat that cross-cousinship and balanced reciprocity pose to chieftainship and tributary relations, and how this apparent 'overcoming' is played out at every meal in every household and every kava-drinking. At the same time, marriage as process transforms sexual love or desire between equals into love that is proper to hierarchical kin relations. It is only in marriage that equal and hierarchical behaviours and the representations to which they contribute confront one another within the confines of the one dyadic relationship. In other words, in a lifetime in which all one's relationships prescribe either hierarchy or competitive equality, only marriage makes it clear that each form contains the possibility of the other. The challenge of this conjunction erupts into personal experience when *veilomani* – mutual compassionate love – is confronted by *veidomoni* – passionate and mutual sexual love.

The passionate love that precipitates marriage

Veidomoni has connotations of desperation, for the root word *domo* figures in terms for obstinacy and courage – *veidomomatuataki, domodomoqa* – and for terrifying or frightening – *vakadomobula*, lit. arousing a lust for life. As a homonym, *domo* means throat, or the sound of a thing. So a woman who laughs loud and high is said to be sexually promiscuous – a notion that connects with a nineteenth-century one that women called their lovers by laughing.[2] Fijians are fond of suggestive puns, so a throat infection I had gave rise to innumerable jokes suggesting that a sore and swollen throat meant that I needed a man. In both these examples female desire is represented as unspoken – so women's feelings are denied even while they are acknowledged. In my own case, sexual frustration was attributed to me because I could not speak; joking apart, it was proper that thwarted desire in a married woman be manifest in an inability to express itself. Even a woman who is said to be sexually promiscuous does not express her desires in speech but in provocative laughter. By contrast, male desire is allowed to be spoken and its association with the throat lies in an analogy between sex and eating. A man's wife – especially while still young and pretty – is often jokingly referred to as *na kena*, 'his to eat'. And uxoriousness in a husband is not referred to as *dodomo*, 'passionate love', which would make him appear faintly ludicrous – one does not fittingly *domona* one's wife – but rather as the desire to eat what is his, *sa via kania na kena*. So far as I know this term is not used reciprocally, i.e. to describe a woman's desire for her husband.

As wife and sex object, a woman is under her husband's command. As an object of desire outside marriage she disposes of herself as she wishes: it is up to her whether or not she assents to a sexual relationship with one of her cross-cousins. But such a relationship is illegitimate, so she cannot freely dispose of herself; a girl's sexuality should be under the guardianship of her father and brothers, held in trust for her husband. On her wedding night her mother formally asks if she is 'truly a girl' (a virgin). If she says she is and fails to prove herself so when the bedding of the wedding night is examined by senior women, then she and her side may be publicly shamed by the presentation of the feast foods that follows consummation – the belly of the cooked pig given to the 'side of the woman' is left gaping open, or a banana thrust into it; had she been a virgin it would have been modestly closed and concealed with leaves.[3] However, this ritual can occur only for marriages arranged by senior kin – those that over the preceding months involve a series of exchanges between both sides and where the wedding ceremony takes place in church.

The usual form of marriage is elopement (*veidrotaki*). This is accomplished when the girl is discovered to have spent the night with the young man in the house of his parents or other close kin. The rituals that follow are to placate the girl's kin and, later, to celebrate the new couple. A church wedding may or may not follow. Couples who elope are usually already lovers; their feeling for one another before marriage is that of *veidomoni*, i.e. 'mutual sexual love' or 'mutual desire'. The term is used reciprocally, but it is noticeable that it is usually the young man who is said to *domona* – desire – the young woman; in other words, both desire and responsibility for the elopement are represented as the young man's. The image one has of the girl in these affairs is that she passively accepts his urgent suit.

Young men are generally assumed to have sexual liaisons; at the same time, girls are assumed by their elders to be chaste. Men compose and sing most Fijian love songs; they often represent desire as a helpless yearning for the woman – *au dodomo ki na nomu vinivo*, 'I love/desire even your pinafore'; or themselves as dependent on a woman's whims – *bogi koya, bogi koya, au a oca na wawa*, 'that night, that night I was tired out with waiting'. Male sexuality is understood to be urgent, difficult to control; so a girl who goes alone to meet a man is said to be culpable if he forces himself upon her. But such an action is considered to be rape and, so far as I know, it is up to the girl herself to decide what she wants. If the young man making the tryst is serious about a girl he will say that he just wants to meet her and enjoy her company, *veitalanoa*, 'telling stories'. However, if a girl allows herself to be alone with a man or men who are drunk on alcohol then she may be raped. A man drunk on alcohol is thought to be in a state of uncontrollable desire, he has to have a woman. A man who is drunk on *yaqona* (kava, the ground root of *piper methysticum* infused in water) is not said to be so aroused, rather, untroubled by desire, he will sleep a dreamless sleep.

The sexual implications of alcohol and dancing

Alcohol is understood to embolden a man so that he can approach the desired woman with sufficient *kaukauwa* – lit. strength, but here meaning sexual magnetism and/or self-confidence – either to gain his end or retire with dignity if refused. The convention is that a man doesn't know what he is doing when drunk and so asking and refusal can be forgotten while asking and acceptance can form the foundation for future meetings. This brings me to the subject of dancing and its connection with sexuality. During my first months in Sawaieke the girls (*gone yalewa*, those who are unmarried, but over 16 or so) often told me how much fun we would have when there was dancing. At last the time came; the chiefs said we might 'stand up' in the hall to the music of the young men. The convention is that a girl or woman gets up, goes to 'touch' a man and returns to the lower part of the room, well below the *tanoa* holding the *yaqona* and at the polar extreme from the area 'above' where chiefs sit. There the man joins her and, side by side, they put their arms about each other's waists and proceed in gentle rhythm back and forth across the floor; this is *taralala*. One can also dance a sedate form of rock 'n' roll, or waltz – provided one holds one's partner at a distance of ten inches or so. I was stunned by the degree of reserve and circumspection that dancing entailed. So far as I could tell only the spectators enjoyed themselves. The dancers remained impassive, gazing over each other's shoulders or into the middle distance. The next day I listened to the girls discussing what a good time we'd had and wasn't it fun, Christina? I agreed, but it was only several dances later that I began to discover why dancing is so much fun and even, from certain points of view, dangerous.

Seating arrangements in any gathering effectively segregate men and women of similar ages. But during dances subtle messages may be sent from one person to another – by brief and careful eye contact or a squeeze of the hand or even, if the lighting is not too good, a rapid verbal exchange. Young men and women expect dancing to lead to sexual liaisons; so do adults and especially church leaders who cannot countenance dancing and must leave the room where it takes place.[4] From a chiefly perspective, dancing is improper because people are standing up in the presence of chiefs.[5] So when dances do occur (and this is rare on Gau) one must not show too much enthusiasm, let alone smile or talk with one's partner. I was often cautioned by elderly men to be careful, for when my husband came to visit me and was told about my dancing I should certainly be punched. My assertion that my husband had never hit me in the previous thirteen years of our life together was considered frankly incredible.

The heavy sexuality that is attributed to dancing finds its truest expression in dances that take place in *na rubbish hall*, lit. 'a rubbish hall'. This is a temporary shelter outside a village; its sides are open, its roof made of unfixed sheets of corrugated iron; the floor is earth and there are no mats to sit on, but planks of wood are fixed to form rough benches along two sides. The dances are to raise money, for example to send the sports teams to Suva for the annual games. No chiefs are present, but two or three married men and women attend as chaperones.

Dancing in the rubbish hall is associated with drunkenness and thus with untrammelled male desire. Sawaieke was 'dry' and 'homebrew' was strictly forbidden; even so, young men managed sometimes to drink alcohol. My first rubbish hall dance was wildly exciting. Nearly all the young men were drunk; the few who were not were playing guitars and singing or looking after the *yaqona*. The latter were doing their best to observe the proper ritual form – a difficult task in the free-for-all fights that erupted among the others during any pause in the dancing. Young men asked girls to dance, slow songs were the most desirable and waltzing de rigueur. Then the dancing became a battle to interpose some little distance between one's own body and the man's. Some girls pushed their partners away, and were most derisive with 'little young men' (*cauravou lalai*, aged up to 19 or so), preferring young men (*cauravou*) in their twenties. Men took the chance to ask for assignations whose object was sometimes implicit but more usually obvious: 'Could we perhaps go together?' to which the standard response is '*Isa!* go together where?'

The sexual implications of dancing are a corollary of the fact that only those who can call each other cross-cousin may dance together, only they may joke and flirt, challenging one another with remarks heavy with sexual innuendo; only they may tease or confront or ridicule. All other categories of relation (ideally, all Fijians are kin to one another) demand varying degrees of avoidance and respect, they are all incest categories – *veitabui*, 'forbidden to each other'. Cross-cousins are potential spouses or siblings-in-law; their relationship is inherently mediated by sexuality (see note 6 of chapter 1). A young person making a tryst always goes with a cross-cousin of the same sex. A girl's female cross-cousin protects her from the suspicions of adults, a young man's male cross-cousin gives moral support or comfort if his suit fails. Girl or boy may ask the cross-cousin to speak for them, if they are shy or want reassurance; sometimes 'double dates' are made.

Flirting (*vosa vakawedewede*, lit. attention-getting talk), joking (*veiwali*) and teasing (*veisamei*) are not only the prerogative of cross-cousins, but even their duty. All the fun of any village gathering depends on the way that those who call each other cross-cousin excite amusement and enjoyment by their jokes and liveliness with one another. The equal relation between them is at once constituted and expressed in these activities and in the competitive and ultimately balanced reciprocity that characterises exchange between them.

The contrast between *dodomo* and *loloma*, between sexual love or desire and compassionate or familial love, is assimilated to an ideal contrast between 'the European way' and 'the Fijian way'. The language of *dodomo* is often English: a young man obsessed by a girl is 'lovesick', his regular girl is his 'dame', a sexually promiscuous girl is a 'bitch', sexual desire is uncontrollable under the influence of alcohol (*yaqona ni vavalagi*, 'European kava'), and both alcohol and sex are linked to European-style dancing in 'rubbish halls' outside the village where one pays money to get in. Here 'the European way' is amoral, without kinship or moral obligations, and implies a wild, uncontrolled, incestuous sexuality. By contrast, the language of *loloma* is Fijian and the behaviour that constitutes it is proper to kinship; contained and legitimate desire is manifest in sedate dances in the village hall where men can be drunk only on *yaqona*, which does not arouse desire and which when presented in its root form is paradigmatic of tribute to chiefs. The ideal contrast between the European and the Fijian ways here refers to an earlier contrast between bush (*veikau*) and house (*vale*). Indeed, illegitimate sex between young people often perforce takes place in garden shelters or temporarily deserted bush houses or school outhouses – all of which lie outside the village proper.

The developmental cycle of love

Uncontrolled sexual desire poses a threat to ordered hierarchy, so the ultimate triumph of the Fijian way over the European way is made possible by the mediation of cross-cousins. Between them *loloma* has an aspect of equality, but when cross-cousins become lovers or when first they marry they discover and submit to the passion of *dodomo*. In time, marriage as process will transform their passion into *loloma* – now become the love proper to hierarchical relations, the love whose very constitution reproduces 'the Fijian way'. With respect to *dodomo* a man seems helpless, the victim of his own desires, but this is represented as the fault of the girl who arouses his passion. A young man resents feeling strongly for a girl; being 'lovesick' is a condition to be avoided if sexual desire is to be thought of as a hunger best satisfied by a wide variety of foods. This notion is common among young men, one of whom – aged 21 and already repenting of his recent marriage – said, 'I have been eating only cassava everyday – today it no longer tastes good to me.' If a young man feels strongly for a woman, his own sexuality is called into question. A man who, when sober, urges his suit so hard that others realise his predicament and his frustration at refusal, is publicly humiliated by his own feelings and blames the woman who aroused them. Young men hold it best to appear indifferent; only when married can a man afford to let his feelings show, for then they can manifest as jealous anger. It is said that girls spurn a man who reveals his love. So women as well as men were appalled to see the explicit devotion displayed by a young Australian visitor for his half-Fijian wife; several elderly women laughed at his desire to be with her all the time and declared his little kisses disgusting; other younger women said he showed a foolish and unmanly fondness for the girl. Men are understood to be depleted by sexual intercourse. During the football season, young men are strictly forbidden to 'go with' girls lest they lose their strength; this is manifest as heat, and football practice is often referred to as *vakatakata*, lit. 'making hot'. That a man can be reduced or humiliated by desire is implicit in notions about sexual liaisons between young men and older women. A young man whose lover is perhaps six to ten years older than he is, is likely to fall ill with *dogai*. He cannot work or do anything but sits at home all day staring into space. Very small things look large to him and if an insect flies his way he ducks to avoid it. He does not know he is sick but one of his close older female kin recognises the illness and cures him with a herbal medicine; the cure, it seems, brings the liaison to an end. *Dogai* is caused by the strength (*kaukauwa*), here implicitly the sexual strength, of the woman; an older woman is more sexually powerful than a young man.[6] This implies that the sexuality of young men and women is of equal strength, but when I asked if this was so, my informant (a young man in his early twenties) said decidedly that it was not; if they are the same age then the man's sexuality is stronger. Fijians of both sexes would, I think, agree with this but while the strength of his sexuality is a young man's boast, it is also his undoing. It puts him at a disadvantage with any girl for whom he feels a powerful attraction, because it makes possible the potential triumph of the girl in refusal.

This accords with the competitive equality that characterises relations between cross-cousins outside marriage, both within and across sex. A male cross-cousin can neither command anything of, nor forbid anything to his female cross-cousin. He can joke, tease, cajole, defy, beg or refuse – but so can she. For example, young men consider smoking their own prerogative and unfitting for girls, and a brother (including a close classificatory brother) is justified in hitting his sister if he discovers her smoking, but girls not only smoke in front of male cross-cousins, they demand cigarettes of them. Also, a girl is allowed to initiate a love affair, although given the double standard she has to be careful to avoid the epithet 'bitch'. Young men may coerce, intimidate or even force themselves upon much younger female cross-cousins, but girls of their own age are able not merely to refuse but to ridicule and humiliate them. This relation between young men and women as cross-cousins is inherent in the process of developing sexuality.

Representations of male and female desire

Little girls are shamed if they touch their genitals or allow them to be seen; toddlers of 2 or so will be smacked and older girls beaten. Boys, by contrast, may be seen naked without too much fuss being made about it.[7] Of a toddler who handles his penis someone may remark, '*Ia*, he takes hold of his *boci*!' (lit. uncircumcised penis) and others present may laugh, but the child is unlikely to be smacked. A boy of 5 or 6 may sit cross-legged, his genitals showing through a hole in his shorts, even after others have laughed and drawn his notice to the deficiency. After all, what other way can he sit that is *vakatagane* – manly?

The concern with covering female genitals even in early childhood is, I think, attributable to Christian conversion and colonisation; in early and pre-colonial Fiji both sexes went naked until the time – often after puberty – when they were ritually clothed for the first time in barkcloth. But Christian puritanism seems to have suited Fijian predilections and the stricter attention to female nakedness to be oddly concordant with the proper mode of sitting *vakamarama*, in a ladylike way, with the knees together and the legs tucked back under the thighs, and with the earlier practice of tattooing girls' thighs, buttocks and vulva, a painful operation performed before puberty and said to make their vaginas *mamaca vinaka* – 'nice and dry'.[8] Men still say that the most desirable state in a woman is when her vagina is 'hot and dry', *katakata ka mamaca*, which suggests that for young women sex is perhaps at best frustrating if not in fact painful.

Judging by what I was told by both girls and young men, a boy's first sexual intercourse occurs around age 17, a girl's around age 15. However, one young man told me that when he was 18 he went with a girl of 11; when I asked him did he not think the girl too young, he said 'No, she knew her own mind'.[9] Thus, a girl's first sexual experience may occur when she is very young and may, despite the views of my informant, be forced upon her. One day when I was walking outside the village I was joined by some little girls, aged between 10 and 12. They kept repeating the words 'nine minutes' in English and giggling like mad, but were reluctant to tell me why this was so funny. At last the youngest – an irrepressible child – revealed that another girl (aged 11) had been surprised by a boy of 14 when she was washing clothes in the stream and forced to have sex with him. The little girls knew all about it from another child who had watched from behind a tree. They placed the blame squarely on the boy, saying that the girl was afraid and that the boy was known to be 'wise in everything bad' (*vuku e na veika ca*); he was always putting his hands up the girls' skirts even if they were only 8 years old. They all joined hilariously in a circumstantial description of the event, making expressive gestures with their hands – a hole with the left hand through which they poked the index finger of the right. They used bizarre words – not Fijian – for the act itself, 'toponi' and 'prish prosh'; nine minutes was the length of time which the boy was overheard to announce as properly spent in the act.

That these acts by males are understood by both sexes to be essentially violent is clear in the foregoing and in the following information, given me by a young man in his early twenties. He had, he said, been slightly injured on his genitals by a girl of about 16 who struck at him with a kitchen knife as he lay sleeping. He was amused by the incident, said of it that the girl 'was joking with me' (*sa veiwali vei au*). Astonished by this story, I asked him why the girl did this – he was asleep and she just came and struck him with the kitchen knife? Yes, he said, 'because we are cross-cousins' (*ka ni keirau e veitavaleni*). When she was younger, he said, he used to touch her genitals even when other people were present. 'She used to be frightened of me then. Now she is not frightened, she jokes with me too, she begins to know that she is grown up.'

Male pride in sexuality and an ability to rationalise violence as an inherent part of it is countered by girls' seeming indifference to sex itself. Where young men are represented as always prey to unsatisfied desire, young women are represented as calm, inhibited, uninterested; at best they passively accept the young man but remain essentially unaroused themselves. Being concerned to redress this imbalance and arouse female desire, young men (especially those who have been in prison) may resort to a form of sub-incision whereby small glass marbles are inserted under the skin of the penis. This practice is said to be a standard one among European gangsters who are known thereby to arouse their women to the very height of desire.

A young man may be concerned to arouse a girl's desire, but he is also concerned that she should desire only himself and no other. So her love is not allowed to be explicitly sexual, for if she desired men as men desire women, she would be a 'bitch'. Young women may feel desire, but it cannot be overtly recognised – even by the girls themselves. In their talks about young men, their schemes for attracting them or for illicit meetings, the notion that they may have sex together or that this is what the girl might want is not, I think, commonly acknowledged. Only one girl, with whom I discussed her love affair with a married man, seemed to feel at ease about sex and to like it, an impression I also had from young matrons of some years standing who talked fondly (or jokingly) of husbands who warmed the bed at night. Sexual desire in young women is only indirectly acknowledged by, for instance, tales of Daucina – 'the Lamp-bearer', one of the old Fijian gods – who spies on young women who bathe alone at night and visits them in their sleep.[10] He takes the form of a handsome stranger or a male cross-cousin; his power makes him irresistibly attractive and the girl can do nothing, only follow where he beckons, there to be taken as his wife. One girl of 19 was regularly visited thus in her sleep and at dusk she had seen Daucina in the form of her boyfriend from another village, crossing the village green; she called her mother's attention to the young man, but when her mother looked up there was no one to be seen and they knew, both of them, that it had been Daucina.

The presumed innocence of girls is such that they may tease and torment a man with their attentions in a public gathering and in doing so, promise nothing. Many times I saw young women in their late teens and early twenties gang up on an unmarried man to whom they were all cross-cousin and fête him with their attentions – they garlanded him with flowers, tucked frangipanis behind his ear, served him bowls of *yaqona*, addressed provoking remarks to him, giggled prettily in his direction and so on. If he was not thus forced to flee the gathering, the young man could only hang his head, overcome by shyness in the face of the onslaught. Consciousness of their power and their ideal inviolability is reflected in young women's body postures when they ask a man to dance. One properly adopts a low, stooping posture when passing among people who are seated and apologises, *tulou tulou*, as one does so. A girl who penetrates a group of men to 'touch' one of them in invitation to dance, adopts this polite, self-effacing posture; however, having touched him and turned again towards the lower part of the room, she walks upright with swinging hips and a proud smile. The very fact that in respectable gatherings in house or village hall a girl flirts and initiates dances is a mark of her ideal chastity and innocence. So, when male visitors are in the village, girls are expected to fête them in this way; it is hospitable and brings praise on the village. Lovers are said to be 'ashamed to look at each other in the light', so publicly flirtatious behaviour should be the best sign of inno-cence; that it is not necessarily so is because 'joking' is also understood to be a prelude to greater intimacy.

Cross-cousin into wife

That girls are supposed to be innocently unconscious of the full effect of their behaviour on men is confirmed by the very circumspection that is expected of married women, and especially of young married women. Married women are assumed both to know what men are and what they risk by behaviour which, before marriage, would have been taken for granted. So young married women do not dance; nor do they flirt, joke, smile or laugh too much in front of men other than their husbands and especially not in the company of their cross-cousins. Villagers take it for granted that married men are jealous and newly-married men the most jealous of all. Jealousy is a recognised motive for a beating; even where the suspicion itself is known to be irrational, the jealousy it arouses is often thought to be the woman's fault. What struck me was that the beatings young married men inflicted on their wives were bound to occur – however impeccably correct the wife's behaviour.[11] One man of 19 beat his wife when she said she was going fishing; some men were also going fishing that day and she might have intended to talk and joke with them. This young couple was only a few months married and the beating prompted the wife to run back to her natal village, for already her husband had hit her so often that she was afraid. She was fetched back by her parents-in-law who went and begged her to return, promising that their son would never beat her again and had undertaken truly to change his ways. But some months later her husband himself had to go to fetch her back from another village nearby; she had run away to avoid his beating her because, in a public gathering, she had politely pledged a bowl of *yaqona* to a male cross-cousin.

Another newly married man beat his wife even for gossiping with the girls because, who knows, she might have been using one of them as a go-between with another man. Two of the girls told me that after his marriage he had instructed his wife as to her behaviour – at the time they were both 21. He said, 'You must not stay up late at night, you must go to sleep early in the evening, don't go about visiting, just stay alone at home ... you are not to dance' and so on. The girls said of this that it was bad, eh? (*sa ca e?*) and then, derisively *i tovo ci!* ('fart-like behaviour'). On the other hand it seemed likely that they would expect similar behaviour from men. As far as I could tell, couples split up only if the woman's kin as well as the woman herself considered the beatings too frequent and too severe as happened with one of the two girls just mentioned and the father of her child with whom she had lived in Suva; he beat her, she told me, at least twice a week and always on Thursdays and when I asked her why said, '*Esi!* I don't know – he was drunk. He got paid on Thursdays. All I knew was that when Thursday came round I would be punched.'

Young men in the first year or more of marriage seemed unable to control their extreme jealousy and anger and from what older women had to say about the early days of their marriages, this was a prevalent pattern. All the women, young and old, with whom I discussed male violence declared it abhorrent and unnecessary. Many old women had fearful stories to tell of dreadful beatings incurred in former days, where for example, a previously pacific and gentle husband on being told that his wife was dancing beat her so badly that she miscarried and, in one case, never again became pregnant. At the same time, most women expected men to be violent and found it hard to believe that I had never been so much as slapped; both sexes considered jealousy to be the most salient cause of violence and took it for granted that 'men are jealous' (*e dau vuvu ko ira na tagane*); one took exception only to too much. Girls however, objected strongly to jealousy in male cross-cousins with whom they were merely *veitau* ('friends'); several times I heard girls speak with contempt of one of their number who acted towards her boyfriend as if they were already married – i.e. she had stopped smoking, given up dancing, was shy (*madua*) in the young man's presence and no fun anymore. It was considered presumptuous in a mere cross-cousin to expect this of a girl though in a regular sexual liaison this pattern might well emerge; such behaviour was often said by girls to be a good reason for not getting married.

The jealousy, the beatings and the anger are all part of the process of turning a cross-cousin into a wife. Whether men admit this I do not know, though the Fijian anthropologist Nayacakalou remarked that men he knew sometimes argued that one should not marry a known cross-cousin because she would be 'difficult to control'.[12] The hierarchy across households that emerges in kava-drinking ritual is reckoned in terms of male household heads, and to be a 'head' one has first and foremost to be seen to be above one's wife. This husbandly superiority is constituted in the wedding exchanges and in every household meal. The wife's labour in the provision, cooking and serving of food is devalued by comparison with her husband's whose own contribution is the 'true food' (*kakana dina*) he labours for on his ancestral land. A wife eats by favour of her husband and his ancestors and this is acknowledged in her seating position *i ra*, 'below', at meals and in her attendance on her husband; she eats after him and her food is often of lesser quality than his. Indeed, she is herself 'his thing to eat'.

The significance of this idiom goes beyond any mere equation between sex and eating, for it was still true in pre- and early colonial Fiji of the mid to late 1800s that one ate one's enemies as an act of vengeful sacrifice;[13] these might be the same people with whom one intermarried. But women were not supposed to eat human flesh.[14] I do not know of any expression that describes legitimate female desire, though it is recognised that married women may properly have sexual feelings. But a married woman's desire should be naturally circumscribed, only for her husband; at least it was suggested to me by older women that a man might want variety, but that a woman can easily curb her desires. I knew of liaisons and of series of liaisons between young men and girls and of adultery between girls and married men, but I never heard of any case of adultery by a married woman. This was unsurprising; a married woman discovered in adultery would have been at risk of severe injury.[15]

A woman is said to become undesirable at some point in her thirties; she is 'old' and past her best. That she may still be desired by young men and regularly making love with her husband is not popularly recognised. So women in their mid-thirties to forties begin to enjoy a new freedom; their youngest children are at school, and they may now 'go about', visit sisters and parents elsewhere, go to weddings and so on – without their husbands. They may also joke with their male cross-cousins in a way that would have meant a beating ten, or even five years, before. By now their relation to their husbands is one of *veilomani*, mutual compassionate and familial love; so when a woman over 40 or so becomes pregnant after a long interval (say when her youngest child is about 6) this is 'disgusting' and her husband is ridiculed behind his back. Sex is proper to marriage, but there comes a time when – especially in the view of rather younger people – it ceases to seem appropriate; for younger persons sex between long-married couples can only be either ludicrous or disgusting, unfitting for those who through their grown-up children (themselves perhaps parents) are now undeniably close kin. In the old days, a man did not properly consume the flesh of any of his close kin for fear his teeth would fall out; by the same token, a man is not supposed to want to 'eat' a woman whom he has himself helped to make a middle-aged wife. A woman thus gains a degree of autonomy only at the point where she ceases to be represented as an object of desire.

This is apparent in the joking behaviour of elderly women (those who are presumably past menopause) which may be aggressively sexual; they may 'stand up' alone without shame or even force a younger man into dancing – with much thrusting of hips and flashing of eyes. This behaviour does not bring into question the desires of the women themselves for they are not represented as having any, rather it displays an amused contempt for the desires of men. Old women fold their hands in the gesture which, in a traditional meke or sitting dance, signifies a spear thrust and thus signify in lewd mime the desires of men towards women. It is they who, at weddings, shame the bride with their remarks and comment loudly on the probable sexual prowess of the groom.

One might compare their behaviour with that of old men, who rarely attain this level of joking with young women and when, on occasion, they are so reckless as to try, earn only the mocking laughter and ill-concealed ridicule of the onlookers. Rather old men solace themselves with stories of witchcraft in the style of the Solomon Islanders (*draunikau vakaSolomoni*) who are said still to know the magic that 'carries away women'. I heard such conversation several times, always in the company of old men. On the occasion I recall here each one had his own story about some ugly old man, skin blackened by the sun, who could get any woman he wanted by use of *draunikau* (magic). One had only to rub one's hands with magically treated oil and then shake hands with the woman or give her something, a box of matches even, it didn't matter what. One had only to touch her and she would turn and follow one as in a dream. It could, I was told, happen to me too. 'Truly, mother of Manuel, it carries women away. You wouldn't know what you were doing. You would just follow. It's such a pitiful thing. It makes the women wretched.' The men described girls who were young and fair, and what a pity it was when they followed men who were old and ugly. *Sa maumau dina!* Truly a waste! they said and shook their heads. One told a story of a remarkably ugly old man whose magic was so strong that he controlled a whole village in this way, the men just passively accepting it. Every morning he called out all the people and chose a woman to massage him and another to make love with him, or he entered a couple's house and took the place of the rightful husband in his own bed while the husband went off to sleep in the kitchen. These stories were greeted with exclamations of True! True! (*Sa dina! Sa dina!*) from the different listeners and *Sa!* – an expression of horrified assent.

It is not, I feel, overly fanciful on my part to find in these stories a desire transformed at last into a wistful projection of remembered violence that here signifies its own final defeat.

And thus began true love

I have tried to show how men and women are represented as situated differently with respect to sexual love, which implicitly poses a threat to hierarchical relations between kin. Unmarried girls may provoke desire in young men even while they are themselves represented as ideally unmoved; unmarried young men and women may joke and tease each other with equal emphasis, but it is usually up to young men to realise the sexual potential of the situation. Female desire remains unspoken. A young man is explicit about his sexual feelings, but it seems that a young woman's desire should await arousal by her husband. After marriage a man's longing for a woman ceases to be represented as sexual love and becomes the legitimate wish to eat what is his. A married woman is assumed to feel desire, but for this very reason she must cease to joke with her male cross-cousins, for the sexuality that was before her marriage only implicit in that relationship is now revealed – but only for the time being – as its motive force. A woman's desire must be only for her husband and rendered subordinate to his – an end that is achieved perhaps in violence, for it is in the earliest years of marriage that a man is most likely to beat his wife. A woman with several children – the eldest already in primary school – is rarely so treated. If her husband comes home drunk she may even be heard loudly berating him for his behaviour – unfitting in the father of her children. Once her oldest children are past puberty and the woman herself in her mid to late thirties, she achieves a certain autonomy. No longer popularly represented as an object of desire and never properly acknowledged as subject to desire, she can again be safely allowed to joke with cross-cousins. The man is understood still to be prey to the sexual desire that has been the sign of his dominance since his youth, so in his mid-thirties and despite an apparently contented domestic life, he may still attempt to seduce young women who laugh at the advances of such 'old men' behind their backs. The older he gets, the more thoroughly is a man undone by desire, for the women who are most desirable in popular belief are those virginal girls whom he cannot have. And in old age, only a magical power could allow him once more to assert his sexuality. Old women, by virtue of their ideal detachment from desire, are able at once to make explicit the covert power that is a young woman's ability to arouse desire without apparently being subject to it, and the covert weakness that makes the man helpless in the face of his need. It is usually at weddings that old women represent this paradox in their own persons by dancing in mime a man's sexual desires and thus rendering him absurd.

Cross-cousins are kin to one another, kin who are potential spouses. For this very reason, if sexual love motivates a man to marry, it threatens the hierarchical relations between the ideal husband and wife with the competitive equality of cross-cousins. Marriage contains sexuality by virtue of the fact that even if sexuality initiates it, this is not represented as its *raison d'être*, which is rather the forging of kinship ties and the reproduction of kinship through the children of the marriage. Nevertheless, people do hold that sexual love is important in marriage, but in terms of married life as it is experienced, marriage as process transforms sexual love between equals (*veidomoni*) into the hierarchy of compassionate love between husband and wife (*veilomani*); when once a woman begins to become thoroughly a wife she can no longer be a source of threat to a man's authority. Then only may 'true love' (*veilomani dina*) begin, for the violence of the man's early desire is itself contained and rendered subordinate to compassion. If, in the first year or two of marriage, violence appears to be a consequence of sexual love, this is because a man's sexuality is at once his strength and his undoing while a woman's sexuality is an unspoken and potential source of power.

I am drawn to speculate on the beginnings of the developmental cycle of love in the manifold relations of childhood, whose interactions at once enter into and are the outcome of love. In the course of their growing up children learn that simple acceptance is the proper response of the junior party to any attention from a senior – whether it be in the form of the giving of food, affectionate gestures, an admonitory lecture, harsh words or ridicule or a disciplinary beating – for love is inscribed in all these acts. All these behaviours are defining attributes of kinship, and particularly of the close and always hierarchical relations within the household, and are encompassed by *veilomani*, mutual compassionate love.

However, not all kinship relations are hierarchical; one has one's peers, but by definition, they are not members of one's own household. Avoidance behaviours do not come into effect before puberty, so a child's peers are not only his cross-cousins, but all others of the same age, irrespective of the kin relation in which they stand to one another. Open, outgoing and lively behaviour is expected among one's peers and it is in this context that one can – and should – assert oneself, joke, play and even fight. Peer relations are fostered early in childhood; many times I saw two mothers, each encouraging the young child in her arms to punch out at the other, both children grinning and crowing with glee until one of them took too hard a blow and began to cry; then he or she was kissed and laughed over by the mother – the children being around eight months or older. These are the very gestures of friendship and love in which the mock punch, the playful knock with the knuckles are common indicators of intimacy and affection, both within and across sex, at least until one is in one's thirties or so. The love knock is not symbolic of a harsh blow; rather it is the opposite end of a continuum of meaning in whose terms love may be framed. So it makes little sense here to distinguish between a violence that is real and one that is symbolic for, in any person's experience, each inevitably implies the other.

Each baby, child, schoolchild, young person, adult and old person plays out her or his own relations with peers and seniors, and observes the relations between others. This experience enters into each one's continuing cognitive construction of the meanings that generate her or his linguistic and other behaviour. And this behaviour itself becomes a constitutive of the meanings that that same person and others construct. This process informs the transformation of meaning over time – be it within a person's mind or the sweep of history – in respect of gender, of kinship, of hierarchy, of competitive equality, of marriage. Marriage generates kinship and so it contains within its own developmental cycle all the forms and expressions of love; here *veidomoni*, sexual love between equals, and *veilomani*, compassionate love that helps constitute hierarchy, are but two moments each of which contains the possibility of the other. In marriage as in other domains one shifts back and forth between relations of competitive equality and hierarchical relations; the alternations produce desire for both kinds of love.[16] In the married man's story that began this chapter, it was *veidomoni* – his own helpless (and unadmitted) sexual passion – that lay behind the beating he gave his wife; sexual love is by definition between equals because it is only allowed between cross-cousins, but it is also the locus of the constitutive violence that produces hierarchy. By contrast, *veilomani* is by definition hierarchical, but is also the site of the possibility of equal relations within marriage – for it is this term that my friend used to denote the 'true love' which began in his and his wife's covert recognition in laughter of what had become at other moments a passionate sexual love. That hierarchical 'compassionate love' comes apparently to dominate 'sexual love' between equals is a function of the fact that the developmental experience of love cannot be abstracted from politico-economic processes whereby the subordination of a woman to her husband within the household generates the patriarchal imagery of Fijian hierarchy. It is a wife's subordination that makes any man a chief in his own house. By the same token, in the image of the collectivity as the household writ large, a chief becomes the father of his people and his wife is simply not mentioned.

Here I point out in passing that this analysis could be extended into the domain of transcendent power, where the Christian god may be represented as having both sexual and compassionate love for his human flock. The imagery is that of marriage, for as one preacher is reported to have said: 'God wants to put a wedding ring on your finger' – an action that would make wives of the congregation.[17] This imagery is a transformation of that which, in the past, informed chiefship and sacrificial offerings to the ancestors and which today is at once constituted and expressed in kava-drinking.

In coming to a conclusion, what strikes me most forcibly is that while I have analysed elsewhere the playing out of the constituent processes of Fijian hierarchy in other guises and with respect to other domains of investigation, it now seems to me that love constitutes the most powerful explanation for the specific nature of that hierarchy. It is perhaps needless to say that it is also the domain that I least understand.

8

COSMOGONIC ASPECTS OF
DESIRE AND COMPASSION IN
FIJI

This chapter concerns the interplay of desire and compassion and how, for Fijian villagers, it informs relations between people and the ancestors, and people and the Christian God. Desire and compassion between people constitute the ideal emotional axis of Fijian kinship; in the more inclusive domain of relations between the Christian God, ancestors, chiefs and people, desire and compassion become cosmogonic. Here desire references the old Gods' oral and sexual desires for people, and compassion is a residual category – one that becomes dominant in the relation between people and the Christian God.

The field data discussed here were gathered in Sawaieke country on the island of Gau, Fiji (see note 1 of chapter 1). To establish the context for my analysis I first summarise some conclusions from earlier papers. I then relate two myths that show how the old Gods' carnal appetites are ultimately cosmogonic. These myths are contrasted with a story of the origin of Sawaieke village and the idea of a compassionate Christian God to show how carnal desire becomes a residual category, partly because it is only implicit in the Christian God's relations with people and partly because it is 'devilish' (*vakatevoro*), a malign aspect of the old Gods. Moreover, Christian notions of God and the supernatural can suggest that hierarchy is an encompassing value. This relatively new idea makes it appear as if the ritual contexts in which hierarchical relations are constituted and expressed are projected on to the Fijian collectivity as a fixed and bounded unit. But Christianity too is being subtly transformed 'in the Fijian way', for when desire as well as compassion is attributed to the Christian God's relation to humans, he becomes associated with competitive equality, which is antithetical to fixed hierarchy and prevents its becoming an encompassing value.[1]

The interplay of compassion and desire in kinship relations

The affective aspect of kinship is constituted in and through the interplay of *veilomani*, mutual compassion, and *veidomoni*, mutual desire (Toren 1994). Fijian kinship relations – and ideally all Fijians are kin to one another – are properly relations of mutual compassionate love. Compassion seems of its nature to be

146

hierarchical, since its paradigmatic reference is to the household, and relations *within* the household are by definition relations of inequality. But *across* households, between cross-cousins, *veilomani* is associated with competitive equality. For while relations between cross-cousins are also informed by *loloma* (compassion, love, pity, mercy), the behaviour expected of them is joking, competitive, intimate, friendly, and exchanges between them are reciprocal and balanced over time – all these behaviours being constitutive of the explicit equality between cross-cousins within and across sex.

Cross-cousins are potential spouses or siblings-in-law; *veidomoni*, mutual sexual love or desire, is proper only to cross-cousins across sex and, like all other behaviour between them, is associated with equality and balanced reciprocity. An incest taboo applies to all other categories of kin, between whom day-to-day relations require varying degrees of respect and avoidance. It is axiomatic that a wife is subordinate to her husband, so when cross-cousins marry (by definition one always marries a cross-cousin) their equal relation becomes a hierarchical one (see note 6 of chapter 1). This shift is evident in betrothal and marriage ceremonies and further established, at least in part, by the young man's periodic violence towards his wife. Not all young married men beat their wives, but violence does seem to characterise the early years of marriage and is attributed by both women and men to male sexual jealousy.[2]

Loloma (compassion) and *dodomo* (desire) tend to be spoken of as independent of each other. This is easy enough, because only in marriage is *veilomani* – the mutual compassionate love proper to hierarchical kinship – confronted by *veidomoni* – mutual desire between equals, within a single dyadic relationship. And only in marriage can each kind of love be seen to be the grounds for the other, such that hierarchical and equal relations can be understood as mutually constituting. In the course of married life, the connotations of the two terms are reversed: the jealous anger fuelled by *dodomo* (passionate desire) is the vehicle of a wife's fear of her husband's violence and helps to create her subordination, the loving trust that emerges in *loloma* (compassionate love) becomes the grounds for a possible, but publicly unacknowledged, equality and mutual respect between spouses. This is important, for the marriage relationship is the crucial site for the constitution of Fijian hierarchy (see Toren 1990: 50–64).

Marriage and hierarchy

Within Sawaieke country (*vanua*), the chiefly village of Sawaieke ranks above seven other villages that owe it tribute; people often describe relations within and across villages as if the heads of ranked households are ranged in ranked clans, in ranked *yavusa* (groups of connected clans), in ranked villages.[3] This notion of a pervasive hierarchy is constituted in *yaqona* ritual, where tribute is made *apparently* to encompass day-to-day exchange relations of balanced reciprocity across households, clans, *yavusa* and villages.

The apparent dominance of tributary hierarchy in the face of thorough-going balanced reciprocity depends on men's being seen to be the heads of households. This is effected by a woman's marrying into her husband's house, where by virtue of age and kinship relation she is subordinate to her husband's parents, and by ritualised aspects of the public face of her relation to her husband. In production and exchange, husbands and wives have equal obligations and are equal partners – with a single important exception: in respect of food products and cooking, husbands' contributions seem to be valued above wives', and at every meal in every house, wives take their places nearest the common entrance *i ra*, below, and wait upon their husbands and eat after them. So 'every man is a chief in his own house' and women refer to their husbands and to other men as 'leaders of households' (*i liuliu ni vale*); whenever I questioned this I was told that 'it is right that [married] men should lead' (*e dodonu me ra liu na turaga*).

The axiomatic ritual subordination of wife to husband is historically attributable to the way that marriage deprived women of direct access to ancestral Gods; but their attendance on the Christian God gave women direct access to divine power on the same basis as men; and they are included too in *yaqona*-drinking, from which they used to be excluded (see Toren 1988). But in *yaqona*-drinking, a woman takes her position with reference to her husband: she sits *i ra*, below, near the common entrance. Even if she be wife to the paramount chief and high-ranking in her own right, she sits *i ra* in the presence of her husband; but as she is of higher status than other women, they all sit below her. So, in *yaqona*-drinking, it *appears* as if all women are below all men, even though, in their natal households, many women as elder sisters not only have a formally higher status than their younger brothers but may also have significant effective authority over them.

Women's status as elder sisters poses a problem for the ranking of households, clans and *yavusa* against one another; but with women as subordinate wives effectively removed from consideration, these collectivities can be ranked in respect of their obligations to chiefs (*turaga*) – a term that can refer to married men, to people of chiefly birth irrespective of gender or, more exclusively, to the chiefs of *yavusa*, also called *na malo*, 'the cloths'. On a day-to-day basis in *yaqona*-drinking, it is with respect to *na malo* and a few other senior and high-status men that elders, married men, young men and women can all apparently be ranked on the above–below axis that describes any space where *yaqona*-drinking takes place. The authority of *na malo* – including the paramount chief – is at once expressed and constituted in *yaqona*-drinking, and especially in the drinking that installs a chief as *yavusa* head, or as paramount of a country (*vanua*).

The presentation of *yaqona* (*sevusevu*) and the drinking of it are paradigmatic of sacrificial tribute: the root is presented raw to the chiefs, under whose aegis it is ritually prepared and re-presented as drink to the people; the *yaqona* cannot now be further transformed. It is, as it were, 'cooked', and must be accepted if one is not to give offence.

In the current politico-economy of rural Fiji, *yaqona*-drinking is crucial for the constitution of the authority of chiefs. Chiefs are held to be essential for the moral well-being of the country at large and for prosperity; they are the locus of exchange across collectivities, and so may seem to give more than they receive and to deserve people's attendance on them. But the material power of the chiefs of small *vanua* is limited; it is the drinking of the installation *yaqona* that makes a chief 'truly effective' (*mana dina*) – because then those who disobey him or are wanting in respect are likely to fall ill and die. By contrast, in pre- and early colonial times, a properly installed chief had the literal power of life and death over his people, and his *mana* was manifest at once in his people's prosperity and in his warriors' victory in war; a truly powerful chief struck terror into his followers according to the strength of his warlike attributes and his carnal appetites. But more of this below.

In the developmental cycle of love, as it emerges from an analysis of representations of what is appropriate at different stages of life, compassion and desire are mutually constituting. *Veilomani*, whose paradigmatic reference is mutual compassion between kin within the hierarchical household, comes into being as the ultimate artefact of the passion of *veidomoni*, which can only describe mutual desire between cross-cousins as equals across households. Thus *loloma* (compassion) and *dodomo* (desire) are opposite ends of a continuum of meaning in which each can be seen to be the grounds of the possibility of the other. This analysis can be extended into the religious domain, for, according to one preacher, the Christian God has both *loloma and dodomo* for his people: 'God wants to put a wedding ring on your finger.'[4]

Here the Christian God's desire motivates the marriage whereby the congregation becomes his wives; the marriage constitutes him as the omnipotent husband and father in a vast, hierarchically ordered household. In this image the Christian God contains within himself the creative tension between *loloma* and *dodomo*, and makes both aspects inform his relation to people. Thus he takes on something of the nature of the old Fijian Gods – in their benign aspect, 'the founding Gods' (*na kalou vu*, lit. origin Gods) or 'the ancestors' (*na qase e liu*, lit. the old ones before), and in their malign aspect 'devils' (*tevoro*). Despite this covert suggestion of syncretism in the imagery of the Christian God's love for humanity, Fijians are able to assert their practice to be eminently Christian. This is because, in an earlier Fijian cosmology, *mana* was manifest less in compassion than in the violence of desire; and compassionate love was rendered a fugitive by-product of a violent and cosmogonic carnal desire.

Cosmogonic desire

Carnal desire was focused in orality as much as in sexuality. To consume a sacrifice demonstrated the power of the consumer; the efficacy, the *mana*, of Gods and chiefs was constituted and expressed in sacrifice. So Sahlins argues that, in myth, the origin of cannibalism is also the origin of culture, and that in his installation a chief becomes at once the feeder of the people and their food

(Sahlins 1983). These ideas are also present in the following story of Tui Delaigau, King of the Heights of Gau (for the original, see the monograph by the Methodist missionary, Waterhouse 1978 [1866]: 379–383).

At odds with their fellow villagers, two men decide not to attend the games at Muana [a promontory near Sawaieke]. Angry at this, their wives go alone to the games. The two men go to picnic elsewhere on the coast and there, while looking for landcrabs to eat with their root vegetables, they see a handsome and gigantic man coming towards them.

When he reaches the beach this man says, 'Arms, go and bathe' and the arms detach themselves and go to wash. Having thus instructed all his body parts, his head goes up into a tree until the parts return and reassemble. Seeing he is a God, the two men follow him to the top of the highest mountain in Gau, where he ascends into a tree.

Next morning the two men take a large root of *yaqona* and present it formally at the foot of the tree. The God appears and asks what they want. The bolder man replies that, having seen and recognised his power, they want him to adopt them as his children and become their God. The God is pleased and tells them to prepare *yaqona for* him. When he has drunk, he summons from the tree a spade, which begins on its own to dig an oven. The men are terrified. The God calls down cooking stones, and wood which ignites itself and heats the stones. When the oven is ready, the God asks which of the two men is to be cooked and eaten. The bolder one says he is, leaps into the oven, is covered by leaves that pour from the tree and earth that is heaped up on the oven by the spade.

Later the God says that all is cooked and calls the spade to open the oven. In it are piles of mats and barkcloth, and under them the man, who jumps out quite unharmed. The God gives the two men all this property and they go home. The next day they return with the product of their own labours – four large baskets of fish, which they leave under the tree as a thank-offering.

The next day the two men go to the games and are insulted by the crowd because they are not well-dressed. One goes to the centre of the dancing-ground, announces that he will make a feast for the chief, and calls above for a spade to dig an oven. A spade descends as before, and the man imitates all the God's commands. His fellow, who was before the onlooker, leaps into the oven, which is covered with earth by the spade. The man then goes to bathe, and returns dressed in the beautiful cloth given him by the God. He calls for the spade to open the oven, revealing a vast number of mats and under them the other man, now dressed superbly in barkcloth with white cowrie shells on his arms and ankles. The property is carried formally to the chief and then the men

150

go home. They have been preceded by their wives and are followed home by other women who also want to marry them, but their wives drive these women away, saying they want no polygamous marriages.

Here the two men's augmented effectiveness results from their willingness to attend on one who is greater than they are, even to the extent of becoming his food. By sacrificing themselves to the God, they are able to become like chiefs. This is evinced by the beauty of their new clothing for, in pre- and early colonial Fiji, the length of a chief's barkcloth train signified his rank, and by the cowrie shells, also a mark of chiefly rank, that adorn the second man's arms and legs. The God's *mana* is manifest in his acts and, more importantly, in the men's very willingness to attend on and to obey him. Cosmogonic power is prefigured by the God's ability to dismember and recreate himself as a new whole; the men's sacrifices oblige him to manifest his power on their behalf.

One current idiom for witchcraft is *sova yaqona*, lit. pouring *yaqona*, which is supposed to take place behind closed doors or in the bush. One who wishes to gain a magical efficacy performs *yaqona* ritual alone, pours a libation to an ancestor God, and asks his aid; the person then has to name a close relative as a sacrifice to the God; the naming itself effects the sacrifice. The God then gives his follower what he or she wants. In the story of Tui Delaigau the two men offer *yaqona* to the God and his acceptance of it is followed by his asking which one of them will become his food. Here the interplay of kinship and oral desire becomes crucial, for the men had asked not only to be allowed to attend on the God, but to become his children. In the Fiji of cannibal sacrifices, the eating of one's close kin was *tabu* and said to cause one's teeth to fall out. The men became the God's children when he accepted their offering of *yaqona*. Thus when the bolder man volunteers to become his food, he shows himself to be truly subordinate even while he relies on the God's compassion for one who is now his son.[5] This man is then able to provide for his own kin, as is his fellow who enters the oven dug on the dancing ground. There is no malign act of witchcraft here; the story reveals the compassion that a good father, a good God and, by implication, a good chief has for those who augment his power by willingly attending on him and doing as he says.

So when the oven is opened, its contents have become those of a grave whose occupant is still living. Today, as in old Fiji, a dead body is dressed, wrapped in barkcloth and fine mats and buried in a grave lined with mats. The grave is dug on *yavusa* or clan gardening land and, when it is filled, the earth is heaped up on it and banked with stones or, today, covered with a concrete platform. In appearance it is a miniature *yavu*, house foundation. In earlier days, and apparently especially in the case of chiefs, the corpse was interred in the house foundation itself. The ancestors are *kalou vu*, 'founding Gods', and the term *yavu* is the base for *yavusa*. That the benign Tui Delaigau has truly adopted the two men as his children is plain in his acceptance of their sacrificial tribute and in his raising them, still alive, from the oven – here made analogous at once to the grave and the house foundation.

House foundations are private to those who have rights in them, and should not be walked across, even if they are not built upon; their names are permanent. The varying height of remaining house foundations still signifies the status of those who live in the houses built on them. Those that are *yavu tabu*, 'forbidden house foundations' are usually situated in the bush on clan and *yavusa* gardening land; their names form the honorific titles of clan and *yavusa* chiefs.

At the outset of the story of Tui DelaiGau the two men hardly appear to be heads of households; their wives are able angrily to defy them and to go off to the games alone. Indeed the women neglect to provide, as is their duty, the *i coi* (the meat, fish or other element of a meal) to go with the cooked vegetables already provided by the men. By the end of the story, having shown themselves to be *mana*, 'effective', the men go home to wives who have, rightly, preceded them; what is implied is that the women will now attend properly on their husbands. The two men are followed by other women, who want too to become willing wifely subordinates. That the men's wives shoo away the other women, saying they want no polygamous marriages, is perhaps the missionary's flourish, but it also suggests that their initial disrespect for their husbands was warranted, and so they can rely on their husbands' forbearance. A wife is *obliged to* attend on her husband only so long as he shows himself deservedly able to command her.

Thus the God's cosmogonic act in transforming the oven at once into grave and house foundation makes it possible for the men, via their marriages, to become the heads of effective, hierarchically ordered households – households in which husbands and wives fulfil their reciprocal obligations to one another, and wives are seen to attend on their husbands.[6]

In the story of Tui DelaiGau, the God's oral desires are overt: the men give him *yaqona* to drink and their own bodies to eat; that he does not eat them does not alter the fact that his *mana is* constituted in the consumption of sacrifices. The great baskets of fish that the men leave as a thank-offering are substitutes for their own bodies and for human bodies in general; men whose clan is that of fishermen (*gone dau* or *kai wai*, lit. seapeople) were, in old Fiji, also often warriors, fishers of men, who provided human sacrifices for both Gods and chiefs. Here the satisfaction of the God's oral desires is ultimately constitutive of the ordered hierarchical household.

The story of the *yavu* (house foundation) called *Na i vinivini* – a great mound covered with stones that stands near the sea front of Sawaieke village – also shows how oral and sexual desire can be *mana*, effective. It was told me by a Sawaieke chief whom I asked to tell me some stories of 'earlier times' (*na gauna e liu*); here I give an outline of it.

At that time Sawaieke country was led by Ravuravu [Killer With a Club – a warrior God, one of the earliest Sawaieke ancestors]. The people went to serve him at his hilltop dwelling near the shore. He was always cold, and they had to drag firewood up there; whole trees like the *dawa*, mango and chestnut were consumed in warming him.

Then a war began between Sawaieke village and one of its tributary villages, Nukuloa. Nukuloa sent a man to ask the help of Radikedike, who was chief of Bua [in Vanua Levu – an island to the north of Gau]. He came to help Nukuloa, but by chance he entered through the reef at the opening near Sawaieke and mistook the *tavola* tree that marked Ravuravu's dwelling for one that was supposed to show where the Nukuloa chief lived.

He came ashore and climbed up the hill, but when he got there no one took any notice of him and he could see he was not expected. Radikedike had brought 100 chestnuts which hung from his arm. He wanted to roast and eat some of his chestnuts, so he went to the house of Ravuravu and asked him for some firewood. Ravuravu said that if he could carry the firewood away, then he was welcome to it, and was astonished to see his visitor take up a whole tree, strip off its leaves and take it away – a tree that had taken fifty Sawaieke people to drag it up the hill. He said to himself, 'I am getting old, I shall give him the country, hand it over to him so that he may lead it.'

So Ravuravu made way for Radikedike. But Radikedike was always wanting women and so asked that he might build his *yavu* at the spot where the ladies ceased to sing *meke* songs on their way home from reef-fishing. So he built his house foundation, *Naivinivini*, there at that spot, which later became the new site of Sawaieke village.

Here, in proper Fijian fashion, an ageing but still powerful chief, recognising a stranger's *mana*, makes him leader of the country. Ravuravu's warlike power is waning, for he has always to be warmed by fire, but the size of the fruit-bearing trees that are consumed in warming him shows his power has still to be reckoned with.[7] Radikedike is in his prime; the man who told me the story said, 'He carried here 100 chestnuts … huge chestnuts – but if 100 hung from his arm, what about the size of this chief, this victorious chief?' Radikedike wants fire-wood, not to spend its fruitfulness in stoking a passion for war, but to roast chestnuts. The chestnuts denote his own fruitfulness, as well as his strength, and eating them gives him the heat that is proper to men, the heat that makes a man desire women.

The leadership of Radikedike and the attendance of the Sawaieke people upon him is implicit in their allowing him to build his *yavu* at the spot where the women ceased to sing as they came home from fishing – the story suggests that he took many wives; moreover, it was in relation to Radikedike's *yavu* that the new village took shape. Today, the house foundations of the old village said to have been under the sway of Ravuravu can still be seen at some distance from the present village of Sawaieke, as can the impressive mound of Radikedike, which stands to one side of the village, beside the road.

In the stories above, the Gods' manifest powers are benign. Tui DelaiGau desires to drink *yaqona* and to eat men and, in return for the men's sacrificial tribute, presents them with superb goods; these make the men both providers of valuables and, implicitly, sexually powerful; so they become effective husbands and household heads. Radikedike, in return for being allowed ready access to many women, accepts the leadership of the country and so enables Sawaieke to retain its paramount position.

Devilish desire

A husband's legitimate sexual desire for his wife is expressed not as *dodomo* (passionate love) but as the desire to eat what is his, *sa via kania na kena*. When people refer to the old Gods as *tevoro*, 'devils', they are usually referring to the Gods' sexual or oral desire to consume humans. *Ko-i-rau-na-marama*, The Two Ladies, are known for both their sexual and cannibal appetites. In Sawaieke they are said to be ancestors of the chiefly *yavusa* Nadawa. They were implicated in one of the two cases of suggested witchcraft that occurred during my time in the field. A man in his late thirties had an apparently incurable illness – one that did not respond to herbal remedies or prolonged Western medical treatment. Speaking of this man's illness, a woman of chiefly birth, aged about 30, said to me:

> It is because of our ancestor Gods; it has been a long time since those two devil women, our ancestor Gods, have appeared. They were seen before Y married and again before Z married [this being at least sixteen years earlier]. Perhaps someone is attending on them, someone wants this man to die.

She said that the sick man was plagued by visions (*rai votu*) of The Two Ladies who took the form of chiefly women whom he knew. Once he heard them say, 'Come, let us throw X outside that he may be killed'; he was sure then that witchcraft had caused his illness, for the ancestor Gods are not usually supposed to act on their own. Speaking of this case, the chief who told me the story of Radikedike's mound, said:

> Those two can't just go and kill a person. There is a reason for it, it may be that someone is doing something in order to kill X. They can't just kill people [on their own account]. Their *yavu* is in the old village at Nadragugasau. Someone has prepared *yaqona* and asked them to do something, perhaps to kill him. Actually they [The Two Ladies] were here last week. My younger brother understood; he was angry, our house smelled bad. He said to me he knew the meaning of it; he was angry – nowadays it's not liked.

In cases of witchcraft-induced illness, an effective cure requires *yaqona* to be drunk in a ceremony where the *dauvagunu* 'giver of drink' – prepares the *yaqona* and calls on the winds to beg the ancestor God to remove the curse; sometimes he or she places a *tabua* (whale's tooth) on a Bible and calls on Jesus Christ as well as on the ancestor God; but whatever the specific form of the ceremony, the tributary offering of *yaqona* is essential.

In the course of the *yaqona*-drinking accompanying a wedding, the man referred to as Z in the woman's remarks above (a married man in his mid-forties) told me, unprompted, about his encounter, about 16 years before, with The Two Ladies. He was returning alone from his gardens when he saw two women whom he greeted politely, though he did not know them; they greeted him in return and began a flirtatious dialogue, remarking on his coming marriage and saying that he would be better off to marry them, at which point he realised they were devils and fell in a faint to the ground. He woke up hours later, knowing that had he gone with them, they would have consumed him.[8] In Sawaieke one can detect their invisible presence by a bad smell for which there is no usual explanation; this smell may hang in the house for days, but one must not remark on it, for if one does The Two Ladies will be offended and misfortune – illness or even death – will strike the household.[9]

The old Gods are held still to visit their malign power upon people and, specifically, to be eager to consume them sexually and orally; to dream of having sexual intercourse is to know that one has been possessed by a God. Several times young women told me they had been visited during their sleep by Daucina (The Lamp-Bearer) in the form of a handsome young man. This God haunts coastlines and possesses women who are foolish enough to bathe alone after dark – a warning of his likely presence is often the subject of a joke directed towards a woman who bathes late. I never heard men's dreams or behaviour in bathing similarly remarked on, though men often say that one of the praiseworthy attributes of *yaqona* is that it ensures a dreamless sleep – which suggests that they are as ambivalent about their dreams as young women seem to be.[10] Young men also tell tales about two female devils (perhaps a manifestation of The Two Ladies) often seen dancing in a Suva night-club – one frequented by villagers on holiday in the capital. Young men have been attracted by their beauty to dance with them, only to realise that they had to be *tevoro* – devils – because their feet did not touch the floor when they danced. The association between sexual intercourse and European-style dancing in night-clubs suggests that these female devils intend to seduce the young men.

That the old Gods are still killers (and cannibals) is implicit in a tale about the first children to board at the Gau Junior Secondary School; the ancestral owner of the site is said to have been angry at the people's temerity in building there (in spite of previous *yaqona* ceremonies to placate his wrath) and to have attacked the children, who woke in terror in the night to find this 'devil' on their chests, trying to choke the life out of them. More ceremonies had to be performed. Thus the old Gods still inhabit the places where once they ruled, though their power is diminished, 'because no one attends on them any more'.

The coming of the light

Attendance on a God or a chief is what actually empowers him. Here one may contrast the story of Radikedike's *yavu* with that of the founding of Sawaieke village as it is today. I was told this story several times; the version below is that of a well-educated commoner in his sixties, much respected for his past achievements and his devout Christianity:

> Before, the people of this village did not live together in the manner of kinship (*vakaveiwekani*). No. Each little village stood alone and there were many quarrels and fights between them. … During the old time, in the time of the devils (*gauna vakatevoro*), the church came here; civilisation came here. It brought the light to us (*vakararamataki keimami*). Before, all the old villages on this piece of coastline had stood alone; then they wanted to be nearer each other because if all the villages moved here it would make easier their attendance on one another (*veiqaravi*, lit. facing each other – their mutual ritual obligations).
>
> The owners of this village, of this land, were *yavusa* Sawaieke Nakorolevu eh? [The Big Village, a name for *yavusa* Sawaieke]. They called the people of the little villages to come here: 'Takalaigau, come here' – and they came; 'Tui Navure, come here' – and they came. And the Voda people came too. The Buli [officer of the colonial administration, usually a traditional chief] decided that house-building should begin. Then they built the church and this was the beginning of true kinship.

Other versions did not mention the Buli, but all agree that the church brought forth the present village of Sawaieke. *Yavusa* Sawaieke, whose chief installs (and some say selects) the paramount, invited the chiefly *yavusa* denoted by Takalaigau to reside on its land along with his landspeople – *yavusa* Navure, and his fishermen – 'the Voda people'. Both priests (*Bete*) and warriors (*Bati*) are conspicuously absent. This may be a function of particular historical conditions, but even so it is fitting that neither figures in the founding of the new village, where chiefs and people dwell in harmony in the sight of the Christian God.[11] For this is no story of cosmogonic carnal desire; rather it recounts the acts of literally enlightened chiefs whose 'attendance on each other' implies their concerted attendance on the Christian God.

The story seems to suggest that Christianity imposed an encompassing hierarchy on 'the little villages'. Before 'the coming of the light they had a certain autonomy; they owed tribute to Sawaieke village, but they might (as Nukuloa did) hope to rebel and to establish the supremacy of their own Gods and chiefs.

So the old stories may tell of Gods making way for Gods and chiefs for chiefs – always on account of acts of *mana* that show them worthy of being 'attended on'. Both Gods and chiefs were represented as striving to establish paramount positions, but the relations between chiefs or between chiefs and people were not fixed, for they were *always and inherently* open to the challenge given by the equality of cross-cousins, a relation that is also played out across countries.

Two countries that attend on the same ancestor God are *veitauvu*, 'of the same root'; Sawaieke and Bua are *veitauvu* because of their common attendance on Radikedike. To be *veitabani* is to be 'mutually branching', and relates countries whose ancestors were cross-cousins. These are both joking relationships, like that between cross-cousins. Even where people say that countries *should* be ranked according to their relative positions in a notional hierarchy, they acknowledge that no such ranking is really possible because people would not agree on what it might be. So, when the Provincial Council for Lomaiviti met in 1982, the seating positions of paramount chiefs in the *yaqona*-drinking that accompanied each day's meeting and the ceremonies that marked each night, shifted as if by mutual but probably unspoken consent; it looked as if each of the chiefs was allowing each of the others a turn in the top, central position of paramount authority. This is a product of earlier times when chiefs (and implicitly their Gods) warred against one another to establish their relative statuses and at the same time gave their sisters in marriage to secure the alliance of some possibly rebellious tributary village. But the hierarchy they vied to establish could never be quite secure – at every level it was challenged by the equality residing in balanced exchange between cross-cousins as affines and equals across generation and across households.

Yaqona-drinking, as an integral part of all *cakacaka vakavanua* (lit. working/doing/acting in the manner of the land), seems to fix hierarchy. But a fixed hierarchy can only be momentarily achieved, for the tributary relation it denotes is manifested only in *yaqona* ritual, where the balanced reciprocal relation between *yavusa* chiefs who stand to one another as 'land' and 'sea' is itself suggested by the order of the drinking (see Toren 1990: 90–118). Thus *yaqona* ritual contains the tension between tribute and balanced reciprocity but does not resolve it; the ritual itself becomes the site of the dynamic play of relationships. That it suggests to a European the image of a hierarchically ordered whole is at once an artefact of European predilections and of the articulation of Christian and indigenous ideas of the relations between humans and Gods.

Church teachings, as given in prayers and often in sermons, make Christianity all-encompassing. So the story of the origin of the present village of Sawaieke makes the church the foundation for the acknowledgement of mutual ritual obligations and for the 'true kinship' that is their product. Like most rural churches, Sawaieke's is built to one side of the village green; it is literally and figuratively at the centre of village life. The Christian God is at the peak of the hierarchy of names derived from sacred places, so prayers often address the Christian God as follows: 'To heaven, to the holy dwelling place, you the true

God, you the God who alone is served.' Further, the speeches for *sevusevu* (presentation of *yaqona*) to chiefs, while they always begin with a recital of the honorific titles of the chiefs – i.e. the names of their *yavu tabu*, lit. forbidden house foundations – often end by expressing the hope that the following of the chiefs and the Methodist minister might 'grow ever greater'.

Death as sacrifice

For nearly a century and a half people have attended on the Christian God. He is supernatural in a sense that was not – and is not – true of the old Fijian Gods. The *kalou vu* were different in quality from humans, but not utterly different in kind; their domains were on earth in known places. So the old paradisal island of Burotu could be moved about at will by its spirit inhabitants, on top of or below the waves, and after death the spirit travelled across known territory and encountered spirits whom he or she now resembled in substance (Hocart 1929: 195; Thompson 1940: 115; Williams 1982 [1858]).

The old Gods were more powerful than humans, but an installed chief himself instantiates godly power by virtue of the installation *yaqona*, which in Gau means that an installed Takalaigau 'has at his back all the ancestor Gods of Gau'. In the installation the high chief becomes at once the object of the people's sacrificial offering of *yaqona* and the sacrifice itself, for when he has drunk he is *mate ni yaqona*, lit. dead from *yaqona* (Sahlins 1983). So his effectiveness (*mana*) is rendered paramount: because the people attend on him, their ancestors are compelled to 'stand at his back'. The power of installed chiefs resides in the godly power they instantiate; in the story of Radikedike's *yavu*, Sawaieke emerged triumphant from an impending war with Nukuloa because its God-chiefs were the more powerful. Winning a war meant that one's own God had (if only temporarily) ousted another.

Today the ancestors are, in their benign aspect, made to attend on the Christian God who, omnipotent and all-knowing, confers chiefship upon men as 'a godly gift' (*na i solisoli vakalou*). So prayers by a church minister are important in chiefly installations, and chiefship seems to have been encompassed by the Christian church. The power to install a chief is itself held to be from God, even though what is conferred with the chiefship is an efficacy whose source is also ancestral. But chiefly installations are rare, precisely because the chiefship is itself open to competition between clan chiefs within the chiefly *yavusa*.[12]

It is death that makes apparent the power of the Christian God and his relation to the indigenous Gods; the Christian God made the world and everything in it and appointed each thing, including humans, to its proper place.[13] He appointed too the day of each person's death, and so each death is implicitly a sacrifice to the Christian God.

In a description of *reguregu*, the last rites for the dead, that forms part of an account of Fijian traditions for secondary school children, it is written that:

In their speeches of offering [lit. of holding in the hand – the whale's teeth or other goods presented by mourning kin] they will emphasise how the living look out for one another, and love one another, and they will emphasise in their acceptance and their invocations their earnest wish that death will delay in coming to us, or that this [death] might be the last of our troubles.

But given that, even while one wants to put it off, each death is a sacrifice, one should not be made angry or resentful by it, partly because it is God's will and partly because in being willed by God each death makes kinship relations across groups take on their proper form 'in the manner of the land' (*vakavanua*). Thus in a speech accepting a *sevusevu* (presentation of *yaqona*) that was part of the initial four days of mourning for a high-status man of chiefly birth, the speaker referred to the occasion of the death as 'that morning that God had concealed from us, it happened so that today the chiefly establishment would have to take form'.

Addressing the assembled chiefs who had brought the body from the capital city, Suva, to Sawaieke, he went on to say:

We know there is a moral that God had already hidden in this day. ... By coming here, you have met with what stood ready for you [you willingly took on your preordained obligations] – this is just according to the chiefly path followed by *yavusa* Nadawa. You were there to meet the trouble when it arrived, it laid on the burden where it was proper that it should be laid, we are very grateful for that. We know this is a thing from God, it followed you, our chiefs, wherever you went – and so I am praising your coming here.

This idea of predestination is likely to be of Christian origin, for while the old Gods could foretell the future or cause particular states of the future to be brought about – as for example in predicting how many of the other side might be killed in a war – there is no suggestion in the old stories that they caused people's futures to be embodied in them on the day of birth.[14] Here I quote a further speech made on the same occasion; a much-respected man of chiefly status was presenting two fine whale's teeth to the land chiefs whose task it is to preside over the mourning ceremonies for the dead of the chiefly *yavusa*:

This is a difficult day, a day we had not appointed ... our father on high knows we are met together in kinship this morning in this chiefly establishment. We greatly respect the chiefs coming here because of our child [chief] who has gone away in atonement and whom you have carried here. ... Different tasks are appointed to us by God. Truly he has said, you did not choose me, only I chose you. ... His [the dead man's] task in our land is already performed; we should rightly be thankful for it. A good-tempered chief and a determined chief, God has called him, we should rightly be very thankful for it.

The idea of death as sacrifice pervades the above speeches and, as with a sacrifice to the old Gods, death makes material the relations between collectivities and gives them form; *yaqona*, whale's teeth and food are amassed according to clan or *yavusa* (*vakamataqali, vakayavusa*) and presented as such by their chiefs to the chiefs of the mourning *yavusa*.

Associated with predestination is the idea that the Christian God chooses his own people. In the speech, God's choice refers to the hearers' 'obligations in the manner of the land' (*i tavi vakavanua*); but the wider implications of the words are that in choosing for them their duties, God has also chosen them as his people; certainly they do not choose him. One might contrast this with the old Gods, on whom people may decide to attend; as far as the Christian God is concerned it seems one has no choice in the matter.

That Christianity is inescapable and all-encompassing is contained in an uncompromising view of the necessity of church membership as represented by a young man of 25 or so:

In the Fijian way, if a person is not a member of a congregation – not a churchgoer – then that person is not a member of a household, not a member of a clan, not a member of a *yavusa* nor a member of a village. The meaning of this is that s/he is not counted as one of the people of this land.

He had asked me about my religious affiliation, and this was his response to my saying that in London I did not go to church. He went on to question the legality of my marriage and my residence in the United Kingdom. Because my husband cannot be described as even nominally Christian and because we are of different nationalities and neither of us is British, my questioner could not credit that either our marriage or our living in London had been properly ratified in any sense with which he was familiar. The young man's demand for consistency in respect of nationality, religious affiliation, marriage and residence was relatively unusual – but it does show how Christianity can be held to be an encompassing value.

On first meeting, villagers in Gau always ask foreigners certain stock questions; these concern one's country of origin, whether one is married, how many children one has, and what church one belongs to. One's acceptability as an adult and moral person is predicated upon marriage and Christianity. One cannot deny being a Christian. People are so dismayed. Once, in the company of a group of women, such a denial on my part met with the shocked response: 'So you live just like that – just anyhow?' I felt compelled to add that as a child I was a Catholic, and this brought sighs of relief and a general relaxation in the tension that had resulted from my earlier denial.

Hierarchy, equality and ritual

Church membership constitutes one domain of social relations, and when Christianity is being talked about it seems to be understood to be a superordinate domain and a superordinate value.[15] But this is true too of kinship and chiefship; it all depends on which domain of relations is presently being made the focus of ritual or discussion. Behaviour according to the church (*vakalotu*), to kinship (*vakaveiwekani*), to chiefs (*vakaturaga*) and to the land (*vakavanua*) are mutually constituting; and in each domain, relations which are either hierarchical or equal are the very grounds of the possibility of the opposing form. In respect of the processes of daily life, any given person is the locus of both the equal and unequal relations which constitute the different domains.

In personal experiential terms, the relation between cross-cousins is essential for passionate relations across sex and for intimate, friendly camaraderie within sex, and is highly valued for these reasons. One can demand anything of a cross-cousin and one should never refuse him or her anything, for one's cross-cousins give zest to life; in other words, this competitive relation between equals is valued as highly as the hierarchical relation between siblings or between parent and child, and is the basis for the possibility of marriage which, in daily domestic life, is constituted as *the* crucial hierarchical relationship.

In their ritual practice Fijians succeed momentarily in the struggle to contain the equal, competitive relation between cross-cousins, and the threat of disorder it sometimes represents, within the bounds of hierarchical kinship. That this struggle is in principle unending is a product of the fact that all dynamic, fertile and affective processes are *founded* in the relation between cross-cousins. Fijians represent social relations in terms, not of fixed structures, but of certain ways of behaving – the chiefly way, the way of kinship, of the land, of the church, of the government, of the law; in so far as each way is associated with certain ritual behaviour (*yaqona*-drinking, meals, life-cycle ceremonies, church services, village council meetings and so on) this behaviour projects particular images of social relations as fixed structures: tributary relations between chiefs and people in *yaqona*-drinking, hierarchical kinship within the household as a commensal unit, the community either as the children of God's cosmic household in church services, or, in council meetings, as the children of chiefs.

But ritual can only momentarily fix social relations as hierarchical, for ultimately, given that all Fijian ritual has recourse to the imagery of the household as the foundation (*yavu*) of all social relations, they suggest too the hidden imagery of the balanced, reciprocal relations between cross-cousins across households, and the dynamic of their sexuality, which is at once permitted and threatening. For the household depends for its very existence on the relations between cross-cousins, who alone can bring into being a new household or ensure the continuance of an existing one.

Today Christianity is taken to be one with 'the Fijian way', and thus *seems* to be an encompassing value. But 'the Fijian way' is being forged in contradistinction to 'the European way', or 'the way of money' (see chapter 1). The contrast operates on difference and hierarchical value in such a way that all that is morally proper is associated with the Fijian way and all that is amoral with Europeans; but if we bring the church into this ideal international contrast it inevitably mediates it by introducing likeness and equality – Fijians as a Christian people alongside other Christian peoples – and suggests relations across boundaries, which are always, at least initially, like relations between cross-cousins. From this perspective Christianity too can be seen as yet another product of the dynamic, cosmogonic play of competition and desire that for Fijians fuels the competitive relations between households, countries, nations, peoples, and underlies their very existence. Here the play of value between dynamic equality and static hierarchy is pushed out beyond the bounds of nations theoretically to encompass the cosmos, where desire and compassion become dual aspects of a new, Fijian, formulation of Christianity.

9

'ALL THINGS GO IN PAIRS, OR THE SHARKS WILL BITE'

The antithetical nature of Fijian chiefship

In his postface to *Homo Hierarchicus*, Dumont argues for a theory of hierarchy as 'the encompassing of the contrary' whereby

> At the superior level there is unity; at the inferior level there is distinction ... complementariness or contradiction is contained in a unity of superior order. But as soon as we intermingle the two levels, we have a logical scandal, because there is identity and contradiction at the same time.
>
> (1980 [1966]: 242)

He contrasts his 'hierarchical schema' with the 'Hegelian schema' where 'transcendence is produced synthetically, instead of pre-existing' (ibid.: 243). Ideas implicate values, and for Dumont 'To adopt a value is to introduce hierarchy, and a certain consensus of values, a certain hierarchy of ideas, things and people, is indispensable to social life' (ibid.: 20). So he implies that human thought is hierarchical in its nature and thus makes hierarchy itself an ultimate value in which other values are nested. His thesis has been influential, particularly in so far as it has given rise to the view that the anthropologist's aim should be to analyse the hierarchy of values that informs the behaviour of people with whom he or she is working.[1]

But what if analysis reveals a profound resistance to the very possibility of an encompassing value? A resistance that itself informs those relations between people we characterise as kinship, political economy, religion, and one that consists precisely in positing contradictory values as equally important? At this point, far from being 'indispensable to social life' and given in the nature of mind, Dumont's 'hierarchical schema' becomes vacuous and the 'Hegelian schema' triumphs.

This essay addresses Dumont's argument with Hegel via an examination of ethnographic material concerning the historical and contemporary nature of Fijian chiefship. In so doing, it deals with hierarchy as a value and with Dumont's theory that values are hierarchically ordered. It does not address his analysis of his Indian data. Rather it argues that in so far as his theory of

163

hierarchy is based on historically specific data and in so far as his 'hierarchy of values' is naive with respect to the model of mind it implies, there are sound reasons to reject its universal application. The essay argues that ethnic Fijians' ideas of the relation between hierarchy and equality are Hegelian rather than Dumontian; that for them, 'transcendence can only be produced synthetically' precisely because complementariness and contradiction cannot, ultimately, be contained.

Fijian ideas of hierarchy are constituted through the transformation in ritual of balanced, reciprocal exchange into tribute. Chiefly ritual *appears* to contain, and thus to render non-threatening, equally powerful notions of equality, such that Fijian villagers come to conceive of hierarchy as given (Toren 1990). However, chiefly ritual does not encompass the whole of life. So, for example, an analysis of representations of compassion and desire as experienced over time by people at different stages of life show that these two most salient forms of love inform and are informed by hierarchical and equal relations within and across sex, such that each kind of love becomes the grounds of the possibility of the other (Toren 1994a). Compassion and desire are rendered cosmogonic in various stories of the old Gods and inform hierarchical and equal relations within and across groups; moreover, Methodism (the religion of the vast majority of ethnic Fijians), which contains its own inherent tension between hierarchy and equality, is taking on a distinctively Fijian form (Toren 1995a).

Equality and hierarchy are the warp and woof of the fabric of Fijian village life.[2] There is an attempt to make hierarchy contain relations of equality and a simultaneous recognition that this hierarchy itself depends for its very continuity on the dynamic of relations of equality which cannot in their nature ultimately be contained by chiefly ritual, but only by raw power – that is to say, by superior physical force.[3] This essay is an historical analysis of this thesis. It concerns political rivalry between Fijian chiefs as this is apparent in the records of the Lands Commission for the *vanua* of Sawaieke, on the island of Gau (see note 1 of chapter 1). The analysis also addresses A. M. Hocart's theory of the development of Fijian hierarchy.

Dualism and the transformation of equality into hierarchy

In his preface to *Kings and Councillors*, Rodney Needham points out that Hocart's first premise is that ritual 'is a practical activity intended to secure life' (Hocart 1970: lxviii). Hocart's general purpose is to argue that government evolves out of ritual organisation such that equality, or a balanced organisation of functions, gives way to centralisation and 'a vertical hierarchy':

> If there is to be government, that is, co-ordination of actions, there must be some to command and a majority to obey ... as the regulation of conduct becomes the main interest rather than the control of nature,

we see the leader become the regulator; groups once equal acknowledge the supremacy of one; a vertical arrangement takes the place of a horizontal one ... '

(1970: 37)

For Hocart this process characterised the development of Fijian chiefship. Later on in the same work, as in others, he discusses what he calls 'the dual organisation' whereby there are two kings or two chiefs – one whose functions are almost purely ritual, and one whose functions are defence and war. He shows how the power of arms allowed the war chief to usurp the position of the ritual chief who had formerly taken precedence over him and how, in Fiji, the *Tui* (King or Ritual Chief) is displaced by the *Sau* (War Chief) (1970: 163–165, 1952: 33–52, 1929: 232–238).

The emphasis on Fijian dualism, on the necessity, in all activities, for there to be 'two sides' pervades Hocart's work; in *The Northern States of Fiji* he quotes a Lauan informant as saying 'In Fiji all things go in pairs, or the sharks will bite' (1952: 57) and later he bemoans the excesses of dualism as

prophetic of decay, for dichotomy was becoming so common as to be cheap ... and was no longer reserved for ritual [occasions]. ... [But] A new and more solemn interest seems to have already encroached upon the old dualism weakened by excess. That new enthusiasm was the service of the chief ... [which] upset the old balance of paired groups. The two sides that used to face each other, equal except in precedence, have begun to break up into units which all face the chief, like planets round the sun.

(1952: 58)

Hocart's work on Fiji is remarkable for its ethnographic richness and its theoretical insights, but 'a vertical hierarchy' is not, I argue, inevitable. Certainly the great war chiefs, like Cakobau, were doing their best to bring a fixed hierarchy into being, but they could suppress the inherent challenge of equal relations between persons and between groups only by force of arms. With pacification under British colonial rule, the ethos of competitive equality that is as important to Fijians as hierarchy reasserted itself, as it was bound to do, for in Fiji kinship implies both kinds of relations and each is predicated on the other. A fixed hierarchy would have required a fundamental shift in kinship and exchange relations, for marriage is predicated on relations of equality between crosscousins across exogamous clans (*mataqali*), not only within, but also across, sex; outside marriage, cross-cousins across sex are one another's equals (see Toren 1990: 50–52).

Hierarchy and equality in Fiji are expressed in terms of disposition in space. So in accordance with one's status one may sit above (*i cake*) or below (*i ra*) others when *yaqona* (kava) is drunk; this above/below axis is constituted out of a transformation in ritual of another spatial construct – *veiqaravi*, lit. 'facing each other' which describes the disposition of houses within the space of the village (see Toren 1990: 74–89, 100–118). With cross-cousins one may be on the same level (*tau vata*, literally 'fall together'); similarly, friends are *veitau*, i.e. equals and in village life, if I refer to someone as my friend (*noqu i tau*), he or she is virtually always my cross-cousin.[4]

All relationships can be conceptualised and referred to as kin relations; at its widest extension one's kin include all other ethnic Fijians. With the exception of the equal relation between cross-cousins, all kinship relations are hierarchical and require varying degrees of respect and avoidance. The antithesis between hierarchy and competitive equality here references that between non-marriageable kin (where the paradigmatic reference is to the hierarchical household and clan) and marriageable kin (who as cross-cousins are equals across households and clans).

The tension between hierarchy and equality given respectively by relations between kin *within* the household and kin relations between cross-cousins as affines *across* households can be historically related to the nature of chiefship. High chiefs are associated on the one hand with relations within the household and on the other with affinity. By virtue of drinking the installation *yaqona* a high chief becomes the leader of the community, whose image in *yaqona* ritual is that of 'the household' writ large. At the same time, in both myth and history, the first high chief is represented as a foreigner from over the sea who married a daughter of the indigenous land chief and was later installed by him as paramount. But the high chief and his descendants rule thereafter only by consent of the landspeople; so the power that lies with the land chief as head of the clan that 'makes the chief' is crucial. He can, and often does, refuse or delay the installation of a putative paramount.[5]

In *yaqona*-drinking the paramount is seen to take precedence over and to be above others just as, within the household, a man is seen to take precedence over and to be above his wife. The perceived subordination of wife to husband itself depends on the ritual transformation of the equality of cross-cousins into the hierarchy of marriage and is effected not only in the marriage ceremonies themselves, but on a daily basis in the conduct of every meal (Toren 1990: 52–64). The exchange relations between spouses are complementary and balanced; but at meals the wife sits below her husband, serves him, and eats only when he has finished. The ritual transformation of balanced reciprocity across households into tribute to chiefs that takes place on a daily basis in *yaqona*-drinking has the appearance of being fully effective only in the ceremony of the installation *yaqona*, in which the chief dies as a man to be reborn as a God 'with all the ancestors at his back' (Toren 1990: 100–118). However, in Gau, while there was, and is, a *named* paramount, Takalaigau, it seems that a putative paramount is often named and never installed and that this was also the case in the past. When I asked people why this was so I received one of two answers: one gave particular reasons to account for particular instances and usually referred to the unfitness of a particular person to take office; the other was contained in the explanation that 'there, is too much *veiqati*', lit. rivalry).

Chiefship and rivalry in the history of Sawaieke

Veiqati, as used by the villagers of Sawaieke, always carried strong connotations of envy and jealousy. It was used especially in connection with political rivalries between chiefs – that is to say, between the chiefs of various *yavusa* (group of closely connected clans) and within *yavusa* between the chiefs of rival *mataqali* (clans).[6]

This jealous rivalry can be understood as a special instance of the ethic of competition that pervades villagers' daily life. *Veiqati* (especially between siblings) is frowned upon as 'not according to kinship' (*sega ni vakaveiwekani*), but friendly competition and brinkmanship is entirely proper between cross-cousins as kin who are affines or potential affines (usually within, but sometimes across, generations) where it routinely takes the form of joking and teasing (*veiwali, veisamei*). This joking and teasing has an aggressive, even confrontational, tone between people who are related as *veitabani* (from countries whose founding ancestors were cross-cousins) or as *veitauvu* (from countries who are descendants of the same ancestor God).[7]

Long-running instances of political *veiqati* are evident in the 'General History of the Country of Sawaieke' (*Na i tukutuku raraba ni vanua ko Sawaieke*) recorded by the officials of the Lands Commission in 1916.[8] The dispute addressed in this essay concerned who had a right to the paramount chiefship, where these persons' ancestors came from, and whether or not they were installed. The record of this dispute at once confirms and throws into question the notion of 'the stranger chief'; it shows the twofold nature of the *vasu* relation between a person and his or her mother's clan, whose focus is the relation between mother's brother and sister's child; it shows how ready certain people may be to challenge even an installed paramount; and above all it makes plain that in both myth and history Fijian hierarchy has always been in tension with competitive equality.

Below I give some extracts from this history whose time-span begins 150 years or so before the Lands Commission and ends at the period that Fiji was ceded to Britain (i.e. between, say, the mid-1700s and 1874).[9] In those days the village was co-terminous with the *yavusa*, the villages attended on each other in ritual and inter-married, but they also challenged and fought each other for precedence. Today, as in 1916, Sawaieke village is made up of several *yavusa*. The 1916 account of the origins of the chiefly *yavusa* Nadawa was given by the leader of Naboginibola, one of its component clans;[10] it is in many respects a classic tale of the stranger chief from over the sea who shows himself to be *mana* (lit. 'effective') and thus gains the daughter of the land chief and later the paramount chiefship which is voluntarily surrendered to him by the older man.

> Our honorific title is Nadawa. The name of our original ancestor (*vu*) is
> Mualevu who came from Nakobuna in Gau. One time NaRai – the

167

leader of the Sawaieke people – wanted to go to a place on the mainland and went to the Nakobuna people that they might sail him there.
So they sailed him there and dropped anchor. Then Mualevu went to
Dravuni in Tai, stayed there a little while and came back ... then all
those who were with NaRai returned to Gau. Afterwards [Mualevu]
returned to Dravuni and was married there, his wife was the child of
KoyamaiDravuni [a chiefly title] and a child was born to them, a boy,
and his name was Bui [*sic*]. Then Biu grew up until he was big and he
was always making the children in Dravuni cry and the fathers of children were angry about this and they pronounced the name of the land
of Biu's father. After that they brought him here to Gau and he went to
stay in his village, Nakobuna, in his clan Waivolita.

One time the Waivolita clan came here ... but when they arrived ...
and the thing was done that they came to do, they were returning to
Nakobuna when they met on the path with NaRai, the leader of the
Sawaieke people, together with his attendants. [The Sawaieke people]
had finished eating [but] there still remained a head of *saqa* and NaRai
called to [Biu and his company] that they should eat the head of that
saqa. But they were afraid to eat it. Then Biu spoke to them: eat the
head of the *saqa*, I take on the responsibility of making a kill with a club
so as to beat down [this challenge]. So they ate it. When they had
finished eating they asked that they might return to Nakobuna where
Biu continued always to think about his speech to NaRai.

Sometimes Biu went as a warrior and killed a few people and
brought them to NaRai. After that NaRai called Bui [*sic*] to go there to
him so the two of them might live together and then Biu was doing a
great deal of work for NaRai. After that NaRai gave his daughter Adi
Tora as wife to Biu and also his High Chief's Comb (*na nona i Seru ni
Sau*) and a piece of land for his village, the name of which was Nadawa,
and so Biu lived there and had children and they were four boys ...[11]

So when these children of Nadawa grew to be many they left Nadawa
and went to make a village at Navasa. They went together with their
father, Biu. After that they each got married and had children ...

And when this band of brothers was living in Navasa and had
become many they asked the chiefs of Burei for a piece of land that
they might build a village ... They made a *yavu* [foundation] for themselves and ... they each built the *yavu* of their houses and they each
settled there. This band of four brothers then divided into three; their
divisions were: 1. Naboginibola 2. Naocomatana 3. Tabaisa ...

The chiefly status of Takalaigau [paramount chief of the eight
villages of Sawaieke country] 'jumps around' (*veiladeyaki*) just to these
three clans. Takalaigau owes allegiance to [*vakarorogo*, lit. listens to] the
High Chief (*Vunivalu*) at Bau ... [See figure 9.1]

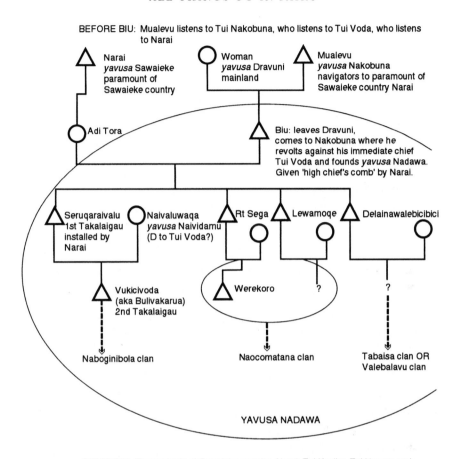

BEFORE BIU: Mualevu listens to Tui Nakobuna, who listens to Tui Voda, who listens to Narai

Narai
yavusa Sawaieke
paramount of
Sawaieke country

Woman
yavusa Dravuni
mainland

Mualevu
yavusa Nakobuna
navigators to paramount of
Sawaieke country Narai

Adi Tora

Biu: leaves Dravuni,
comes to Nakobuna where he
revolts against his immediate chief
Tui Voda and founds *yavusa* Nadawa.
Given 'high chief's comb' by Narai.

Seruqaraivalu
1st Takalaigau
installed by
Narai

Naivaluwaqa
yavusa Naividamu
(D to Tui Voda?)

Rt Sega

Lewamoqe

Delainawalebicibici

Vukicivoda
(aka Bulivakarua)
2nd Takalaigau

Werekoro

?

?

Naboginibola clan

Naocomatana clan

Tabaisa clan OR
Valebalavu clan

YAVUSA NADAWA

AFTER BIU: These chiefs of Sawaieke country: Narai, Tui Koviko, Tui Navure and
Tui Voda listen to Takalaigau who listens to the Vunivalu (paramount) at Bau

Figure 9.1   Origins of *yavusa* Nadawa

Fijian chiefship, Hocart argued, was concerned to bring about and to maintain prosperity and the story shows Biu to be an effective warrior and provider. He accepts the challenge to eat the head of the *saqa* (a fish whose eating is the prerogative of chiefs) and shows himself a capable warrior and able to further the prosperity of his people, for NaRai gives him land to found a new village, Nadawa. However Biu's living together with NaRai and the 'great deal of work' he does for him seem to suggest bride service – observations which do not fit with an assumption of the stranger-chief's inherent superiority (Sahlins 1985: 78). Moreover the marriage makes the foreigner son-in-law to the reigning chief, to whom he thus owes the utmost respect and obedience, and cross-cousin – and equal – to his wife's brothers. His children will be sister's children to his wife's brothers and *vasu* to her clan; this *vasu* relation is twofold in that it demands respect and obedience from the sister's child (and more saliently from the sister's son) to the mother's brother and at the same time allows the sister's child as *vasu* 'to take without asking' from the mother's people (cf. Lévi-Strauss 1984: 172).

However, Biu – whose name means 'rejected' – is not really a stranger.[12] Indeed he has every right to be in Sawaieke *vanua* where his father came from and where he thus has patrilineal rights in land. Further Biu belongs to a clan that can be classified as 'sea' and in this respect stands in an exchange relation of balanced reciprocity to the clan of NaRai, 'leader of the Sawaieke people', who is 'land'.[13] The founding ancestor of landspeople clans was given in 1916 by NaRai (once the title of the paramount and today the title of the chief of lands-people clans) as Rokotaloko from Vuya, Bua, Vanua Levu.

Indeed, the records of the Lands Commission investigation show that all the ancestors of all the people of Sawaieke country came from elsewhere.[14] But there is no suggestion in the records that an ancestor of the NaRai who created the first paramount to hold the title Takalaigau had wrested the chiefship from an earlier incumbent who was the chief of another, possibly, indigenous people. Oral traditions, however, suggest that this was so.[15] The NaRai who figures in the story of Biu is also referred to as *Na Sau*, a title which Hocart says was that of the war chief who was second in precedence to the ritual chief or *Tui*. The chief of Biu's clan and *yavusa*, whom he apparently revolted against, was Tui Voda who may, at that time, have been the 'ritual chief' alongside NaRai as 'war chief'.[16] Today, in Sawaieke, the title *Tui* is accorded to the heads of three of the village's component *yavusa*, all of whom owe allegiance to (*vakarorogo vua*, lit. 'listen to') Takalaigau, who is also referred to as *Na Sau* (cf. Hocart 1952: 34–37).

In 1916 Takalaigau, the paramount chief of Sawaieke country (*vanua* i.e. eight villages of which Sawaieke is the chiefly village), was Ratu Tomasi Tokalauvere of the chiefly Tabaisa clan (see figure 9.2). In his evidence to the Lands Commission, he at first referred only to his Sawaieke ancestry and he was challenged by a man in a rival chiefly clan as follows:[17]

> During the time that the late *Buli* [Fijian official of the colonial admin-istration] was living we had already gathered together [i.e. several little villages had come together to form a single chiefly village of several component *yavusa*] and it was explained to the high chief and told to him that his line (*nona kawa*) came from Lasakau in Bau – that's how it is. We said therefore that our paths were two [divided]; he comes from Bau, we do not, but it appears from the high chief's account that we are just one.

Ratu Tomasi countered this by saying that he was indeed related to the Sawaieke people through his father's father's father's mother who had married into a Bauan family and that his father's father, Ratu Damudamu, was of the Matanivanua in Bau. Then another of Ratu Tomasi's rivals, the chief who had

YAVUSA Nadawa
MATAQALI (clan) Tabaisa

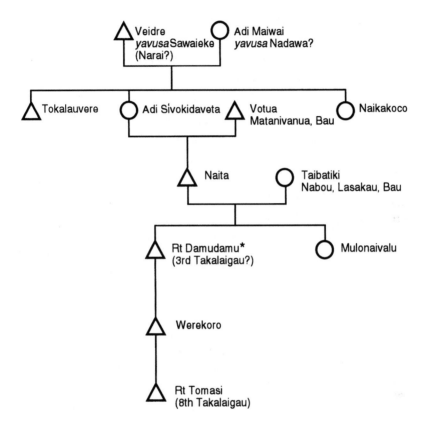

Figure 9.2   Origins of *mataqali* Tabaisa
Notes
*Rt Damudamu comes to Gau. Lives with his FMF Veidre in Nadawa with 'the chiefs' to Navasa and, again with 'the chiefs' to Lomanibuca. The name of his *yavu* (house foundation) in Lomanibuca was Tabaisa.

Holders of the title Takalaigau

Seruqaraivalu	clan Naboginibola
Vukicivoda (Bukivakarua), son of above	clan Naboginibola
Damudamu (?)	clan Tabaisa
Bokoinaca	clan Naboginibola
Loma	clan Valebalavu
Rt Meli Vodosiro	clan Valebalavu
Rt Laita Lewanavavua	clan Naboginibola
Rt Tomasi Tokalauvere	clan Tabaisa

told the story of Biu with its account of the origins of the chiefly Nadawa clan, asserted that Tabaisa – Ratu Tomasi's clan – could not be recognised as a chiefly, Nadawa clan. 'The Tabaisa clan is of different origins (e ra kawa tani),' he said. The dispute continued and Ratu Tomasi told how his ancestor Ratu Damudamu had come to Gau and been taken in by his grandfather Veidre (FMF) who, it is implied, was then NaRai, chief of the landspeople, and able to install the paramount.18 Ratu Tomasi asserted that his grandfather had installed Ratu Damudamu as Takalaigau and that because of this there was a quarrel; Ratu Damudamu and his supporters had fled to a neighbouring village and from there called to his kin in Bau for support:

> Then Ratu Damudamu proclaimed war and called on Bau [to help him], then the warships went from Bau. Then [the chiefs of two rival clans in the chiefly *yavusa* and the land chief] went there to intercept [the warships] at the opening in the reef and there they performed the atonement with a reed [in order to prevent war], so that they might drink (*yaqona*) together to bring about peace. Then Ratu Damudamu was confirmed as Takalaigau...
>
> The chiefs (*malo*, cloths) of the [chiefly] Nadawa people are [the leaders of the component clans] Tabaisa, Lomanibuca, Naboginibola and Valebalavu.

Ratu Tomasi had already described how, when presentations of feast food (*magiti*) were made to the chiefly *yavusa*, Tabaisa clan along with Valebalavu and Naboginibola were 'accorded their share from the village green' (*e votai mai rara*). Since this was infallible evidence that Tabaisa was recognised as a clan in the chiefly *yavusa*, his apparent rival, the Naboginibola chief, had to admit that Ratu Tomasi's account of the composition of the *yavusa* and the ritual duties of its component clans was correct.[19] However, Ratu Tomasi's other evidence was again disputed, again by a member of a rival chiefly clan:[20]

> My *mataqali* is Naboginibola. Lomanibuca, Navakaotisau and Vanuayalewa are our *yavu* (house foundations) in Naboginibola and were made significant through the murders of Biu. The meaning of Navakaotisau is that the reign of Raitena was over. Vanuayalewa is because of Biu's challenge to those above him. Lomanibuca is because their village stood in the centre of the *vanua*. Those in Tabaisa have only the one *yavu*, Tabaisa. Buliruarua [a.k.a. Vukicivoda, the grandson of the founding ancestor Biu] was Takalaigau when Damudamu arrived here. Tabaisa dropped anchor at an opening in the reef. Damudamu was not installed as Takalaigau.

This account was verified by the then leader of landspeople clans, that is to say, by the man who as holder of the title NaRai was able to install a paramount chief.[21]

> Ratu Damudamu was not installed. He just came here and lived with the chiefs. Those chiefs looked down on him and they quarrelled. Then he spoke with our elders, who moved him to [a neighbouring village]. Then war was declared and the Sawaieke people had no energy for it. We gave in. We returned here, then Damudamu died in Sawaieke. Ratu Tomasi is already installed as Takalaigau. When [the previous Takalaigau] was about to die, he declared Ratu Tomasi his successor, and so he was installed.

At the end of this dispute it is clear that Ratu Tomasi's claims that his *yavu* (house foundation) and clan were legitimately part of the chiefly *yavusa* and that he was himself a properly installed paramount chief were accepted as correct by the officers of the Lands Commission. The points to be noticed here are, firstly, that Tabaisa (the name of the house and clan of which Ratu Tomasi is head) is said to have 'dropped anchor at an opening in the reef'; this suggests a cynical and very successful opportunism on the part of Ratu Tomasi's ancestor Ratu Damudamu.[22]

Secondly, an attempt is made to use Ratu Tomasi's foreign origins against him; indeed it appears from the early part of the Lands Commission record that those who gave evidence to it may have thought that to make good their claims to land they had to have a founding ancestor who was born in Gau.[23] Certainly Ratu Tomasi seems to have thought that this was what was required.

Thirdly, it appears from information not quoted here that previous to Ratu Tomasi there had been some seven holders of the title Takalaigau, the first being Seruqaraivalu, the son of Biu whose story was told above and who received 'his High Chief's Comb' from the then paramount NaRai; when the genealogies are matched to the places where specific incidents took place, it would seem that Ratu Damudamu from the island of Bau was a contemporary of the second Takalaigau, Buliruarua, the son of Seruqaraivalu.[24] If we allow any given Takalaigau a generous ascendancy of some twenty years, then the title came into being some 100 to 150 years before the Lands Commission investigation. This makes sense, for it accords with the dates when Bau was asserting its power in Lomaiviti (central Fiji, where Gau lies) and the title Takalaigau is originally that of Bau's representative in Gau.[25] In the Lands Commission records Takalaigau is said 'to listen to' (owe allegiance to) the paramount chief in Bau.

Fourthly, and given Ratu Tomasi's emphasis on his Bauan ancestor's descent through a woman who was daughter to a landspeople chief in Sawaieke country, it seems very possible that Ratu Damudamu made his claim on his grandfather as a *vasu* (sister's child, even if at several removes); the privilege of the *vasu* is to 'take without asking' from the mother's people and if 'grandfather Veidre' indeed held the title NaRai, as Ratu Tomasi's account suggests he did, then what he had to give was the paramount chiefship – for only NaRai can install a paramount in office, however he cannot be compelled to do so, except perhaps by the threat of superior force of arms. Indeed this may be what happened; it is suggestive that the Takalaigau who was in office when Ratu Damudamu arrived is referred to as Buliruarua or Bulivakarua – meaning 'Twice Installed' – who is elsewhere identified as being Biu's son's son, Vukicivoda; perhaps his reign was interrupted by Ratu Damudamu who died while Vukicivoda was still alive, so allowing him to be installed a second time.

But what allowed Ratu Damudamu to be adopted into the chiefly Nadawa clan so that all his descendants became legitimate members of it? The record does not tell us, but it does suggest that he lived with 'the chiefs in Navasa' before he went to live with his grandfather, the chief of landspeople clans. He may have married into the Nadawa clan, but it is more likely that he was related to the Nadawa people via the female line since Bau where his own mother came from and the mainland village of Dravuni where Biu's mother came from are near to one another. But, whatever the case, he certainly had close kin in Sawaieke.

Finally, the records reveal that members of another chiefly clan appeared to have no compunction about using the Lands Commission's investigations to undermine – and perhaps even to try to oust – an installed paramount chief. Certainly the 1916 dispute contains no challenges from persons outside the chiefly *yavusa*, but then they would have nothing to gain because the position of paramount can go only to a member of a chiefly clan. Further, the then land chief, while he is not against Ratu Tomasi as paramount, is prepared to contradict and to correct him.

When one analyses these records it becomes apparent that Fijian chiefship had retained its dual nature, that in their rise to power the war chiefs (*Na Sau*) had not yet managed to render hierarchy absolute, for, as I show below, it was still predicated on its antithesis – equality between persons who relate to one another as cross-cousins across households, and within and across clans and other larger collectivities.

Antithetical duality and its transformation

That hierarchy in Fiji is *not* an encompassing value is apparent in the words of Hocart's Lauan informant: 'In Fiji all things go in pairs, or the sharks will bite.' Here 'sharks' can refer to fishes, to the ancestor gods as manifest in that form, or to chiefs as dangerous and warlike persons. The saying emphasises the duality of 'all things', but what is most important here is, I suggest, the antithesis that is captured by this duality. In other words, 'things' have to be related to one another in a reciprocal form that allows hierarchy and equality to be *at one and the same time* implicated in that relationship. This is because in Fiji the fundamental organising concept is that of 'the household' which by definition depends on the existence of other households for its continuing existence. People relate to one another as kin, but while kin relations *within* the household are axiomatically hierarchical – husband above wife, older sibling above junior sibling – kinship *across* households references the equal relationship between cross-cousins. Further, all exchange relations are competitive and ultimately those of balanced reciprocity even while the rituals of chiefship render them as tributary and apparently unequal.[26]

In the story of Biu, his marriage to NaRai's daughter is a stage in his progress towards the paramount chiefship; it does not render him superior to his father-in-law to whom he owes obedience and respect, but it does provide him at once with a household of his own and a wife who is subordinate to him. In the exchanges on betrothal and marriage and at the birth of the first child, 'the side of the man' must give more than 'the side of the woman'; this points not to the inherent superiority of wife-takers but to the fact that the woman and her future children are part of what is given by 'the side of the woman', for what I was told of these exchanges is that if the man's side does *not* give more, they will be 'ashamed' (see Toren 1990: 52–56, 85–89, cf. Sahlins 1976: 24–46).

However, within the marriage relationship itself, the effective alienation of the woman from her natal household and clan renders her subordinate to her husband, for she eats food that is provided by the fertile power of his ancestors whose land he gardens and whose power sends her the fish she catches; indeed her own fertility is implicitly sacrificed to the same source; thus, as Fijians say, 'every man is a chief in his own house' and a wife attends on her husband and receives his largesse. Nevertheless, in terms of the division of labour, of produc-tion and exchange, husband and wife are in a reciprocal and equal relation of demand – he must produce root crops and she must fish, he must build the house and she must weave mats to furnish it, and so on; this reciprocal and balanced relation of interdependence is undoubtedly important for the nature of the transformations that are evident in the marriage relationship. Before marriage a woman is the equal of her male cross-cousin and, by definition, all marriages are between cross-cousins. After marriage she is axiomatically subordinate to her husband – a subordination which is rendered apparently complete by the young husband's almost routine violence towards his wife. However, over time, this rela-tionship is transformed yet again so that it becomes implicitly a relation between equals, even while it is said to be hierarchical (Toren 1994a).[27]

In marrying out a woman is, as it were, unfairly deprived of her birthright, and this is implicit in the way her rights in her natal clan devolve upon her chil-dren who, as *vasu*, may 'take without asking' from the men of their mother's clan. If one leaves the woman herself out of the reckoning, one can argue that what the *vasu* takes is his or hers by virtue, not of what the mother has given up, but of the massive prestation of goods to the mother's kin that secures recogni-tion of the *vasu* in the ceremony of *kau mata ni gone* (lit. 'carrying the face of the child') (see Sahlins 1976: 29–32). But this is to ignore the twofold nature of the relation between mother's brother and sister's child which combines the licence that is usually proper only to people or groups who relate to one another as cross-cousins, with the extreme respect, avoidance and obedience that is properly shown by a real or classificatory son-in-law to his father-in-law. The prestation of goods compensates the woman's clan for the loss of her child who carries the blood of their ancestors too, and so secures recognition of the child in his or her own person; but the *vasu*'s subsequent 'snatching', the 'taking without asking' surely signifies a recognition of the enforced loss through her marriage of the mother's natal rights and her inalienable claim to them – an observation that is borne out by the fact that no other, similarly massive, prestation across groups entails any similar entitlement just to take what one wants in return (cf. Lévi-Strauss 1984: 176). 'Taking without asking' is, however, an implicit possibility between cross-cousins, between persons who relate to one another as *veitabani* or *veitauvu* (two countries – *vanua* – whose ancestors were cross-cousins or who have their founding ancestor in common), and does in fact occur.[28] And this is so even though no previous prestation has 'secured' such a right on behalf of particular persons and is indeed entirely unnecessary – precisely because they should be treated as 'equal owners' in the house or village of their opposite numbers; the sister's child is affiliated to its father's clan and identified with him and it is only by virtue of a similar identification between *mother* and child that the child at once retains its junior status as child and becomes an 'owner' in the mother's natal household on the same footing as her brothers.[29]

One finds a similar set of transformations between people who relate to one another as 'land' and 'sea', where exchange relations are again at once reciprocal and balanced and where again, from one point of view they are regarded as one another's equals, while from another 'sea' appears to be superior to 'land'. The classification is not co-terminous with that which distinguishes chiefly from commoner *yavusa*; thus, while chiefly *yavusa* are always 'sea', certain commoner *yavusa* are also 'sea'. In central Fiji the relationship also obtains across countries, e.g. in relation to the people of Batiki, all the people of Sawaieke *vanua* are 'land'. When sea and land people are eating together, seapeople cannot eat fish and landpeople cannot eat pork, freshwater shrimp etc.; each makes available to the other the product of their labour.

'All things go in pairs, or the sharks will bite.' And given that all things go in pairs, a totality consists of a pair of pairs, which explains why, in Fiji everything really goes in fours.[30] Thus, even while people relate to one another as 'land' and 'sea', they *simultaneously* relate to one another as 'chief' and 'commoner'. A member of the chiefly clan is by definition 'sea' while a member of the clan that installs the chief is by definition 'land'. A putative paramount chief cannot properly claim precedence and ritual superiority over the land chief who is to install him. This is evident in the story of Biu who is challenged by the land chief to show he is *mana*, 'effective'; when Biu accepts NaRai's challenge he locks the land chief into a competitive exchange of *mana* that culminates with the land chief's apparently final defeat since the supreme act of *mana* that is open to him is that of installing a paramount – an act that renders him ritually inferior to the other man.[31] Thus, as the present NaRai told me:

The making of the chief is my task alone ... that is a godly gift that is made to me ... it is in the blood ... that is the power that is mine ... but if the *yaqona* is given to him [Takalaigau – the putative paramount] everything in the manner of the land is encompassed therein. It does not matter that the *yaqona* is given to him, I am still chief, but after I have given him the *yaqona* I shall address him as *saka* ['sir'], I shall act with great respect towards him. That is after I have given the *yaqona*, after I have made him drink. ... After that I shall attend on him, everything he tells me I shall shoulder as a burden, nor shall I try to make myself great by refusing to follow him. Everything he wants done in this country will be told to me. ... I shall then order it to be done.

At first reading this statement suggests that NaRai becomes unambiguously inferior to the installed Takalaigau; but even while NaRai says that the paramount chiefship encompasses everything, he also says that the installation 'does not matter' for he is 'still chief'. He is prepared to show great respect and to attend on the installed paramount, but at the same time implies that he could, if he wished, refuse to 'follow' him and in so doing make himself 'great'. Further it is apparent that an installed paramount cannot himself order things to be done, for it is NaRai's prerogative to give orders. As Hocart pointed out, the function of an installed paramount is just to be, so that he may receive and re-distribute the people's feasts and thus promote prosperity. Moreover, in exalting the other man to a paramount position, NaRai simultaneously exalts himself. The paramount now 'has at his back all the ancestors of Gau' but as the one who gives orders, NaRai too commands a greater and more effective power than he had before. That NaRai retains his effective power and even augments it is apparent in the Lands Commission records where the man holding the title in 1916 is called as an authority and gives evidence that is accepted and only *partly* in favour of the paramount chief, Ratu Tomasi. He is not cowed by his counterpart's precedence in ritual.

Of course the question remains as to why a chief who is able to do so does *not* install a putative paramount. I had previously thought that this was because the paramount would thus attain an unambiguously superior position with respect to the installing chief. However I now think that this reluctance arises in circumstances where the rivalries between particular persons in the chiefly clan itself are as important as the relationship between the land chief and the putative paramount. In other words, the land chief's relationship with other members of the chiefly clan and with the chiefs of other clans governs his decision to install or not to install a particular person.

Here it is interesting to look at the story of Biu as 'stranger chief' alongside the story of Damudamu as 'stranger chief' and the attitudes and effective powers of the persons who gave evidence to the Lands Commission. That Biu was indeed paramount and his son the first Takalaigau is accepted, but Ratu Tomasi's claim that his ancestor Ratu Damudamu was installed as paramount remains in question with conflicting evidence being adduced by everyone concerned. If Ratu Damudamu was installed it seems he must have gained the chiefship by virtue of being able to call on his Bauan kin to aid him in war; he is not said to have performed any acts that were *mana*, 'effective'. Those opposing Ratu Tomasi represent Ratu Damudamu as an illegitimate claimant precisely *because* he came from elsewhere and tried to usurp the title by force; they ignore the fact that he could be classified as *vasu* to the land chief, NaRai, and that he was clearly related to the chiefs of Nadawa. Thus the opponents of Ratu Tomasi are implying that he, as Damudamu's descendant, cannot himself be regarded as a legitimate Takalaigau even though he is already installed. Ratu Tomasi has great difficulty in countering these implications and has to rely on his counterpart, the land chief, to support him; this the land chief does – but only up to a point.

One asks oneself what Ratu Tomasi lacks to make good his claim and the answer is clear – he lacks warriors, he commands no physical force, no terrifying reputation. The colonial administration had long done away with both warriors and the priests whose godhead, in the dual person of the land chief and the installed paramount, demanded cannibal feasts. Ratu Tomasi had his ancestors to call on, as does any installed chief, whose power automatically punishes any dereliction from duty on the part of those who owe allegiance to him, but these ancestors were now under the sway of the Christian god and 'no one attended on them anymore'.[32] Further Ratu Tomasi could not now call on *his* Bauan kin to support him in war against any rival claimant. He was an installed chief and as such he would have received all those ritual attentions that were still possible, be seen to take precedence over others and to sit above them in *yaqona*-drinking, to receive feasts whose distribution was presided over by his counterpart the land chief, and to be accorded all the formal appearances of respect. Ratu Tomasi reigned, but he could not rule; only command of physical force would allow him to rule, because the dual nature of Fijian chiefship inevitably works against the institution of 'a vertical hierarchy'.

The main point here is that, when the records of the Lands Commission for Gau are analysed in light of relations within and across groups, it is apparent that in 1916 hierarchy could not be said to be an encompassing value; it is not Dumontian in its nature because it always simultaneously implies competitive equality as an equally important and antithetical value. Here my view differs from that put forward by Sahlins in his various works, and more particularly in Sahlins (1985) and (1991). In the latter essay, where he develops his notion of Fijian history as 'heroic' he writes:

> Of course everybody's actions signify, are meaningful. But what distinguishes social-historical individuals is that their acts transcend self-reference – by far and in a twofold way. Their acts engage social totalities, in the first place by virtue of the structures of hierarchy in which as chiefs they encompass others. This is logical as well as socio-

logical; the chief represents the logical class of which the people are members (Dumont 1970).

(Sahlins 1991: 63)

Up to a point I agree with this, the great chiefs of the large confederations did manage to encompass others, but this was not by virtue of the 'structures of hierarchy', for Fijian hierarchy was never simply that, it never became 'a vertical hierarchy' for it was always, even in Bau, in tension with the antithetical value of equality. It was force of arms and terror that allowed the various *Sau* (war chiefs) to usurp the *Tui* (ritual chiefs) in the first place and it was terror and force of arms that allowed them to maintain and consolidate their position. Certainly, had their rise to power not been interrupted by European imperialism, they might have managed over time to achieve an instituted vertical hierarchy that, at least within their own countries, not only effectively contained notions of equality across persons, and clans, but even rendered Fijian social organisation as 'caste-like'. That they had not nearly achieved this is evident not only in my own material, but in Hocart's remarks, quoted above, on what he regarded as a degenerate efflorescence of dualism, whereby ritual practices of competitive equality were extended into other activities.

This efflorescence of practices of competitive equality may, I suggest, be attributed to the chiefs' loss of their warrior forces. Freed from the terror that was inspired by cannibalism and endemic warfare, people in general – including those who, as members of chiefly clans, were classified as chiefs and those who were chiefs of the various clans and *vanua* – were able once again to assert the dual nature of their values, to show that balanced reciprocity and competitive equality are as salient, and as important, as tribute and hierarchy.

But if hierarchy is not and cannot be an encompassing value for Fijians, neither can equality achieve the ascendancy, for equal relations too always implicate their opposite value. Marriage is predicated on the equal relation between cross-cousins, but marriage brings the household into being and with it the hierarchy of husband and wife, the authority of the first-born, and the seniority of siblings. The logic of Fijian social relations, of the relation between land and sea, husband and wife, brother and sister, cross-cousins, mother's brother and sister's children, commoner and chief, is always a twofold logic where hierarchy and equality are in tension with one another and dependent on one another for their very continuity. The rituals of chiefship are explicitly understood to promote prosperity, but they do so by virtue of projecting onto the collectivity – the *vanua* (country) – an image of the hierarchical household; this image implies the necessity for its own transformation because marriage is not possible within but only across households; in other words one has always to posit the existence of at least two households 'facing each other'. So Fijian chiefship *has* to be dual, *has* to be made up of land and sea, of the executive powers of the land chief and the ritual precedence of the paramount; only thus can it project an image of the hierarchical household as existing *alongside* other households in the relation of

179

balanced reciprocity and equality that makes marriage possible. In other words, the logic of Fijian chiefship is such that it can promote prosperity only if it is dual.[33]

If balanced reciprocity and equality are denied, then powerful war chiefs can 'bite' as they evidently did during the late eighteenth and nineteenth centuries. They ceased merely to preside over the re-distribution of feasts and began to extract them, they exploited the rights of the *vasu*, they promoted not general prosperity but sought to augment the power of their own house and clan, but even so they could not eradicate equality and balanced reciprocity, for these are enshrined in the very same ritual practices that constitute hierarchy: *veiqaravi*, which denotes 'attendance on chiefs' means literally 'facing each other' or 'attendance on each other'. Hocart's informant was undoubtedly right; 'in Fiji all things go in pairs, or the sharks will bite'.

Conclusion

Dumont's representation of the argument between himself and Hegel asserts that he is concerned with 'structure' while Hegel is concerned with 'dialectic'. However, Dumont does not address the implicit suggestion that while Hegel could be said to be concerned with the analysis of the nature of the categories of mind as a function of historical shifts, Dumont is only implicitly concerned with mind as a function of 'ideology'. Hegel's *Phenomenology* contains an implicit notion of progress in respect of the 'historical development' of categories of mind, and this is surely disputable; nevertheless he was just as surely right to emphasise history and to insist that mind constitutes its categories and is constituted by them. In this perspective, transcendence is given by Hegel's notion of mind as the totality that is materially manifest in its products, even while this very notion cannot be posited in the absence of an antithesis between mind and matter.[34]

Hegel's ideas remain useful precisely in so far as he attempted to come to grips with the subject/object relation between persons and their historically constituted notions about the world they inhabit; by contrast Dumont avoids this challenge by implicitly locating categories that are the product of mind in some abstract space *between* persons. In so doing, he makes 'ideology' the source of the categories, but 'an ideology' only comes into existence as the artefact of sociological analysis and as such it cannot be assumed to allow transparent access to the workings of mind.

My point here is that mind can be located only in the embodied cognitive processes of particular persons whose cognitive constitution of meaning is mediated by their relations with one another; thus meaning is never received 'readymade' (for cognitive processes are inherently dynamic) but neither can meaning be made in isolation. Rather the categorical products of mind have always to be constituted anew by particular persons and this process is always informed by the meanings already made by those particular others with whom any given person interacts. So meaning is inevitably historically constituted and inevitably transformed. This suggests that Dumont's 'ideology' as a system of hierarchically ranked values has little explanatory value, for it implies that meaning is received; indeed he takes ideology to be immanent in language and language itself to be transparent, to declare its own meaning and thus implicitly to be ahistorical: 'It is obvious that there is a basic ideology, a kind of germinal ideology tied to common language and hence to the linguistic group or the global society' (1980: 343).[35]

But when we focus on the person in relation to other persons, it becomes clear that any given person is the locus of the relations in which he or she engages with others, and that in the course of this engagement the nature of any given relationship is itself cognitively constituted by each of the persons involved.

Any Fijian person is the locus of relations that are mutually constituted as either hierarchical or equal; however, given their different histories as particular persons, each one has somewhat different ideas about the nature of those hierarchical or equal relationships, and any given person's engagement in such relationships begins at birth. For the Fijian child the very process of 'learning kinship' constitutes relations with non-marriageable kin as hierarchical and with marriageable kin as equal. Further, this process does not implicate an axiomatic distinction between power and status, for material power is inherent in the process in and through which any given child learns that this person's status is manifest in command over him or her and that person's status in a mutual, competitive equality. Neither is there any point at which one can say that, for any given Fijian person, hierarchy acquires a greater value than equality – for, on an everyday basis, one may even say from moment to moment, the person is engaged in constituting the one and the other as equally crucial to the nature of existence. Further, given that it is through inter-subjectivity that the notion of the self as subject is constituted, it becomes apparent that *both* hierarchy and equality will be implicated in Fijian notions of self and personhood. It is precisely this antithesis that makes it possible for a person to be *yalo qaqa* (of determined mind, courageous) and so respond to a challenge that comes from one who is far superior in status and power; thus Biu, in the story with which I began, is able as a young man to rise to the challenge from the then paramount NaRai and, over time, prove himself worthy of the paramount chiefship, even though his initial structural position would seem to disqualify him from doing so.

NOTES

INTRODUCTION: MIND, MATERIALITY AND HISTORY

1 For example, Maturana and Varela (1980 [1972] and 1988), Johnson (1987) and Varela, Thompson and Rosch (1991) give us different perspectives on this fundamental idea.

2 See Thompson, Palacios and Varela (1992).

3 See for example the continuing debate on colour vision; in 1992 an anthropologist (MacLaury) and a team composed of a philosopher, a biologist and a neuroscientist (Thompson, Palacios and Varela) published comprehensive theories of colour vision, each of which was treated to extensive published peer review in major journals. MacLaury argued for an objectivist model and denied the possibility of a viable phenomenological explanation, while Thompson *et al.* suggested that 'colors are not already labelled properties in the world which the perceiving animal must simply recover (objectivism) ... [but neither are they] internally generated qualities that the animal simply projects onto the world ... colors are properties of the world that result from animal environment codetermination ... the world and the perceiving animal determine each other, like chicken and egg'. This co-determination is a function of the nature of the animal's *activity* in its environing world. Human activity is mediated by inter-subjectivity; thus the varying complexity of colour terminologies in different languages is not 'an evolutionary sequence' as MacLaury maintains, but a function at once of the history of people's relations with one another in the world and the processes in and through which they make meaning.

4 See Maturana and Varela (1972) and (1988); my account of autopoiesis is derived from these two fascinating works.

5 See Trevarthen (1987).

6 The description of Piaget's cognitive scheme is derived from his book *Structuralism*. First published in 1968, when he was 72, this is a succinct statement of Piaget's key ideas as they apply to mathematical and logical structures and also to 'structures ... whose transformations unfold in time' (1971: 15).

7 See Piaget 1971: 63 and 71 from which I took the formal description given in this and the succeeding paragraphs, adding examples of my own in order to clarify the technical terms.

8 Piaget's scheme, by contrast, provides intrinsically for structure and process, continuity and transformation; neither is there any mystery about its being a function of embodied mind. Cf. the schema as 'representation' or 'cultural model' that figures in works by Holland and Quinn (1987 – esp. the editors' introduction), D'Andrade (1995 – esp. the discussion in chapters 6 and 7), and Shore (1996 – esp. chapter 2), who gets into something of a muddle trying to distinguish between 'conventional

models' and 'personal models'; as should be plain by now, the conventional and the personal are bound to be aspects of one another.

9 For an overview of connexionist theory, see Clark (1990).

10 See Mehler and Dupoux (1994) for an overview.

11 'In humans, some one hundred billion interneurons connect some one million motorneurons that activate a few thousand muscles, with some ten million sensory cells distributed as receptor surfaces throughout the body. Between motor and sensory neurons lies the brain, like a gigantic mass of interneurons that interconnects them (at a ratio of 10:100,000:1) in an ever-changing dynamics' (Maturana and Varela 1988: 159).

12 See, for example, the papers by Sperber, Carey and Spelke, and Keil, in Hirschfeld and Gelman (eds) (1994). Jerry Fodor was the first, and remains the most influential, contemporary cognitive psychologist to propose a modularity theory (see Fodor 1983). In a review of Plotkin (1997) and Pinker (1998), however, Fodor argues against the idea of massive modularity in large part because 'eventually, the mind has to integrate the results of all those modular computations and I don't see how there could be a module for doing that' (Fodor 1998: 12).

13 Interestingly enough, Merleau-Ponty held the chair of child psychology and pedagogy at the Sorbonne from 1949 until 1952 and was succeeded by Piaget (Johnson and Smith 1990: xxiv).

14 What middle-class British, Australian or American parents may take to be a natural stage of child development – the why? stage – is not observable in Fijian children; indeed, given the high value placed by middle-class Western parents on the idea of the intelligent child as an inquiring child, it seems likely that we actively foster this why? stage.

15 For example, the awareness that another, a stranger to oneself, is angry or upset or afraid or lying etc. even when there are no overt signs to justify one's certainty that this is so.

16 He appears not to have read his contemporary Volosinov's brilliant *Marxism and the Philosophy of Language* (1929), which argues against Saussure's distinction between *langue* and *parole*, and for an analysis of 'the utterance' as a social phenomenon.

17 For an excellent psychological discussion of this aspect of Vygotsky's work, see Wertsch and Stone (1985).

1 DRINKING CASH: THE PURIFICATION OF MONEY THROUGH CEREMONIAL EXCHANGE IN FIJI

1 Gau is the fifth largest of the 332 islands of Fiji. It is about 140 square kilometres in area and in 1981–1983 had a population of around 3,000. The population of the chiefly village of Sawaieke was 260; this was among the largest of the eight villages of Sawaieke country (*vanua ko Sawaieke*) which had a population of about 1,250 to 1,400. By 1990 the population of the *vanua* had risen to 1,700–1,800 and of the village to around 290. The economy is mixed subsistence (gardening, and small numbers of pigs, cows and poultry) and cash-cropping; in 1981–1983 copra was still a viable cash crop, by 1990 it had been largely replaced by *yaqona* which had become much more lucrative. Fiji's population in 1983 numbered over 634,000; by 1990 it had risen to 750,000. Indo-Fijians (the descendants of indentured labourers brought to Fiji in the late nineteenth and early twentieth centuries to work the sugar plantations of British colonists) make up almost half the population of Fiji, but on smaller islands the population is often almost entirely Fijian. There was no Indo-Fijian community on Gau. Given salient differences in social relations, I do not wish to claim that my analysis

will hold good for the northern and western areas, though it should be applicable to central and eastern Fiji.

2 I translate *yavusa* as 'clan' and *mataqali* as 'lineage' to distinguish higher and lower levels of integration; the terms are often used in this sense, though *mataqali* may refer to either level. Within *mataqali*, *tokatoka* are ranked against each other on the model of elder brother and younger brother.

3 Chiefs are able to give more because they get more and in giving more they are seen to deserve their status, but chiefs are not necessarily better off than others; they cannot easily accumulate because they should, ideally, re-distribute all they receive. This is not to say that an economic advantage over others may not be manipulated so as to achieve higher status than one might otherwise have obtained.

4 In Sawaieke, traditional obligations to chiefs are stressed at *yavusa* level. In the central government model of the Fijian village the *yavusa* is said to be co-terminous with the village, but in Sawaieke there are five *yavusa*. See France (1969) and Clammer (1973) on the distortions produced by the colonial administration's standardisation of what had been different principles of land tenure. It is not clear, however, that the apparently unusual situation in Sawaieke is a direct product of the Lands Commissions' investigations. Oral history/myth attributes the large number of *yavusa* to an amalgamation of what were once separate villages, the remains of which are still to be seen.

5 Eating together on a routine basis defines the domestic group; food exchange is also a defining marker for groups at a higher level of integration. Thus Hocart (1952: 22) defines *mataqali* (lineage) as 'an assessment unit for feasts'; note too that in Lau the *tokatoka* (sub-lineages) are called *bati ni lovo*, 'sides of the oven'.

6 Kinship terminology is Dravidian; both the terminology and marriage preferences in the district of Sawaieke largely accord with descriptions given by Nayacakalou (1955) for Tokatoka, Tailevu, by Sahlins (1962: 147ff.) for Moala, and by Hocart (1929: 33–42), Thompson (1940: 53–65) and Hooper (1982: 20–23) for Lau. All ethnic Fijians are ideally kin to one another; kinship is classificatory and thus allows for the extension of kinship terms. So, for example, anyone my mother addresses as sister, I call mother; anyone she addresses as brother, I call father-in-law. Similarly anyone my father calls brother, I call father; and anyone he addresses as sister, I call mother-in-law. The children of anyone I call mother or father are my siblings, and the children of anyone I call mother-in-law or father-in-law are my cross-cousins. I cannot marry anyone I call sibling, but marriage is possible with one whom I call cross-cousin. Spouses are cross-cousins by virtue of marriage, even if their relation to one another before marriage is unknown. So, within generation, one ideally relates to any other as 'sibling' or as 'cross-cousin'; across sex this means that a woman relates to a man either as his sister or as his spouse or potential spouse. A man must avoid and respect his sister and if she is his elder sister he is also bound to consult her in any matters of importance. As a wife and irrespective of relative age, this same woman is axiomatically subordinate to her husband. One may marry someone to whom no actual kin relation can be traced, but in this case the in-marrying spouse, usually the wife, learns to address her husband's kin as if the two of them had been cross-cousins before marriage.

7 The giving of food is also important for 'the way according to kinship', but *yaqona* is the primary ritual object of gift and tribute and so I concentrate my analysis upon it.

8 For eastern Lau, Knapman and Walter (1979/80) make a sharp empirical distinction between 'the way of the land' and 'the path of money' that presumably corresponds to an indigenous contrast. The status of *yaqona* as commodity has not, in Sawaieke, introduced the 'decline in custom and the rise of cash' that they describe with respect to the cash cropping of copra in Mavana (see p. 207). Neither is it the case, in Sawaieke, that '[c]eremonial has become largely divorced from the hard realities of

the new economic life and diminished in social and cultural importance' (ibid.) even though, like Mavana, Sawaieke is unquestionably involved in the monetary economy.

9 Indo-Fijians are routinely distinguished from Fijians who refer to themselves as *i taukei* (owners) when making the distinction between them.

10 I prefer the term amoral because practices such as polygamy, witchcraft and cannibalism are often said to have occurred because the ancestors 'did not know the light'.

11 See Walter (1978/79).

12 Cf. MacNaught (1982b), who views 'Fijian culture' as having been 'lost' as a result of the impact of colonialism and a monetary economy.

13 *Yaqona*-drinking stalls are run by Indo-Fijians in the markets of large towns and a generation ago *yaqona* saloons were, I was told, common in the capital Suva; here bowls of *yaqona* are paid for. Apparently one or two of these saloons still exist. Neither market stall nor saloon existed on the island of Gau during the period of my fieldwork, nor did I ever hear that they had ever existed there.

14 Apparently buying for oneself alone may occur in the stalls or saloons mentioned in note 13 above. This context may mediate between 'traditional' and 'market' contexts in that I suspect that men in groups would each in turn 'buy a round' much as one does in a pub. This is emphatically not the case in *gunu sede*.

15 I do not know when it began, but was told by various informants that this method of money-raising was already common in the 1940s. One said that a similar practice applied to dances, until this was banned by church authorities who considered it more than unseemly; apparently one paid for someone else to dance with a particular person. Note that only cross-cousins would have been able to dance with one another.

16 The *vasu* relationship is formally established at any time from infancy onwards by the ceremony of *kau mata ni gone* (lit. carrying the face of the child) when the child or adolescent is formally presented by its father's kin to its mother's kin. See Hooper (1982: 199–218) and Hocart (1915 and 1929: 40).

17 The *yavu* as named house sites within the village are distinguished from *yavu tabu* (sacred yavu) on clan and lineage gardening land and old village sites and associated with the ancestor gods (*kalou vu*); this association apparently being derived from the fact that traditionally the dead were buried in the *yavu* of the house.

18 The importance of affinity as the 'hidden' third term that mediates between 'the Fijian way' and 'the European way' is amply borne out by the earlier practice of selling dances, mentioned in note 15 above.

19 In Sawaieke there is said formerly to have been a prohibition on marriage between immediate cross-cousins, but today this is not the case; rather, if one can call someone cross-cousin, that person is marriageable. Cf. Walter (1975).

20 Today the *vasu* does not often avail him or herself of the privileges that are said to be his due. Most persons with whom I discussed this matter said either that they had never done so or related what seemed to be considered a 'daring' incident of their youth. Only once did I myself see an instance of the *vasu* seizing property from his mother's brother.

2 MAKING THE PRESENT, REVEALING THE PAST: THE MUTABILITY AND CONTINUITY OF TRADITION AS PROCESS

1 All relations of equality are joking relationships and in some sense cross boundaries. The cross-cousin relation typically obtains *across* domestic groups.

2 The 'man's side' in marriage exchanges *must* give more than the 'woman's side' lest they be 'ashamed'. This implies that the exchanges are balanced – i.e. that the bride is part of what is given by her side. Sahlins (1976: 24–46) asserts wife-takers to be

superior to wife-givers in Moala. My data from Gau suggest that the two sides are notionally equal; the wedding exchanges constitute the superiority of the man over his wife, not that of his side over hers.

3 On the above/below axis marked by the cloth, a man is clearly superior to his wife – her seat defines the pole below. This does not mean that the senior woman of the household always sits at the pole below; e.g. a widow of chiefly birth who lives with her son sits a little below him and above his children. But if man and wife are resident together, she always sits at the pole below.

4 In other respects, women's labour is as highly valued as men's and, in exchange, women's 'valuables' are as important as the men's 'feast'. Men garden and women fish, but men are not 'land' and women, 'sea'; rather each sex has both land and sea attributes. So women as makers of mats (from pandanus) and barkcloth (from the paper mulberry tree) are associated with the land, and men as fishers for turtle and for big fish (such as the *saqa*, whose eating is the prerogative of chiefs) with sea. Sahlins (1976: 26–42) explores these associations in some detail; however, where I take the relation between sea and land to denote balanced reciprocity in exchange relations, he takes sea to be above land and nests it within an opposition between nobles (*turaga*) and land (*vanua*, i.e. the people).

5 Ranking is given by the nature of the reciprocal traditional obligations that obtain between clans (*yavusa*). This pattern holds for ranked relations across lineages (*mataqali*); within lineage the ranking of sub-lineages (*tokatoka*) is referred to the relative seniority of the set of brothers who were the original founders of the lineage. Clan affiliation is patrilineal, but kin relations are reckoned bilaterally; a child has certain rights in his or her mother's lineage (see e.g. Hocart 1915 and 1929: 40 and Sahlins 1962: 169, 185).

6 So 'landspeople' do not eat pig, shrimp and other 'land' foods when they eat in the company of 'seapeople' who do not eat fish; each group symbolically makes available to the other the products of its labour.

7 Sahlins (1976: 32–33) drawing on data from Hocart (1929) makes the sea-door/land-door distinction isomorphic with the above/below axis of the internal space of the house. My data suggest that the sea/land distinction is irrelevant for people's disposition inside a house. I equate the relation between 'sea' and 'land' with that between cross-cousins as affines and equals and thus with relations across domestic groups. By contrast, above/below in the internal space of the house constitutes hierarchical relations within the domestic group.

8 A herbal remedy is *mana* (effective) in curing illness; so is the clan chief whose *mana* installs a paramount in office; so is the speech that accompanies a *sevusevu*. Here, the formula *Mana ... e dina* expresses the notion that the words of the speechmaker have by their pronunciation brought about the peace and prosperity to which they refer.

9 The witch who 'drinks kava on his own' initiates the flow of *mana* only to misdirect it for selfish ends; the *mana* of the chiefs of old was supposed to be for the good of all in so far as it resulted in prosperity or victory in battle.

10 If only women are drinking kava, those of highest status sit above as may very high status women visitors in a mixed gathering, but only if their husbands are not present.

11 E.g. the speech for *sevusevu* may end with the words: 'And may the following of the elders (chiefs) and the minister grow ever greater.'

12 On infanticide, see Williams (1858: 181), Waterhouse (1866: 328); widow strangling, Waterhouse (1866: 197–201); presentation of women to chiefs and forced marriage, Williams (1858: 40, 41). On women's exclusion from kava-drinking and consumption of human sacrifices, see Waterhouse (1866: 314, 419) and Williams (1858: 232).

13 It was considered unfitting in Deuba (Viti Levu) in the 1940s and is still so in Fulaga, Lau (Geddes 1945: 18; Herr 1981: 344).

14 See also Bott and Leach in La Fontaine (ed.) (1972). Certain aspects of my argument recall Leach's re-analysis of Bott's material. Cf. Turner (1986) for an analysis of Fijian kava-drinking that builds on Leach's notion of kava ritual as sacrifice.

3 SEEING THE ANCESTRAL SITE: TRANSFORMATIONS IN FIJIAN NOTIONS OF THE LAND

1 For example: 'Our founding ancestor is Ro[ko]taloko, this ancestor I heard came from Nakauvadra [Pandanus-tree], then went to Vanualevu [Great-Land] and to Dama in Bua [Frangipani-tree] then came here to this island of Gau [Middle] and made a village here, Nukubolo [Sand-strewn-with-coconut-leaves] near to Navukailagi [Flew-to-the-sky]. After that they went up higher to live in Qilai [Branches-pulled-down-with-a-forked-stick] – an empty spot ... ' These place names tend to refer to features of the land or to events that occurred there.

2 I owe this insight to Nancy Munn, who made this point in a seminar discussion during the 1992 conference of the Australian Anthropological Association. See Munn (1986) for an extended analysis of how spatio-temporal concepts inform cultural praxis on Gawa, in Papua New Guinea.

3 This distinction is implicit in villagers' insistence on the validity of direct personal experience as opposed to second-hand knowledge derived from what other people have told one. However, from an analytical point of view no experience can ever be unmediated, as indeed is clear from the ethnography that follows.

4 Regarding burial of the dead in the *yavu*, see e.g. Williams (1982: 191), Capell (1973: 186), Waterhouse (1978: 43), Hocart (1912: 448; 1929: 182), Thompson (1940: 222).

5 In previous publications I have translated *yavusa* as clan and represented it, as Fijians often do, as a patrilineal descent group. However, see Toren (1994c) for an analysis of Fijian social organisation in terms of the relations between houses along the lines suggested by Lévi-Strauss (1983: 163–187). Cf. Sayes (1984: 87) who argues that 'the idiom of descent is used to disguise a power relationship. The true formation process would appear to be one in which the different co-residential groups have been drawn together by intermarriage and ... the dominance of one of the component groups.'

6 So Thomas Williams describes attempts to effect success in war by attendance on particular ancestors who had not, previous to the threat of war, been the object of any particular attention (Williams 1931, ii. 282, 516). Similarly, a paramount chief becomes *mana* (effective) through the attendance of the people upon him in the installation ceremony, where he is 'made to drink' the installation *yaqona* (kava) by the installing chief, who is also chief of 'landspeople'.

7 For accounts of missionary activity in Fiji, see e.g. Calvert (1858) and Clammer (1976); the latter attributes the success of missionaries to their policy of establishing a widespread literacy whose objects were religious texts. In Sawaieke country there is virtually 100 per cent adult literacy, but reading matter is largely confined to the Methodist Prayer and Hymn Book, the Bible and, sometimes, religious tracts. Villagers read newspapers and books relatively rarely.

8 These two ancestors are probably those goddesses who are known elsewhere as *ko i rau na marama*, 'the two ladies'. What I was told about these two by a 30-year-old woman implied that my informant took them to be ancestresses of her own *yavusa*, but I may be mistaken here.

9 The colonial administration tried to make people bury their dead in designated graveyards (apparently for reasons of hygiene) but, as far as I can tell, the practice was not followed for people of high status and today seems to have been completely discontinued.

10 The graves in the graveyard are unmarked and the identity of those buried on gardening land may be known only to people who witnessed the burial.

11 Dening (1980: 53) argues for traditional Marquesan society that 'to know the *tapu* was to know a social map of Te Henua [the landscape]'. Bradd Shore (1989: 143), in his fascinating paper on *mana and tapu* in Polynesia, remarks that Dening's reading of *tapu* distinguishes the noble from the common. Certainly one could say for old Fiji that to know the *tabu* was to know a social map of the *vanua*, land or country, but the *tabu*, while it may have been the prerogative of chiefs, was not confined to those who came from chiefly *yavusa;* I was told that any *tabu* imposed on the use of lands, streams, sea, etc. was the prerogative of the chief of those *yavusa* classified as 'land' (i.e. commoners). The *tabu* on the salt water that I refer to in the text was imposed by a man who was, at the time, 'acting land chief'.

12 My informant distinguished this kind of *tabu* from one announced by persons who do not want others to take fruit or watercress etc. from their land; these are dependent for their effect on goodwill and people may not take much notice of them; they are not *mana* – effective – as is the *tabu* that is announced, under the proper circumstances, by one with traditional authority.

13 For an extended account of the significance and uses of *tabua*, see Hooper (1982).

14 In *yaqona*-drinking in Sawaieke, 'sea' is above 'land' when the high chief (sea) drinks before the chief of the *yavusa* whose prerogative it is to install him (land); but 'land' is above 'sea' when the chief of the landspeople *yavusa* drinks before the chief of the seapeople *yavusa*.

15 Note that *bukete*, meaning 'pregnant', is derived from *bukebuke*, meaning a mound of earth on which yams are planted or, possibly, from *bu*, green coconut, and *kete*, belly – both yams and coconuts being male products.

16 Chiefs are empowered by *yaqona*-drinking, but today this legitimate, collective, drinking is under the auspices of the Christian God.

17 Thomas (1991: 35–82) discusses the gift/commodity distinction in the Pacific; for Fiji, he argues that while the objects of gift exchange were alienable, ceremonial exchanges 'create a lien, and in that sense have "inalienable" ramifications' (p. 67).

18 For a detailed description of these processes in contemporary village life, see Toren (1990: 50–64, 90–118, 238–244).

19 In accepting a *tabua* (whale's tooth) the speaker sniff-kisses it (*reguca*) several times and continues to hold and gaze at it as he speaks. Given that *tabua* are chiefly products given in exchange against tributary products of the land, this behaviour suggests that the speaker is implicitly consuming an intangible chiefly substance that inheres in the tooth.

4 SIGN INTO SYMBOL, SYMBOL AS SIGN: COGNITIVE ASPECTS OF A SOCIAL PROCESS

1 This consideration of kava-drinking and household meals is not meant to suggest an opposition between a public and a private domain. Meals are public in that they are taken in full view of passers-by, all doors of the house being open, and passers-by are always invited in to eat. Conventionally one politely refuses the invitation, but this does not negate the general kinship obligation that is inherent in the invitation.

2 This notion of ritual as rule-governed appears to clash with that of tradition (*cakacaka vakavanua*, under which 'ritual' is subsumed) as processual, a notion I have explored elsewhere (Toren 1988). As I showed in that paper, it is the very fact of being made explicit that 'fixes' what is done, thus history is understood as unchanging and tradition as flexible, processual. In other words, what is not explicit in ritual, or about ritual, is allowed to change; what is explicit is held to be immutable.

NOTES

5 MAKING HISTORY: THE SIGNIFICANCE OF CHILDHOOD COGNITION FOR A COMPARATIVE ANTHROPOLOGY OF MIND

1 See, for example, Bowerman (1982) who shows that the development of meaning takes place largely before and outside the acquisition of language forms, and that children have gradually to work out the categories of meaning implicit in the structure of their language on the basis of experience with language itself. Bowerman's work suggests that semantics – i.e. meaning in language – is not isomorphic with an embodied, but inarticulable, understanding of the world.

2 Cf. Merleau-Ponty (1964: 20) who argues that the movement of history 'is of the same order as the movement of Thought and Speech, and, in short of the perceptible world's explosion within us'. Cf. Sahlins for whom cultural categories are received readymade only to be 'risked' in practice (1985: 144–151). But meaning is never 'received', it is always the product of a process of cognitive construction in particular persons that is mediated, but cannot be determined, by each person's relations with others. Sahlins' implicit distinction between cognition and practice reifies his cultural 'system' as an ultimately all-encompassing and ahistorical model of possibilities.

3 Cf. Ingold (1990a) 'every human infant comes into the world already situated within a field of social relations, and becoming a person is a matter of gathering those relations into the structures of consciousness'.

4 Cf. Csordas (1990) who attacks the mind/body and subject/object distinctions via a reflexive theoretical synthesis of the work of Merleau-Ponty (1962) and Bourdieu (1977). My own argument has been similarly informed and I agree with most of what Csordas has to say; I am concerned, however, to go further and to collapse distinctions like biology/culture and individual/society that work to preclude a genuinely anthropological theory of mind.

5 Cf. Merleau-Ponty 'whenever I try to understand myself the whole fabric of the perceptible world comes too and with it come the others who are caught in it' (1964: 15).

6 Thus the children's eventual understanding of above/below as expressive, rather than constitutive, cannot be merely a function of their understanding of metaphor. Conversely, their early understanding of above/below as constitutive cannot be explained away as an inability to comprehend it as metaphorical.

7 This observation explains why 'It is because subjects do not, strictly speaking, know what they are doing that what they do has more meaning than they know ...' (Bourdieu 1977: 79).

8 See Phylactou and Toren (1990) and Hirschfeld (1990).

9 Hirschfeld notes that '[r]ace and racism ... are ... not separate and contingently allied predicates for the young child, as conventional wisdom would argue, but one and the same predicate' (1988: 624). I would argue that it is precisely the conventional (and untenable) notion of 'race' as denoting essential biological differences that makes any 'racial' category itself racist.

10 I am thinking here of examples of what is or is not proper for women to do or be, such as 'women can't be artists' said by a 5-year-old who actually knows well a number of women artists. In other words, children are likely to make generalisations that are sexist even if their parents do not, because, by the age of 4 or 5, their experience of the world at large has allowed them to constitute such notions as valid.

11 See Trevarthen (1987) for a psychological study of inter-subjectivity between caregivers and infants.

12 Cf. Ingold (1986: 292).

13 Freeman's findings on olfactory perception in rabbits have implications for models of human neurology since they are compatible with 'neural net' psychological models of human nervous system function (which are currently replacing the earlier, linear information-processing models). Neural net models imply (as Freeman's findings have shown) that we should make no hard and fast distinction between pre- and post-cortical neurology (e.g. between 'perception' and 'cognition'). Neural nets are computer models of cognitive processes that attempt to simulate neurological functioning and as such they include a determinedly biological perspective; but because they rest on the distinction between biology and culture, they implicitly assume 'culture' to be a separable aspect of human cognition that resides in language (see e.g. Clark 1990: 114).

14 See Piaget (1971: 113). My use here of Piaget's idea of the scheme does not entail any allegiance to his general stage theory – his view that the end point of learning is known, his assumption that child cognitive development is largely unmediated by relations with other people, etc.

15 Cf. Merleau-Ponty (1962: 15) 'sensation and images ... never make their appearance anywhere other than within a horizon of meaning, and the significance of the percept, far from resulting from an association, is in fact presupposed in all association'.

16 Here, as throughout this article, I am allowing Merleau-Ponty's ideas on perception and language to inflect my own attempts to derive a theory of cognition as a micro-historical process (see Merleau-Ponty 1962; 1964: 3–35, 84–97; 1974: 196–226).

17 See also Strathern and Toren in the debate edited by Ingold (1990b); see Ingold (1991).

18 For example, in the Vygotskian perspective, children are initially 'biological' beings who become 'cultural' by virtue of learning language and the cultural knowledge that is immanent in language. This is a misleading distinction, but see Vygotsky (1978, 1986) and e.g. Rommetveit (1985) for useful accounts of how language informs the child's constitution of knowledge.

19 Cf. Valerie Walkerdine's (1990) study of children's cognitive construction of mathematical concepts; her more sophisticated use of 'discourse' is derived from Foucault and her analysis includes a Lacanian perspective. The problem remains, however, of how 'discourse' is constituted and where it is to be located.

20 Cf. Merleau-Ponty (1962: 15) 'the perceptible is precisely that which can haunt more than one body without budging from its place. No one will see that table which now meets my eye; only I can do that. And yet I know that at the same moment it presses upon every glance in the same way. For I see these other glances too.'

21 This is not meant to suggest that psychoanalysis is not a useful therapeutic method; I think it is. My argument here is against its efficacy as a universal explanation of human experience (cf. Rubin 1975).

22 Thus Ross (1981) attributes to culture the 'attribution error' whereby an observer assumes that a person's mistakes are attributable to his or her disposition (e.g. he tripped because he's clumsy) rather than to the situation (e.g. he tripped because that toy was in his way). Even so, he fails to question his own 'dispositional bias' which is apparent in his assumption that universally people can be characterised as 'intuitive scientists'.

23 No doubt Holland and Quinn are well aware that language is an historical phenomenon, but their assumption that culture is immanent in language implies otherwise. Their privileging of language and their (critical) use of Schank and Abelson's (1977) information-processing model of mind suggests that the embodied nature of cognitive processes – many of which materialise in action rather than articulation – is of little or no concern. But while they are correct in criticising Schank

(1982) for failing to recognise how much knowledge is communicated in language (rather than through 'firsthand experience'), they seem not to realise that the expectations a person has of a situation he or she has yet to experience are a function of that person's own history.

24 That the social is extraneous to most psychological models of mind is perhaps in part a function of a taken-for-granted distinction between structure and process – itself an artefact of the mind/computer analogy. Cf. Maturana and Varela (1988) and Piaget (1971) where structure and process are facets of each other. The structure/process distinction bedevils theorising in cognitive psychology even where it has been identified as a salient problem (see e.g. Keil 1984). The new 'connexionist' models of mind are, however, at least attempting to take human biology into account (see e.g. Clark 1990: 61–80).

25 Johnson (1987) includes a fascinating theoretical analysis of the way in which embodied experience prefigures one's understanding of the logical relations inscribed in language.

6 RITUAL, RULE AND COGNITIVE SCHEME

1 This paper focuses on the hierarchical aspect of Fijian social relations, but the reader should note that relations of competitive equality between peers are just as important.

2 Fijian village houses usually contain one or two chairs, but these are rarely used and then only by the owners of a house; such behaviour would be highly presumptuous in a guest. But if one is seated in a chair when someone arrives, it is proper to move to a place on the floor so as to be on a level with the guest. Only old and high-ranking men may retain a chair when a guest is present, and then only if the visit is likely to be brief and involves one or two younger people of lower rank. There are no chairs in village halls but churches are provided with pews. For further information on the valuation of space in village buildings, see Toren (1990: 29–39, 107–118, 131–137).

3 The noticeable differences in the extent to which people incline from the vertical when walking *lolou* tend to correlate with their status relative to those in the same company.

4 'Imitation' is used here in its Piagetian sense, to refer to the young child's cognitive accommodation to the practices of others in its immediate milieu. In other words, while certain forms of imitation in neonates suggest that a 'body schema' is innate (see Mehler and Dupoux [1990] 1994: 100–103; Meltzoff and Moore, 1985), imitation in infants and older children is the outcome of a process of cognitive constitution (see Piaget 1962 [1946]: 78–86).

5 The data are derived from children's drawings of a gathering in the village hall and their commentary on them, and from their responses to a variety of prepared drawings of meals and *yaqona*-drinking.

6 Children are not admitted to *yaqona*-drinking, though a toddler or two may be present on informal occasions, especially at home. Even so, any lively gathering in house or village hall attracts small groups of children, who range themselves outside the building and peer in at the proceedings through chinks and crevices in the bamboo slats or other material that form the walls. School-age children may have to penetrate a *yaqona*-drinking group to deliver a message or suchlike. So, despite their formal exclusion from *yaqona*-drinking and other adult activities, children are in a position to form their own ideas about their nature.

7 Boys tend to make gender a factor in that for them only a high chief or a few clan chiefs can be above; however wives of men below the status of clan chief are said to be on a level with their husbands. By contrast, girls are much more likely to make gender entirely irrelevant by saying that any woman is necessarily on the same level

(i.e., of the same status) as her husband. In either case, this description virtually never accords with a child's empirical experience – wives do *not sit* beside their husbands at home, in church, or in a village hall.

8 The clap, or *cobo*, is performed with the palms crossed and slightly cupped to give a soft, hollow sound. The *cobo* is a feature of Fijian politeness and is used to express thanks in all kinds of situations, but especially in ceremonial performances and in the drinking of *yaqona*.

9 Here I follow Lewis's (1980: 11) formulation that, '[i]n all those instances where we would feel no doubt that we had observed ritual we could have noticed and will notice whether the people who perform it have explicit rules to guide them in what they do. ... What is always explicit about ritual and recognised by those who perform it, is that aspect of it which states who should do what and when.'

10 The idea of good breeding sets a contempt for ambition and status-striving (this attitude being associated with both the upper and working classes) against the smug achievements of the bourgeoisie.

11 See Piaget, 1971 [1968]: 62 (italics in original).

12 So, in sixty-seven drawings of *yaqona*-drinking in the village hall produced by all the children attending the Sawaieke District School in 1982, a total of thirty-seven different oppositions could be distinguished concerning who sat below, and who above. Looking at the poles of the opposition above–below as they varied together, the thirty-seven different types could be further broken down into ten distinct types of drawing. It is in terms of these ten oppositions that I was able to show reliable group differences across age and sex with respect to children's understanding of status distinctions.

13 See Piaget 1971 [1968]: 113.

14 So Bloch (1974) argues that when language is a feature of ritual, its propositional content is inevitably restricted and its illocutionary force emphasised.

15 See Bloch (1974; 1986: 178–195).

16 Take for example, table manners. A Euro-American child who asks *why* it should not put its elbows on the table, and who continues to pursue the question through a series of quasi-explanations such as 'because it's not nice' or 'because it looks ugly', may ultimately be told by an exasperated parent to take his or her elbows off the table 'because I said so'.

7 TRANSFORMING LOVE: REPRESENTING FIJIAN HIERARCHY

1 Here I am indebted to Maria Phylactou for an enlightening discussion.

2 Williams (1982 [1858]: 182) refers to the *dredre kaci*, the 'call by laughing' as bringing a severe beating upon a married woman.

3 Cf. Brewster (1922: 197); Lester (1940: 283); Quain (1948: 339). Geddes (1948: 192) says that the virginity of chiefly women was especially guarded.

4 MacNaught (1982a: 106) tells how the *taralala* 'spread like an epidemic' through the Fiji of 1925, to the horror of both chiefs and missionaries.

5 This violates the hierarchical spatial relations whereby a chief should always be above others; thus the internal space of house, church, and village hall has an area called 'above' where chiefs sit and an area called 'below' that is the place of women and/or young men.

6 Thomson (1968 [1908]: 24) gives *dogai* as 'what is called "broken heart" by Europeans'. I also thought the symptoms similarly suggestive and asked the young man who first told me about it whether *dogai* was the same as being broken-hearted – an expression that is used in popular songs (*kavoro na utoqu*, 'my heart is broken'). But I

was told this was not the case. It seems likely therefore that Thomson was relying on his own reading of the symptoms. Cf. Brewster (1922: 198) who refers to *dogai* in Nadarivatu, north Colo, as an ancestral punishment for illicit love affairs before marriage, especially with reference to 'youths'.

7 Cf. Quain (1948: 317–318) who says that neither boys nor girls in Nakoroka, Vanua Levu, have to bother about concealing their genitals from view until puberty.

8 See Thomson (1908: 219). For other references on tattooing of girls see, for example, Williams (1982 [1858]: 160); Seeman (1862: 113); Brewster (1922: 184–187); Quain (1948: 315). Cf. Hocart (1929: 149–150) on the confinement of Lauan girls of chiefly birth at puberty. Gell (1993) contains a fascinating comparative analysis of tattooing practices in Fiji, Samoa and Tonga. In Fiji boys were not tattooed; they were circumcised, as they are still today, see, e.g. Williams (1958: 166), Waterhouse (1978 [1866]: 341), Quain (1948: 134), Sahlins (1962: 187).

9 *Sega. Sa tu vei koya na lewa i loma vakaikoya*, lit. 'No, it was up to her [to make] the decision in her own mind.' Because sex before marriage is illegitimate, there seems to be no explicit notion of an 'age of consent', but I think it probable that adult men and women would consider sex between a young man and a girl so young to be an act of rape.

10 Quain (1948: 320, 321) notes that sexual experience in dreams is considered to be intercourse with devils and the souls of the dead, see also Herr (1981) who argues that, for Fijian women, 'sexual feelings are inextricably tied ... with notions of being consumed and devoured and also of death'.

11 Cf. Amratlal *et al.* (1975) where a young woman is told by her father that 'her new boss was her husband and that she must listen to him' (p. 44). Also, 'it was normal and accepted that a husband sometimes beat his wife' (p. 47); 'women's position especially in the home has not changed that much – women accept that men should lead' (p. 59).

12 See Nayacakalou (1955: 48).

13 See Williams (1982 [1858]: 210) and Henderson (1931: 57), who remarks that Tanoa, chief of Bau, had as his kava toast *sese matairua* [or perhaps this should be *saisai matairua?*], 'a spear with two points', apparently a metaphor for the breast of a virgin which Henderson says was a favoured delicacy. It seems possible that Henderson confused the sexual usage of 'eat' with the literal one. Williams (1982 [1858]: 211) says that, with respect to the epicurean properties of human flesh, it was the upper limbs, heart, liver, etc. that were praised. However, Tanoa's toast is interesting in respect of its sexual connotations, for here the virgin becomes at once that which slays and that which is 'eaten'. Cf. Sahlins (1983: 76; 1985: 89).

14 See Williams (1982 [1858]: 211); cf. Clunie (1977: 40) who says that while human flesh was generally *tabu* to women, they did sometimes eat of it.

15 Hocart (1929: 158) records that adultery and divorce were common in Lau apparently on the part of wives as well as husbands and Thompson (1940: 58) says that 'the discovery of adultery on the part of one's spouse usually causes only temporary friction'. Perhaps Wesleyanism has wrought a change here, though I find it difficult to believe that in the past wives were allowed such licence; Williams (1982 [1858]: 182) makes it clear that Bauan women were not, while Seeman (1862: 192) says that those discovered in adultery were put to death.

16 I am indebted for this point to Marilyn Strathern.

17 See Peck (1982: 348).

8 COSMOGONIC ASPECTS OF DESIRE AND COMPASSION IN FIJI

1 In Fiji, hierarchy is what Dumont would call a 'value' and is routinely evinced in people's disposition *vis-à-vis* one another inside any village building. A spatial axis whose poles are given by the terms 'above' and 'below' (in reference to a single plane) is mapped onto internal spaces; people of higher status are always seated above those of lower status. So, when gathered together in any space, villagers are always seated such that their relative status (derived from an interaction between rank, gender and seniority) is apparent. This and other ritualised behaviours have led analysts such as Hocart and Sahlins to describe Fijian hierarchy as if it is Dumontian in form – that is to say, as if 'chiefliness' is the ultimate encompassing value in a hierarchy of values where an opposition between 'chiefs' and 'people' generates all other sets of binary opposing values. I argue that, on the contrary, hierarchy in Fijian social relations can never become an encompassing value because it is always and inevitably opposed by competitive equality as an equally important and antithetical value.

2 From the analyst's view, male violence in the early years of marriage may be attributed to any one of a number of causes; however, it seems significant that jealousy is the usual reason given by villagers.

3 The *yavusa* is made up of clans that are closely connected by affinal and ritual-cum-political ties. In pre-colonial times the *yavusa* was co-terminous with the village; today Sawaieke contains five *yavusa*.

4 This observation was made by Pamela Peck, who worked in Lovu, another village in the *vanua* of Sawaieke, and is quoted in her doctoral thesis (Peck 1982).

5 One could not eat close kin; cross-cousins might be close kin, so in earlier days marriage was allowed only between second cross-cousins (a notion that is still in force in many parts of Fiji, but not in Sawaieke). The marriage taboo itself suggests the degree of relationship where 'eating' might perhaps begin, so there is a covert suggestion here that the god is initially to be thought of as perhaps a cross-cousin to the two men. But the God's manifest *mana* is such that the men cannot approach him as his peers, for then he might eat them; they disavow the possibility of cross-cousinship and opt for the hierarchical parent–child relationship.

6 The very dwelling of Tui DelaiGau implicates the domestic life; his home is reported by Waterhouse to be 'a very lofty cowrie tree'; this is the *dakua*, which grows to great heights and whose wood was used for many everyday and yet important purposes. Thus Seeman says '*Dakua* is used for mats, booms, spars, for flooring houses and for all those purposes for which deal is usually employed by us.' Its gum was burned as a torch, or used to fuel lamps, and a dye made from the burning gum was used for the hair, for printing barkcloth, and for tattooing the skin of women not of chiefly clans (Seeman 1862: 358–360).

7 Heat connotes anger and a warlike spirit. The old Fijian Gods often have their abode in trees, whose nature and uses always accord with the nature of the God who lives there, or whose dwelling is marked by the tree's proximity. A *tavola* tree marks Ravuravu's dwelling; its wood is used to make the great slit drums with which, in pre- and early colonial times, the people of one group might challenge another to war and beat out the rhythms of their success in killing and eating the enemy (Seeman 1862: 363; Clunie 1977: 25, 27).

8 His tale accords with one related by Waterhouse (1978 [1866]: 387–388), where The Two Ladies are said maliciously to kill all solitary travellers in revenge for having been poorly treated by the people of Vione (a Gau village – not part of the *vanua* of Sawaieke), whose chief one of them had married and to whom she had born a son.

9 Shortly afterwards I remarked on this in conversation with a young man of 23, unthinkingly telling him that oddly enough, I had noticed a bad smell in my own house during the previous few days and been unable to find out what was causing it. He was angry and hissed at me sotto voce not to talk about it; 'Those two will hear you,' he said.

10 Dreams are often accorded validity in that they are considered either to be 'messages' from God or the ancestors or to be 'out of the body' experiences. See Herr (1981).

11 *Yavusa* Koviko, which traditionally supplied both priests and/or warriors to the Sawaieke chiefs had, for many years before this story was told me, been subsumed as a clan (*mataqali*) within the chiefly *yavusa* Nadawa; it was reconstituted as a *yavusa* in its own right in 1982.

12 See Toren (forthcoming e).

13 The old Gods are held to have created particular areas in Fiji and to have given form to the country itself. Perhaps the Christian God delegated to them this task, or perhaps they indeed formed the land and the Christian God revealed himself later as the true source of their power; I have heard both views expressed by different people, and on two different occasions by the same person.

14 The ancestors are the source of one's identity as a member of a particular clan, etc.; they are also often said to be the source of various powers, abilities, etc. with which people are born, but this refers to what particular ancestral sources can pass on to their own descendants; these are not notions of predestination.

15 Virtually all Fijians (as opposed to Fiji Indians) are practising Christians, the overwhelming majority being Wesleyans; 'the church' (*na lotu*) denotes Christianity in general. Sawaieke villagers held explicitly that while they were all Wesleyans, other forms of Christian practice were perfectly acceptable; what was important was that one professed oneself to be of some Christian denomination. For accounts of early missionary activity in Fiji, see, for example Williams (1982 [1858], Clammer (1976). Missionary success was assured when the powerful paramount chief Cakobau converted to Wesleyanism in 1854; his conversion (like that of lesser paramounts) led to mass conversions by those who were subject to him. Calvert (1982 [1858]: 401) quoted in Geddes (1948: 334) claimed 54,000 conversions by 1856 – one-third of the population. Cf. Burton (1910:127), who described the Fiji of his times as only 'nominally' Christian – despite its 80,000 Methodists in a total population of 86,000 Fijians.

9 'ALL THINGS GO IN PAIRS, OR THE SHARKS WILL BITE': THE ANTITHETICAL NATURE OF FIJIAN CHIEFSHIP

1 See Barnes, de Coppet and Parkin (eds) (1985) for a debate on this issue. Dumont's thesis has also informed analyses of political hierarchy outside India – see e.g. Sahlins (1985 and 1991) on Fiji and Valeri (1985) on Hawaii; other scholars of Austronesia have argued against it (see e.g. Mosko and Jolly, forthcoming).

2 So, for example, the ritualised drinking of *yaqona* (kava) and of alcohol refer to the antithesis between hierarchical and equal relations, between tribute and balanced reciprocity (Toren 1994b). Here the contrast suggests that these equal relations are 'not Fijian' – a sleight of hand that is evident too in the contrast drawn between 'the gift' and 'the commodity' (Toren 1989) – and which is possible because neither alcohol drinking nor commodity exchange can take on the form of chiefly ritual.

3 Cf. Jolly (forthcoming) who, in her comparison of hierarchy in Vanuatu and Fiji, remarks that 'Hierarchy is a pervasive feature of both symbolic systems and of sociopolitical relations, but there is no overarching principle which establishes the

hierarchical ordering of all elements in any social "whole".' My own position is rather different, for I am arguing here that, at least for Fijians, hierarchy and equality are always and inevitably posited together and counterposed such that the existence of each is dependent on that of its opposite, and neither hierarchy nor equality can become an encompassing value.

4 *Veitau* is also used to denote friendly competition as in *veitau cici*, a foot-race; cf. *veiqati* which denotes a more jealous rivalry.

5 In the country (*vanua*) of Sawaieke, chiefs are usually no richer and no poorer than commoners and this is so even if we use 'chiefs' in its narrowest sense to refer only to those men who are chiefs of *yavusa* (*na malo*, lit. 'the cloths') – a *yavusa* being a group of clans connected by affinal and ritual-cum-political ties; in pre-colonial days the *yavusa* was co-terminous with the village.

6 In previous works I have translated *yavusa* as 'clan' and *mataqali* as 'lineage'; here the latter term is translated as 'clan' while *yavusa*, derived from *yavu* (house foundation), denotes a group of related 'houses'. In part I agree with Shelley Sayes' thesis that *yavusa* are not so much 'descent groups' as 'a group of *mataqali* who have remained together in the same locality ... kinship through intermarriage often might have been their only ties' (Sayes 1982: 87). However, in Fiji marriage is the foundation for the constitution of kinship, just as kinship (i.e. the relation between brother and sister) creates the possibility of marriage (i.e. between the respective children of the brother and sister, or their children's children, who are affines). In other words, affinal ties are explicitly encompassed by kinship.

7 I was told many times in Sawaieke that a person with whom one is *veitauvu* was 'just the same as an owner of the village' and that his or her every want would not only be attended to at once, but even anticipated; however, when people spoke of visiting places where they were *tauvu*, they always emphasised how reluctant they were to be recognised as such because of the aggressive, if welcoming, attention this recognition entails.

8 Enquiries into land holdings began in the late nineteenth century but those that were ultimately recognised were established by the Lands Commission of 1912 onwards. I am grateful to the present Takalaigau, Ratu Marika Uluinadawa, who gave me access to his personal copy of the records for Gau, which are also held in the *I Taba ni Veitarogi Vanua* in Suva.

9 To avoid the confusion produced by too many unfamiliar names, I have at times paraphrased the text.

10 Ratu Marika Lewanavanua, then the *Buli* for Gau. This office was created by the British administration; in any given area, the *Buli* was usually selected from the chiefly clan.

11 The name of Biu's first son, Seruqaraivalu, means 'Comb Warrior' or, more literally 'Comb facing war' and the name of Seruqaraivalu's son, Vukicivoda, means 'Revolted against Voda'. Seruqaraivalu, as one whose father gained status through his warlike prowess, was the first holder of the title Takalaigau; the name of his son refers to Biu's revolt against the chief of his own *yavusa*, Tui Voda. Till today, children may be named after an important event in the lives of their parents or grandparents.

12 In the *I tukutuku raraba ni vanua ko Sawaieke* Biu's name is also sometimes given as Bui, but I take this to be a typing error since Bui means 'grandmother' and Biu meaning 'rejected' is consistent with the story of his dismissal by his mother's people.

13 As Na Sau, the paramount, NaRai would initially be 'sea', as would Biu who 'went to stay in his village Nakobuna, in his clan Waivolita'. The Nakobuna chief 'listened to' (*vakarorogo vua*, i.e. owed allegiance to) Tui Voda – then and today the chief of fisher-people clans – whose founding ancestor is recorded as having come from Kaba, Tailevu. The story shows that the Nakobuna people were navigators to the Sau – war

chief – NaRai (also known as Na Raitena); Nakobuna village still existed in 1916, though not today. NaRai's giving of the chiefship transforms him into 'land' and makes Biu take on the association with 'sea' that belongs to the paramount.

14 A similar point is made by Deryck Scarr (1976) for Bau and by Shelley Sayes (1982: xxviii, 36, 57ff., 65, 74, 87) in her history of the Cakaudrove chiefship; see also Nicholas Thomas (1986).

15 Rokotaloko, the founding ancestor of the Na Raitena people, is sometimes referred to as the owner of Na i vinivini, a large mound that stands on the outskirts of Sawaieke village – the foundation of a *bure kalou*, god house, 'in the time of the devils' (*e na gauna vakatevoro*). For an analysis of the story of Radikedike, a.k.a. Rokotaloko, see Toren (1995a). Rokotaloko is variously said to have come from Vuya or from Dama, in Bua, Vanua Levu; Radikedike is said to have come from Dama.

16 The story makes it appear that NaRai as *Sau* may have taken precedence over Tui Voda, but this may be an artefact of the accounts being given by a chief whose ideas of the ritual duties of the two *yavusa* are those of 1916, rather than of an earlier era.

17 Orisi Qaraiwalu, of Naocomatana; the paramount Ratu Tomasi had asserted that Naocomatana was a subdivision of Naboginibola clan, rather than a clan in its own right. The speaker, Orisi Qaraiwalu was at the time *turaga ni koro* – 'village chief', a position created by the colonial administration. The post is not a high-status one and today is often held by a relatively young man in his thirties or forties, who is elected by his fellow villagers.

18 At one point, Ratu Tomasi says that Veidre (whom he had first stated to be his *vu* or founding ancestor) was himself installed as Takalaigau, but since other evidence suggests that Veidre was a land chief (not a member of the chiefly clan) this seems unlikely to have been the case.

19 The Naboginibola chief also leaves another chiefly clan, Valebalavu, out of his account. This suggests he saw Valebalavu as a threat and that another clan, Naocomatana, which his account implicitly exalts, were his allies.

20 Akariva Beraateri.

21 Vilikesa Kalou.

22 Chiefs may be identified with *na vesi* or *na waqa vakaturaga* – both terms for the chiefly canoe.

23 This is clearly the case for the Naboginibola chief who tells the story of Biu; in fact, Biu's father, Mualevu turns out to be the only *vu* who is said to have come from Gau; but if we accept the story of Biu, then Mualevu's own origins have to be those accorded to the Waivolita people in Nakobuna – i.e. his *vu* is from Kaba in Tailevu.

24 In calculating the genealogies, I have allowed for a use of the term 'grandfather' to refer to anyone who is senior in the line of FF or FM.

25 See Capell (1973: 213). By the early 1800s Bau had achieved ascendancy throughout much of central and eastern Fiji (Scarr 1976).

26 Cf. Thomas (forthcoming) who argues that '[e]ncompassment is ... not a structural condition – a one to one identification between king and society – but an effect of efficacy that is open to being undermined or challenged'.

27 All children take 'mother' to be below 'father' within the household, but those who have begun to have an enlightened understanding of status distinctions simultaneously take husbands and wives to be one another's peers within the collectivity at large (Toren 1990: 202–205). Yet older children, those who have constituted the 'mature' concept of hierarchy as arising out of an interaction between gender, rank and seniority, represent women as an undifferentiated group with a lower status than married men; however, while for boys women may generally be said to be 'lower' even than young (i.e. unmarried) men, for girls married women have a status that is higher or equal to that of young men.

28 Persons who relate to one another as cross-cousins, or as *veitabani* or *veitauvu*, are not explicitly said to be able to 'take without asking' from their opposite numbers, but I was told of many instances of such behaviour, especially between cross-cousins. When the telling was a complaint and I asked why my informant had made no protest, he or she would routinely say that it would not be right to protest 'because we are cross-cousins' (or *veitabani* or *veitauvu*) (cf. Hocart 1952: 41–46).

29 The sister's child is cross-cousin to mother's brother's children, and while today marriage is possible between immediate cross-cousins it used not to be so, thus with respect to mother's brother's children, the sister's children were neither in an incest category nor in a marriage category, neither within the same household nor fully outside it; they mediated between marriageable and non-marriageable kin and so their rights as *vasu* reference the relation between brother and sister in the ascending generation and that between cross-cousins in ego's generation.

30 Thus Sahlins (1976: 28) notes that 'Four is the Lauan numerical concept of a totality'; cf. Hocart (1952: 29).

31 Given that NaRai was 'leader of the Sawaieke people' at the time of the story of Biu, he would himself have been 'sea', as were the Nakobuna people who were his navigators; other clans, such as Navure, would have been classified as 'land' in relation to the Sawaieke clan as 'sea'. But the sea/land distinction is inherently transformable, so when Biu comes on the scene as the 'stranger from over the sea' he is 'sea' and the indigenous chief NaRai becomes 'land' by virtue of the outcome of their subsequent encounter.

32 Attendance on a god or a chief is explicitly said to empower them; note that everyone has ancestors to call on and that witchcraft consists in the solitary offering of libations of *yaqona* to one's own or someone else's ancestors, in order at once to empower them and to direct this power to one's own selfish ends.

33 The apparent success of parliamentary democracy in Fiji and the inevitability of the coups of 1987 can be explained by virtue of this same logic. Democracy worked well enough when it was seen to be under the aegis of Fijian chiefs, but the egalitarian ethic could not be allowed to become an encompassing form as it would be if chiefs can no longer be seen to take precedence in government (see Toren forthcoming e).

34 Given that cognitive processes are inevitably micro-historical and dynamic and that each one of us manifests the biology of cognition as historically located subjects, this antithesis between mind and matter can be collapsed.

35 This passage from Dumont is a slippery one; it implicitly refers to Saussure's distinction between *langue* and *parole* with *langage* as the product of their interaction. I follow Volosinov (1986) [1929] in rejecting the formalism of Saussurean theory and its anti-phenomenological and anti-materialist stance.

REFERENCES

Amratlal, J. *et al.* (1975) *Women's Role in Fiji*, Suva South Pacific Social Sciences Association, in association with the Pacific Women's Conference.

Barnes, R. H., Daniel de Coppet and R. J. Parkin (eds) (1985) *Contexts and Levels: Anthropological Essays on Hierarchy*, JASO Occasional Papers No. 4, Oxford.

Bloch, M. (1974) 'Symbols, song, dance and features of articulation: is religion an extreme form of traditional authority?', *Archives Européenes de Sociologie* 15: 55–81.

—— (1985) 'From cognition to ideology', in R. Fardon (ed.) *Power and Knowledge: Anthropological and Sociological Approaches*, Edinburgh: Scottish Academic Press.

—— (1986) *From Blessing to Violence*, Cambridge: Cambridge University Press.

Borofsky, R. (1987) *Making History: Pukapukan and Anthropological Constructions of Knowledge*, Cambridge: Cambridge University Press.

Bott, E. (1972) 'Psychoanalysis and ceremony', in J. S. La Fontaine (ed.) *The Interpretation of Ritual*, London: Tavistock.

Bourdieu, P. (1977) *Outline of a Theory of Practice*, Cambridge: Cambridge University Press.

Bowerman, M. (1982) 'Reorganizational processes in lexical and syntactic development', in E. Wanner and L. P. Gleitman (eds) *Language Acquisition: The State of the Art*, Cambridge: Cambridge University Press.

Brewster, A. R. (1922) *The Hill Tribes of Fiji*, London: Seeley, Service and Co. Ltd.

Brown, P. and Tuzin, D. (eds) (1983) *The Ethnography of Cannibalism*, Special Publication, Society for Psychological Anthropology.

Burton, J. W. (1910) *The Fiji of Today*, London: Charles Kelly.

Calvert, J. (1982) [1858] *Fiji and the Fijians 2, Mission History*, Suva: Fiji Museum.

Capell, A. (1973) [1941] *A New Fijian Dictionary*, Suva: Government Printer.

Case, R. (1984) 'The process of stage transition: a neo-Piagetian view' in P. J. Sternberg (ed.) *Mechanisms of Cognitive Development*, New York: W. H. Freeman.

Clammer, J. R. (1973) 'Colonialism and the perception of tradition in Fiji', in T. Asad (ed.) *Anthropology and the Colonial Encounter*, London: Ithaca Press.

—— (1976) *Literacy and Social Change*, Leiden: E. J. Brill.

Clark, A. (1990) *Microcognition: Philosophy, Cognitive Science and Parallel Distributed Processing*, Cambridge, MA: MIT Press.

Clunie, F. (1977) *Fijian Weapons and Warfare*, Bulletin of the Fiji Museum, Suva.

Csordas, T. J. (1990) 'Embodiment as a paradigm for anthropology', *Ethos* 18: 5–47.

D'Andrade, R. (1985) *The Development of Cognitive Anthropology*, Cambridge: Cambridge University Press.

REFERENCES

Davidson, J. W and Scarr, D. (eds) (1976) *Pacific Island Portraits*, Canberra: Australian National University.

Dening, G. (1980) *Islands and Beaches: Discourse on a Silent Land, Marquesas 1774–1880*, Honolulu: University of Hawaii Press.

Derrick, R. A. (1974) [1950] *A History of Fiji*, Suva: Government Press.

Dumont, L. (1980) [1966] *Homo Hierarchicus The Caste System and its Implications*, Chicago, London: The University of Chicago Press.

Fodor, J. A. (1983) *The Modularity of Mind*, Cambridge, MA: MIT Press.

—— (1998) 'The trouble with psychological Darwinism', *London Review of Books*, 20 (2): 11–13.

Forge, A. (1970) 'Learning to see in New Guinea', in P. Mayer (ed.) *Socialization*, London: Academic Press.

France, P. (1969) *The Charter of the Land*, Melbourne: Oxford University Press.

Freeman, W. J. (1991) 'The physiology of perception', *Scientific American*, Feb. 34–41.

Geddes, W. R. (1945) *Deuba: A Study of a Fijian Village*, Wellington: Polynesian Society.

—— (1948) 'An analysis of cultural change in Fiji', unpublished Ph.D. Thesis, London School of Economics and Political Science.

Gell, A. (1993) *Wrapping in Images: Tattooing in Polynesia*, Oxford: Clarendon Press.

Gow, P. (1989) 'The perverse child: desire in a native Amazonian economy', *Man, The Journal of the Royal Anthropological Institute* (NS) 24: 299–314.

—— (1991) *Of Mixed Blood: Kinship and History in Peruvian Amazonia*, Oxford: Clarendon Press.

—— (forthcoming) *A Man Who Went Under the Earth: The History of an Amazonian Myth*, Oxford: Oxford University Press.

Henderson, G. C. (1931) *Fiji and the Fijians* (1835–56), Sydney: Angus and Robertson.

Herr, B. (1981) 'The expressive character of Fijian dream and nightmare experiences', *Ethos* 9 (4): 331–352.

Hirschfeld, L. A. (1988) 'On acquiring social categories; cognitive development and anthropological wisdom', *Man, The Journal of the Royal Anthropological Institute* (NS) 23: 611–638.

—— (1990) 'Acquiring social categories', *Man, The Journal of the Royal Anthropological Institute* (NS) 25: 146.

Hirschfeld, L. A. and Gelman, S. A. (eds) (1994) *Mapping the Mind: Domain Specificity in Cognition and Culture*, Cambridge: Cambridge University Press.

Hirschon, R. (ed.) (1984) *Women and Property, Women as Property*, London: Croom Helm.

Hobsbawm, E. and Ranger, T. (eds) (1983) *The Invention of Tradition*, Cambridge: Cambridge University Press.

Hocart, A. M. (1912) 'On the meaning of *Kalou*', *Journal of the Royal Anthropological Society* 42: 437–449.

—— (1915) 'Chieftainship and the sister's son in the Pacific', *American Anthropologist* 17: 631–646.

—— (1929) *Lau Islands, Fiji*, Honolulu: Bernice P. Bishop Museum Bulletin 62.

—— (1952) *The Northern States of Fiji*, Occasional Publication No. 11, London: Royal Anthropological Institute.

—— (1970) *Kings and Councillors: An Essay in the Comparative Anatomy of Human Society*, edited and with an introduction by Rodney Needham, Chicago and London: University of Chicago Press.

Holland, D. and Quinn, N. (1987) *Cultural Models in Language and Thought*, Cambridge: Cambridge University Press.

Hooper, S. P. (1982) 'A study of valuables in the chiefdom of Lau, Fiji', unpublished Ph.D. thesis, University of Cambridge.

Ingold, T. (1986) *Evolution and Social Life*, Cambridge: Cambridge University Press.

—— (1990a) 'An anthropologist looks at biology', *Man, The Journal of the Royal Anthropological Institute* (NS) 25: 208–229.

—— (ed.) (1990b) *The Concept of Society is Theoretically Obsolete* (text of a debate between M. Strathern & C. Toren and J. Peel & J. Spencer), Manchester: Group for Debates in Anthropological Theory, Manchester University.

—— (1991) 'Becoming persons: consciousness and sociality in human evolution', *Cultural Dynamics* 4: 355–378.

Johnson, G. A. and Smith, M. B. (1990) *Ontology and Alterity in Merleau-Ponty*, Evanston, IL: Northwestern University Press.

Johnson, M. (1987) *The Body in the Mind: The Bodily Basis of Meaning, Imagination and Reason*, Chicago: Chicago University Press.

Jolly, M. (forthcoming) 'Hierarchy and encompassment: rank, gender and place in North Vanuatu and Fiji', in Mark Mosko and Margaret Jolly (eds) *Transformations of Hierarchy.. Structure, History and Horizon in the Austronesian World*.

Keil, F. C. (1984) 'Mechanisms in cognitive development and the structure of knowledge', in P. J. Sternberg (ed.) *Mechanisms of Cognitive Development*, New York: W. H. Freeman.

Kessen, W. (1983) 'The child and other cultural inventions', in F. S. Kessel and A. W. Siegel (eds) *The Child and Other Cultural Inventions*, New York: Praeger.

Knapman, B. and Walter, M. A. H. B. (1979/80) 'The way of the land and the path of money: the generation of economic inequality in Eastern Fiji', *Journal of Developing Areas* 14: 201–222.

La Fontaine, J. S. (ed.) (1972) *The Interpretation of Ritual*, London: Tavistock.

Lakoff, G. (1987) *Women, Fire and Dangerous Things*, Chicago, London: University of Chicago Press.

Lave, J. (1988) *Cognition in Practice*. Cambridge: Cambridge University Press.

Leach, E. (1972) 'The structure of symbolism' in J. S. La Fontaine (ed.) *The Interpretation of Ritual*, London: Tavistock.

Lester, R. H. (1940) 'Betrothal and marriage customs of Mbau, Fiji', *Oceania* 10: 273–285.

Lévi-Strauss, C. (1981) [1971] *The Naked Man*, London: Jonathan Cape.

—— (1983) [1979] *The Way of the Masks*, London: Jonathan Cape.

—— (1984) *Anthropology and Myth: Lectures 1951–1982*, Oxford: Basil Blackwell.

Lewis, G. (1980) *Day of Shining Red: An Essay on Understanding Ritual*, Cambridge: Cambridge University Press.

MacLaury, R. E. (1992) 'From brightness to hue: an explanatory model of color-category evolution', *Current Anthropology* 23 (2): 137–186.

MacNaught, T. J. (1982a) *The Fijian Colonial Experience: A Study of the Neo Traditional Order Under British Colonial Rule Prior to W. W. II*, Canberra: Australian National University.

—— (1982b) 'We are no longer Fijians', *Pacific Studies* 1–2: 15–24.

Maturana, H. P., Uribe, G. and Frenk, S. (1968) 'A biological theory of relativistic color coding in the primate retina', *Arch. Biologia Med. Exp.* (Suppl. 1) Santiago, Chile.

Maturana , H. P. and Varela, F. J. (1980) [1972] *Autopoiesis and Cognition: The Realisation of the Living*, Dordrecht: D. Reidel.

201

—— (1988) *The Tree of Knowledge*, Boston, London: New Science Library, Shambhala.

Mead, M. (1932) 'An investigation of the thought of primitive children with special reference to animism', *Journal of the Royal Anthropological Institute* 62: 173–190.

Mehler, J. and Dupoux, E. (1994) [1990] *What Infants Know*, Cambridge: Blackwell.

Meltzoff, A. and Moore, M. (1985) 'Cognitive foundations and social functions of imitation and intermodal representation in infancy', in J. Mehler and P. Fox (eds) *Neonate Cognition*, Hillsdale, NJ: Lawrence Erlbaum.

Merleau-Ponty, M. (1962) [1945] *Phenomenology of Perception*, London: Routledge and Kegan Paul.

—— (1964) [1960] *Signs*, Evanston, IL: Northwestern University Press.

—— (1974) *Phenomenology, Language and Sociology* (ed.) J. O'Neill, London: Heinemann.

Middleton, J. and Edwards (1990) *Collective Remembering*, London: Sage Publications.

Miller, D. (1987) *Material Culture and Mass Consumption*, Oxford: Blackwell.

Mosko, M. and Jolly, M. (eds) (forthcoming) *Transformations of Hierarchy, Structure, History and Horizon in the Austronesian World*.

Munn, N. (1986) *The Fame of Gawa*, London: Cambridge University Press.

Nayacakalou, R. R. (1955) 'The Fijian system of kinship and marriage', *Journal of the Polynesian Society* 64: 44–56.

Ouroussoff, A. (1988) 'Public company: an anthropological study of the relationship between management belief systems and social organization in two British factories', unpublished Ph.D Thesis, London School of Economics.

Peck, P. J. (1982) 'Missionary analogues: the descriptive analysis of a development aid program in Fiji', unpublished Ph.D Thesis, University of British Columbia.

Phylactou, M. and Toren, C. (1990) 'Acquiring social categories', *Man, The Journal of the Royal Anthropological Institute* (NS) 25: 144–145.

Piaget, J. (1962) [1946] *Play, Dreams and Imitation in Childhood*, New York: Norton.

—— (1971) [1968] *Structuralism*, London: Routledge and Kegan Paul.

Pinker, S. (1998) *How the Mind Works*, London: Allen Lane.

Plotkin, H. (1997) *Evolution in Mind*, London: Allen Lane.

Quain, B. (1948) *Fijian Village*, Chicago: University of Chicago Press.

Ricoeur, P. (1978) 'The metaphorical process as cognition, imagination and feeling', *Critical Inquiry* 5: 143–159.

Rommetveit, P. (1985) 'Language acquisition as increasing linguistic structuring of experience and symbolic behaviour control', in J. V. Wertsch (ed.) *Culture, Communication and Cognition*, Cambridge: Cambridge University Press.

Ross, L. (1981) 'The "intuitive scientist" formulation and its developmental implications', in J. H. Flavell and L. Ross (eds) *Social Cognitive Development*, Cambridge: Cambridge University Press.

Routledge, D. (1985) *Matanitu: The Struggle for Power in Early Fiji*, Suva: University of the South Pacific.

Rubin, G. (1975) 'The traffic in women: notes on the "political economy" of sex', in R. Reiter (ed.) *Toward an Anthropology of Women*, New York: Monthly Review Press.

Sahlins, M. (1962) *Moala: Culture and Nature on a Fijian Island*, Ann Arbor: University of Michigan Press.

—— (1976) *Culture and Practical Reason*, Chicago: Chicago University Press.

—— (1983) 'Raw women, cooked men and other "great things" of the Fiji islands', in P. Brown and D. Tuzin (eds) *The Ethnography of Cannibalism*, Special Publication, Society for Psychological Anthropology.

—— (1985) *Islands of History*, Chicago: University of Chicago Press.

—— (1991) 'The return of the event, again; with reflections on the beginnings of the great Fijian war of 1843 to 1855 between the kingdoms of Bau and Rewa', in Aletta Biersack (ed.) *Clio in Oceania. Towards a Historical Anthropology*, Washington and London: Smithsonian Institution Press.

Sayes, S. A. (1982) 'Cakaudrove: ideology and reality in a Fijian confederation', Ph.D Thesis, Canberra, Australia National University.

—— (1984) 'Changing paths of the land', *Journal of Pacific History* 19: 3–20.

Scarr, D. (1976) 'Cakobau and Ma'afu: contenders for pre-eminence in Fiji', in J. W. Davidson and D. Scarr (eds) *Pacific Island Portraits*, Canberra: Australian National University.

Schank, R. (1982) *Dynamic Memory: A Theory of Reminding and Learning in Computers and People*, Cambridge: Cambridge University Press.

Schank, R. and Abelson, R. (1977) *Scripts, Plans, Goals and Understanding: An Inquiry into Human Knowledge Structures*, Hillsdale, NJ: Lawrence Erlbaum Associates.

Seeman, B. (1862) *Viti: An Account of a Government Mission to the Vitian or Fijian Islands*, Cambridge: Macmillan and Co.

Shore, B. (1989) '*Mana* and *tapu*', in Alan Howard and Robert Borofsky (eds) *Developments in Polynesian Ethnology*, Honolulu: University of Hawaii Press.

—— (1996) *Culture in Mind. Cognition, Culture and the Problem of Meaning*, Oxford: Oxford University Press.

Sperber, D. (1980) 'Is symbolic thought pre-rational?', in M. Foster and S. Brandes (eds) *Symbol As Sense*, New York: Academic Press.

Strathern, M. (1984) 'Subject or object? Women and the circulation of valuables in Highland New Guinea', in R. Hirschon (ed.) *Women and Property, Women as Property*, London: Croom Helm.

—— (1988) *The Gender of the Gift*, Berkeley: University of California Press.

Thomas, N. (1986) *Planets Around the Sun*, Sydney: Oceania Monographs.

—— (1991) *Entangled Objects: Exchange, Material Culture and Colonialism in the Pacific*, Cambridge, MA: Harvard University Press.

—— (forthcoming) 'Kingship and hierarchy: transformations of polities and ritual in Eastern Oceania', in M. Mosko and M. Jolly (eds) *Transformations of Hierarchy: Structure, History and Horizon in the Austronesian World*.

Thompson, E., Palacios, A. and Varela, F. J. (1992) 'Ways of coloring', *Behavioural and Brain Sciences* 15: 1–26.

Thompson, L. M. (1940) *Southern Lau, Fiji: An Ethnography*, Honolulu: Bernice P. Bishop Museum.

Thomson, B. (1968) [1908] *The Fijians: A Study of the Decay of Custom*, London: Sawsons of Pall Mall.

Toren, C. (1984) 'Thinking symbols: a critique of Sperber (1979)', *Man, The Journal of the Royal Anthropological Institute* (NS) 18: 260–268.

—— (1987) 'The chief sits above and the ladies sit below: children's perceptions of gender and hierarchy in Fiji', in G. Jahoda and I. M. Lewis (eds) *Acquiring Culture: Cross-cultural Studies of Childhood*, London: Routledge.

—— (1988) 'Making the present, revealing the past: the mutability and continuity of tradition as process', *Man, The Journal of the Royal Anthropological Institute* (NS) 23: 696–717 (reprinted as chapter 2 of this book).

—— (1989) 'Drinking cash: the purification of money in ceremonial exchange in Fiji', in J. Parry and M. Bloch (eds) *Money and the Morality of Exchange*, New York and London: Cambridge University Press (reprinted as chapter 1 of this book).

—— (1990) *Making Sense of Hierarchy: Cognition as Social Process in Fiji*, LSE Monographs in Social Anthropology 61, London: Athlone Press.

—— (1993a) 'Making history: the significance of childhood cognition for a comparative anthropology of mind', *Man, The Journal of the Royal Anthropological Institute* (NS) 28: 461–478 (reprinted as chapter 5 of this book).

—— (1993b) 'Sign into symbol, symbol as sign: cognitive aspects of a social process', in P. Boyer (ed.) *Cognitive Aspects of Religious Symbolism*, Cambridge: Cambridge University Press (reprinted as chapter 4 of this book).

—— (1994a) 'Transforming love, representing Fijian hierarchy', in P. Gow and P. Harvey (eds) *Sexuality and Violence. Issues in Representation and Experience*, London: Routledge.

—— (1994b) 'The drinker as chief or rebel: yaqona and alcohol in Fiji', in M. McDonald (ed.) *Gender Drink and Drugs*, Oxford: Berg.

—— (1994c) ' "All things go in pairs or the sharks will bite": the antithetical nature of Fijian chiefship' *Oceania* 64 (3): 197–216 (reprinted as chapter 9 of this book).

—— (1994d) 'On childhood cognition and social institutions', *Man, The Journal of the Royal Anthropological Institute* 29: 976–981.

—— (1995a) 'Seeing the ancestral sites: transformations in Fijian notions of the land', in E. Hirsch and M. O'Hanlon (eds) *Anthropology of the Landscape*, Oxford: Clarendon Press (reprinted as chapter 3 of this book).

—— (1995b) 'Ritual, rule and cognitive scheme', in Paul Wohlmuth (ed.) *The Crisis in Text, Journal of Contemporary Legal Issues* 6: 521–533, University of San Diego (reprinted as chapter 6 of this book).

—— (1995c) 'Cosmogonic aspects of desire and compassion in Fiji', in D. de Coppet and A. Iteanu (eds) *Cosmos and Society*, London: Berg (reprinted as chapter 8 of this book).

—— (1998) 'Cannibalism and compassion: transformations in Fijian concepts of the person', in V. Keck (ed.) *Common Worlds and Single Lives: Constituting Knowledge in Pacific Societies*, London: Berg.

—— (forthcoming a) 'The child in mind', in H. Whitehouse (ed.) *New Perspectives in Cognitive Anthropology*, Cambridge: Cambridge University Press.

—— (forthcoming b) 'Compassion for one another: constituting kinship as intentionality in Fiji', 1996 Malinowski Lecture, *Journal of Royal Anthropological Institute*, in press for June 1999.

—— (forthcoming c) 'Becoming a Christian in Fiji', in F. Cannell and M. Green (eds) *Power and Transformation in Local Christianities*.

—— (forthcoming d) 'Space–time coordinates of subjectivity in Fiji', in G. Bennardo (ed.) *Linguistic and Cultural Perspectives on Space in Oceania*, Special Issue, *Pacific Linguistics*.

—— (forthcoming e) 'Why Fijian chiefs have to be elected', in J. Pina Cabral (ed.) *Succession in Elite Contexts*, London: Berg.

Trevarthen, C. (1987) 'Universal cooperative motives: how infants begin to know the language and culture of their parents', in G. Jahoda and I. M. Lewis (eds) *Acquiring Culture: Cross-cultural Studies in Child Development*, London: Croom Helm.

Turner, J. W. (1986) 'The water of life: kava ritual and the logic of sacrifice', *Ethnology* 25: 203–214.

Valeri, V. (1985) *Kingship and Sacrifice: Ritual and Society in Ancient Hawaii*, Chicago: University of Chicago Press.

Varela, F. J., Thompson, E. and Rosch, E. (1991) *The Embodied Mind*, Cambridge, MA: MIT Press.

Volosinov, V. N. (1986) [1929] *Marxism and the Philosophy of Language*, Cambridge, MA: Harvard University Press.

Vygotsky, L. S. (1978) [1936] *Mind in Society*, Cambridge, MA: Harvard University Press.

—— (1981) 'The genesis of higher mental functions', in J. V. Werstch (ed.) *The Concept of Activity in Soviet Psychology*, Armonk, NJ: Sharpe.

—— (1986) [1934] *Thought and Language*, Cambridge, MA: Harvard University Press.

Wagner, R. (1986) *Symbols That Stand For Themselves*, Chicago: University of Chicago Press.

Walkerdine, V. (1990) *The Mastery of Reason*, London: Routledge.

Walter, M. A. H. B. (1975) 'Kinship and marriage in Mualevu: a Dravidian variant in Fiji?' *Ethnology* 14: 181–195.

—— (1978/79) 'An examination of hierarchical notions in Fijian society: a test case for the applicability of the term "chief"', *Oceania* 49: 7.

Waterhouse, J. (1978) [1866] *The King and the People of Fiji*, New York, AMS. (Reprint of the 1866 edition published by the Wesleyan Conference Office.)

Wertsch, J. V. and Stone, C. A. (1985) 'The concept of internalization in Vygotsky's account of the genesis of higher mental functions', in J. V Wertsch (ed.) *Culture, Communication and Cognition: Vygotskian Perspectives*, Cambridge: Cambridge University Press.

White, G. M. and Kirkpatrick, J. (eds) (1985) *Person, Self and Experience*, Berkeley: University of California Press.

Williams, T. (1982) [1858] *Fiji and the Fijians*, ed. G. S. Rowe, Suva: Fiji Museum. (A reprint of the 1858 London edition.)

—— (1931) *The Journal of Thomas Williams, Missionary in Fiji, 1840–1853*, ed. G. C. Henderson, Sydney: Angus and Robertson.

INDEX

accommodation 9
adultery 141
affines 40
affinity 42
alcohol 133–135; and *yaqona* 135
analytical categories 4–6, 16
ancestors 49, 70–71, 81; 178
ancestor Gods 34, 54, 72, 146, 150–156;
    and desire 139, 149–156
ancestral powers 73–77
assimilation 9–10, 125
autonomy 6
autopoiesis 6–12, 108, 121
avoidance 50, 144

babies 7; *see also* neonates
balanced reciprocity 43, 53, 65, 147, 157
barkcloth 62
behaviourists 112
binary distinctions 109
biology and culture 4, 5
Bloch 63, 84, 98, 100, 122
bodily comportment 116
body scheme 11
Borofsky 45, 63
Bourdieu 23, 94, 100, 123

cannibalism 36, 48, 60, 62, 151, 155, 178
ceremonial exchange 32
chiefly ritual 76, 164
chiefly village 72
chiefs 33, 53, 89, 148; installation of 33,
    37, 49–50, 60–61, 79, 166; and tribute
    34
chiefship 163, 166–176
child, ideas of 110–114
children 16, 18–20, 90, 144; Abelam 103,

106; and gender 91–94; as informants
    83, 85; Euro–American 103, 106–107;
    Fijian 91–101, 104–105; Manus Island
    103, 105–106; *see also* babies, neonates
children's drawings 85, 91–93
Christian God 49, 54, 70, 145, 146,
    148–149, 157–160
Christianity 36, 37, 45–50, 62, 156–160;
    and development 77–79
church services 70
Clammer 48
Clunie 72
cognitive construction 12, 82, 86, 87–88,
    91–101
cognitive modules 12
cognitive processes 68
cognitive scheme 9–12, 109, 121
cognitivist 24
colonial encounter 25, 37, 43
colonisation 36, 57
commodities 78
commodity exchange 28–32
competition 167
conditioning theories 112
connexionist models 11
consciousness 12–14
consumption 80
conversion 46, 48, 64–65, 81
cooking 51
core symbols 99–100
Council of Chiefs 49
cross-cousins 29, 42, 50, 55, 69, 135–139,
    143, 157, 161, 166, 175, 179
cross-modal matching 12
cultural categories 64
cultural construction 110
cultural models 11, 13, 114

WITHDRAWN

60 4058645 6